Standards in the Classroom

HOW TEACHERS AND STUDENTS NEGOTIATE LEARNING

Standards in the Classroom

HOW TEACHERS AND STUDENTS NEGOTIATE LEARNING

John Kordalewski

FOREWORD BY CATHERINE G. KRUPNICK

Teachers College Press
New York and London

Published by Teachers College Press, 1234 Amsterdam Avenue, New York, NY 10027

Library of Congress Cataloging-in-Publication Data

Kordalewski, John.
    Standards in the classroom : how teachers and students negotiate learning / John Kordalewski ; foreword by Catherine G. Krupnick.
        p.   cm.
    Includes bibliographical references and index.
    ISBN 0-8077-3947-2 (cloth : alk. paper)—ISBN 0-8077-3946-4 (pbk. : alk. paper)
        1. Education—Standards—United States. 2. Educational tests and measurements—United States. 3. Teaching—United States. I. Title.

    LB3060.83.K67   2000
    371.27'1—dc21

00-020157

ISBN 0-8077-3946-4 (paper)
ISBN 0-8077-3947-2 (cloth)

Printed on acid-free paper
Manufactured in the United States of America

07   06   05   04   03   02   01   00   8   7   6   5   4   3   2   1

Contents

Foreword

Debates about classroom standards or "the standards movement" are perpetuated by the public's scant knowledge of classroom practice. The rhetoric of school reform is often too passionate, theoretical, and empty of content to apply to the context in which students acquire—or refuse—learning. Actual reports of contemporary classroom transactions are rare, perhaps because so few people can write them. Teachers and students, busy in their own worlds, do not have time to spend on major research projects. Other potential reporters lack the participant-observer status necessary for good classroom research and interviews. John Kordalewski's STANDARDS IN THE CLASSROOM: HOW TEACHERS AND STUDENTS NEGOTIATE LEARNING addresses a gap in our knowledge. It is a substantial achievement, the result of meticulous research by the right person in the right place at the right time.

"Official standards initiatives," Kordalewski notes, "produce standards on paper which their advocates hope will have an impact on classrooms. [But meaningful] standards within a classroom relate directly to students' and teachers' actual performances."

Kordalewski observed, and participated in, the classroom lives of students and teachers while employed as a teacher and ethnographer by "Earl Powell" High School. A conspicuous feature of these classroom lives, he discovered, was the ongoing negotiation of standards for acceptable academic work. That such negotiations occur will surprise many readers, and it will disappoint those who believe that schools can be improved by imposing rigorous external standards on students—and punishing schools when students fail to attain those standards.

One of the strengths of STANDARDS IN THE CLASSROOM is its discussion of diverse definitions of academic standards. From the definitions that produce standards on paper to those that "influence the kind and quality of work pursued by . . . students and teachers," Kordalewski examines intentions and results. This discussion alone makes the book useful.

What makes STANDARDS IN THE CLASSROOM invaluable is Kordalewski's portraits of students. Each of four portraits demonstrates how academic standards developed over the course of a year in the life of the student. All of them illustrate the interaction between teachers' aspirations and students' development. Teachers, generally, hope their students will internalize standards that can lead them to master increasingly complicated skills. Students sometimes, but not always, share this hope. Inspiring students to raise their standards is one of the key challenges of classroom instruction.

Powell High's teachers created a program of study driven, in part, by students' interest in gaining the respect of their peers. Each student was required to deliver four oral presentations a year. These presentations were based on independently chosen and researched humanities topics, often a historical issue, or a contemporary social studies issue. Whatever the topic chosen, however, the student was allowed considerable freedom in defining its scope. Students and teachers often began with widely differing notions of good work habits and products, which served as starting points for ongoing negotiations about standards that continued over the course of the marking period. Learning was possible, most possible, through negotiation of the standards themselves.

At Powell, then, much of classroom life could be characterized as negotiation about standards. Perhaps there is as much negotiation over standards at other schools as there is at Powell, but the pedagogy and favorable teacher-student ratio at Powell made this negotiation particularly transparent. This permitted Kordalewski to draw a clear picture that can facilitate our understanding of how standards affect students' learning.

The portraits of individual students (and extensive quotes from other students and teachers) provide the answers. They show how learning standards evolve (or stall) in the lives of individuals, and in interactions between students and teachers. We cannot understand how standards operate in students' lives without the kind of data Kordalewski provides. Where and from whom do endogenous standards evolve? How are standards communicated? Understood? Legitimated? Met? Discarded? Exceeded? How do students decide when they are meeting, or exceeding, a given standard for written or oral presentations? What are accomplishments that students value but teachers fail to appreciate?

STANDARDS IN THE CLASSROOM is a substantial achievement. Among its most important contributions is providing a language and framework for discussing the relationship between classroom standards and student learning. I doubt that any single policy prescription will emerge from this book. Nevertheless, demonstrating the value of the ethnographic approach to classroom research is a start. For those of us who believe no standard is meaningful when removed from its social context, Korda-lewski's ethnographic approach to the study of standards is the best way to begin a discussion.

Catherine G. Krupnick
Harvard Graduate School of Education

Standards in the Classroom

HOW TEACHERS AND STUDENTS NEGOTIATE LEARNING

1

Overview

In current discussions about reforming public schools, the word *standards* appears with great frequency. School improvement is often framed as a matter of raising standards. And many reform proposals and initiatives revolve around the establishment of official standards—for a school, a district, a state, or the nation.

With such emphasis being placed on standards in relation to teaching and learning, I believe it is worthwhile to take a close look at how standards form and operate within classrooms. The standards in a classroom relate directly to students' and teachers' actual performances. Official standards initiatives, by contrast, produce standards on paper, which their advocates hope will have an impact in classrooms.

Classroom standards, broadly, are the kind and quality of work valued and pursued by classroom participants—that is, by students and teachers. These standards will exist in students' and teachers' minds and/or become manifest through their actions.

This book differs from most treatments of standards because it emphasizes students' role in standard setting. As is demonstrated here, students have ideas about what is important. Those ideas, which do not simply follow from what teachers present to students, affect the nature of students' efforts and products. Students' efforts and products, furthermore, signify what is being accomplished by the collective classroom enterprise.

By no means does this emphasis on students relegate teachers to the sidelines. Classrooms are interactive environments, and classroom standard setting is an interactive process. In that process, teachers influence students to pursue new standards and show students how to attain them. At the same time, teachers' ideas and decisions are subject to the influence of their students.

Given this joint input into classroom standards, I assert that those standards develop through a process of *negotiation*. This book offers a portrait and an analysis of that process.

This study does not examine contemporary initiatives featuring official standards; rather, the focus is on phenomena and processes that are internal to classrooms. Nonetheless, the ideas and evidence presented here should evoke skepticism about standards strategies that have been in vogue among educators and politicians alike during the 1990s. By looking within classroom communities, I show that standards are much more—and much more complex—than official declarations of what students should do. I also suggest that the processes of creating and negotiating standards within classrooms are fundamental to learning and teaching—that they cannot be short-circuited. Official standards may have some impact, both stimulative and diversionary, on those processes. There is also much that official standards do not address. Certainly, they are not solutions to issues of educational attainment as proclaimed by their crudest rationales; for instance, "National standards . . . will ensure that no child leaves our schools without mastering the basics" (Clinton, 1997, p. 1371).

WHAT ARE "STANDARDS"?

The word *standards* has several meanings and shades of meaning. Unwitting shifts among those meanings can cloud conversations about standards. Prior to a discussion of classroom standards, I consider it necessary to clarify what those meanings are and how they will apply.

Classroom standards, broadly defined above as what classroom participants value and pursue, are an inclusive concept: one that encompasses several more particular definitions of *standards*. Examining classroom standards does not entail choosing one of these definitions; rather, it involves recognizing interrelationships among different forms of standards. A series of definitions, and how each pertains to classroom standards, are described below.

In some of its more common uses, *standards* means both official requirements and numerically determined thresholds of acceptable performance. Reports of how educational and other institutions are "toughening standards" often refer to standards of this nature: SAT scores required for college admissions, for instance. In individual classrooms, scores on tests and other quantified performances (e.g., attendance, assignments completed) constitute this sort of standard when, for instance, they determine whether students pass a course.

Official requirements and performance thresholds need not be based on numeric measures. The "standards" used in court proceedings are a good example. Legislation, the Constitution, and case law establish requirements in the form of principles; for instance, race-based admissions quotas at publicly funded schools must serve a "compelling government interest" in order to be legally allowed. Human judgment, with various criteria and precedents serving as references, then comes into play in decisions regarding whether a specific act or set of acts meets such a standard.

Standards underlie unofficial as well as official judgments, and unofficially, too, individuals and groups generate standards that revolve around principles. In classrooms, students' and teachers' conceptions of good work—their thoughts as to what qualities characterize it—are often standards of this nature.

When standards indicate what is treated or viewed as acceptable or good work, they also imply that a certain kind of work is valued by an individual or community. In some uses of the word, *standards* means one's system of relative values. The National Council of Teachers of Mathematics (1989) introduces its published "curriculum and evaluation standards" with the claim, "Standards are statements about what is valued" (p. 2). Classroom standards include teachers' and students' ideas about what is worth doing, thinking about, or celebrating; these are instances of valuing.

Along with values, *standards* can refer to a person's commitment to acting in accordance with those values. Grant Wiggins (1991) writes, "When we speak of persons or institutions with standards—especially when modified by the word *high*—we mean they live by a set of mature, coherent, and consistently applied values evident in all their actions" (p. 20). With the key phrase "live by," this definition emphasizes actions as well as thoughts. In a classroom context, it points to individuals' habits and pursuits.

Standards, in another sense, are meanings that the experiences of individuals or communities give to relative, evaluative concepts. A sportscaster's remark during a basketball game illustrates: When there was 1 minute left in the game and the home team trailed by six points, he said that there was "still plenty of time by NBA standards." The history of games in the National Basketball Association, in other words, had rendered it quite conceivable that a team could make up six points in 1 minute of play. In other contexts, or to another person's frame of reference,

1 minute would be far from "plenty of time." Similarly, what is considered by a student or teacher to be a "good" student paper—or, to focus on particular qualities, an "informative" or "clear" one—varies depending on that person's experience.

Concepts of good work are sometimes embodied in benchmark performances. In classroom-based as well as large-scale assessment procedures, selected pieces of student work can serve as reference points: They demonstrate what characteristics mark an "A" product, a "B" product, and so forth. Informally, also, students can evaluate their performances by comparing them to those of classmates. At times, the benchmark is itself called a *standard,* with the word meaning a measuring stick or basis of comparison.

One particular kind of benchmark is the exemplar—a performance that represents the highest level of excellence. When someone is said to have "set the standard" or "set a new standard," an exemplary performance is often indicated. Exemplars frequently come from outside a community; they may be the work of leading practitioners in a field of endeavor. In such cases, the exemplar may represent a level of accomplishment that people aim toward without necessarily expecting to attain.

The adjective form of *standard* carries yet another meaning. It refers to usual practices, as in "standard operating procedure." This meaning intertwines with the others. Usual practices reflect the requirements, values, and commitments in a community. The kind of work that is "standard" in a classroom, furthermore, establishes the context of experience out of which concepts of quality emerge.

In looking at classroom standards, this book focuses on certain phenomena, to which the above definitions apply in overlapping fashion. The discussions of standards center around students' and teachers' ideas about what constituted good work, students' purposes as they did their work, expectations that teachers projected to students, and patterns of individual and collaborative activity and achievement. These discussions highlight standards as principles, values, commitments, meanings rooted in experience, and usual practices. At times, they also touch on formal requirements, thresholds of acceptability, benchmarks, and exemplars.

FIVE THEORIES OF STANDARD SETTING

How do classroom standards form and develop? Implicit in various educational practices, and in various writings about teaching and learning or about standards, are a set of five theories that address this question.

These theories point to processes of *demanding, informing, teaching, negotiating,* and *arising.*

The processes highlighted by these theories intertwine with each other in practice. Each process, however, has distinct qualities. In addition, those who promote each theory do not necessarily claim that one process is exclusively responsible for the creation of classroom standards. The theories nonetheless represent different emphases, which appear both in analyses of how standards are formed and in approaches to classroom practice.

The term *standard setting,* as used elsewhere, often denotes the process whereby committees, or perhaps faculties, determine among themselves what students should know and be able to do. In this book, the term refers to the establishment of standards in classrooms: in the thoughts and actions of students as well as teachers.

Demanding

The demanding theory figures prominently in the movement for national standards and similar efforts on state and local levels. The National Council on Education Standards and Testing (1992), a panel convened in 1991 pursuant to the President's Education Summit with the Governors, states, in its rationale for a new system of national standards,

> What has [heretofore] been demanded is insufficient in that it covers far too little of the knowledge and skills students need to succeed in the modern workplace and to participate in the democratic process. Such low expectations shortchange students and ill-serve the country. (p. 12)

Implicit in this statement is a belief that demands will result in behavior that conforms to them—and that higher student achievement will occur if demanded. Those are the central premises behind the demanding theory.

Not all groups that propose national, state, or school district standards emphasize this demanding function. For instance, national subject-area organizations (e.g., the National Council of Teachers of English [1996] and the National Council of Teachers of Mathematics [1989]) have compiled standards documents and billed them as references, which schools and teachers can use in devising their own policies and pursuing support for them. Nonetheless, the notion of demanding undergirds many contemporary large-scale standards initiatives.

Many standards initiatives and proposals include assessment programs with consequences attached to students' and/or schools' performances. Some expand the application of negative outcomes, such as re-tention for low-performing students and receivership for low-performing schools, while others feature new sets of rewards, such as advanced certificates for students who perform well. Such consequences are intended to provide force behind a given set of demands.

In the case of national, state, or school district standards, those doing the demanding are people outside of schools. The demanding theory can also be framed with teachers occupying that position. This is illustrated in the following statement by Grant Wiggins (1993):

> Accountability begins with teachers not accepting work that is shoddy: it isn't done until it's done right. . . . Consider . . . requiring every faculty, team, or academic department to formulate policies that ensure that quality work is not merely an *option.* (pp. 284–285; emphasis in original)

Like the other four theories, the demanding theory, on the classroom scale, highlights particular teacher behaviors. It suggests that teachers establish standards by insisting on certain performances from their students. It assigns importance to the qualities that make a teacher effective at insisting: consistency of purpose and action, for instance, and strength of will and presence. Demanding may also involve assessment procedures, and teachers passing students only if they perform at certain levels.

The classroom-scale demanding theory emphasizes teachers' role in the process of standard setting. Students' input is not considered nearly so crucial a variable as teachers', since students' behavior is expected to change in response to the demands. Also, the standards themselves originate entirely with the teachers or with other adults.

Informing

The national standards movement makes use of the informing theory as well as the demanding theory. Ray Marshall and Marc Tucker (1992), for instance, stress that under their proposed system of assessments tied to national standards, "students, their parents, and their advocates will be armed for the first time with clear information about what they have to do to succeed [and about] how well they are doing as they progress through school" (p. 150). In essence, the informing theory asserts that if students know clearly what it is they are being asked to do, they will focus their attention and effort on those goals.

Like the demanding theory, the informing theory has classroom-scale versions as well as appearing in broader-scale policy proposals. In a study of practices in individual schools, for instance, Linda Darling-Hammond, Jacqueline Ancess, and Beverly Falk (1995) state that "authentic" assessment activities involve well-articulated performance standards. These are openly expressed to students ... rather than kept secret in the tradition of fact-based examinations. ... Learning and performance are both supported when ... students know ahead of time that an assessment will focus, for example, on students' demonstrated ability to evaluate competing viewpoints and use evidence in developing a persuasive essay concerning a topic of social importance. (p. 12)

In a discussion of grades, Wiggins (1993) asserts that information can both guide and motivate students. He emphasizes students' having access to grading criteria, and teachers' designating criteria that pertain to transparent qualities or recognizable results of one's work, so that students can "both self-assess and self-correct" (p. 149). He further states that "clear and worthy standards combined with the measuring of incremental progress always provide incentives to the learner, even when the gap between present performance and the standard is great" (p. 153).

There are a variety of ways in which teachers can inform students about standards for a given activity. When those standards are embodied in assessment procedures, and when student performances are not evaluated simply according to numbers of correct answers, such information can be conveyed through sample performances, presented in the form of rubrics that spell out scoring criteria, or communicated through other verbal means. In addition, teachers can design situations in which students observe assessment processes in action. For instance, at some schools where seniors defend portfolios of their work before graduation committees, younger students attend older students' committee sessions, where they can see how adults respond to student work. Informing about standards also occurs when teachers articulate expectations to students without regard to assessment procedures—through instructions for an assignment, perhaps, or individual conferences about work-in-progress.

Like the demanding theory, the informing theory of standard setting views standards as existing independently of the student. Target performances may be more or less precisely defined and more or less subject to ongoing revision by teachers; nonetheless, there is information about what students need to do that is, at some point, established fact. The theory suggests that teachers or other adults establish standards in classrooms by providing students with clear, consistent, and thorough information. Students' responses are expected to follow.

Teaching

For the most part, the teaching theory of standard setting, like the demanding and informing theories, sees standards as originating from teachers or other adults. What distinguishes it is the emphasis it places on the process whereby students come to internalize those standards. The demanding and informing theories do not focus on this process, implying that it results naturally from strong demands or pertinent information, or perhaps that it is insignificant.

Deborah Meier, founding director of Central Park East Secondary School in New York City, provides an example of the "teaching" perspective on classroom standards: "After four years of lots of conversation around your work, hopefully kids can say, 'I understand what [teachers are] trying to get at,' and they're buying it" (quoted in Darling-Hammond et al., 1995, p. 49). This statement suggests that students form standards in their minds by "buying" what teachers are "trying to get at"—and that this is a process that involves ongoing interaction ("lots of conversation").

Thomas Wilson (1996) presents a similar concept:

> We want our children to perform on . . . standards of excellence set in their minds, habits and work, not on [standards set by government]. . . . Implanting and nourishing standards of excellence for good work is a major challenge for good teaching. (pp. 223–224)

Wilson locates standards in students' minds and actions. He also suggests that those standards are "implanted and nourished" by teachers.

Teaching standards to students involves providing information; it also involves activities through which students become acculturated to certain standards, gain understanding of them, and put them into practice. Ron Berger (1991), for instance, describes peer review routines in his writing classroom as instilling standards. Here, the standards being taught concern ways of working and thinking: the habit of giving input to other writers and the use of certain vocabulary to discuss writing. Berger establishes formal procedures through which students share and comment on each other's papers. When his students eventually begin critiquing each other's work informally and on their own, "that signifies to me the real adoption of the culture of high standards" (p. 35). Wiggins (1993) describes how certain assessment practices can teach standards in a manner similar to Berger's peer review routines. He says that when work is graded according to criteria that are made public, and students can dialogue with teacher-assessors around how their performances meet those criteria, students gain appreciation for the standard that decisions are to be based on rules of evidence and argument, as well as for the more specific "adult standards" used in a given assessment.

Standards are taught through a range of interactions between teachers and students. As in Wiggins's example above, teachers can model for students the principles they believe are important. They can explain, encourage, and cajole. When coaching students in individual and group activities, teachers guide students toward doing their work in certain ways. Teaching standards to students also encompasses teaching students how to do the work in question, since students' ability to realize standards in their own performances contributes to their internalization of those standards.

The teaching theory of standard setting recognizes students' active role in the construction of classroom standards. It also suggests that young people acquire standards—as they learn many things—through adult guidance. This theory places great importance on teachers' skills, as teachers do not simply pass on the standards but rather create conditions under which they become real to their students.

Negotiating

If classroom standards are established through negotiation, students help to *determine* the standards. They do not simply internalize or respond to teachers' standards. Rather, the standards become defined through teachers' and students' interactions, and they reflect the input of both parties.

One form of negotiation that has been observed by some commentators involves implicit bargains between teachers and students. These bargains are marked by teachers' reducing the amount and quality of work they expect, and students' giving compliance in return: attending class, for instance, and not behaving disruptively (Powell, Farrar, & Cohen, 1985). The student input that leads to such bargains is often characterized as resistance to teachers (McQuillan, 1998). In this scenario, students' influence is viewed as having a negative impact on standards.

A second form of negotiation occurs when teachers invite student input and thereby make aspects of their curriculum and/or requirements deliberately negotiable. This teacher strategy can be employed to various extents. Students might simply be given options or a voice in selected instances: a choice of essay topics, for example, or a chance to suggest categories for a scoring rubric. Alternatively, a teacher may embark on a more pervasive effort to share power in the classroom. Whatever the extent of student input solicited, the teacher is likely to establish some boundaries as to what is negotiable and what is not.

Those who promote this approach assert that student collaboration in setting the purposes and direction of classroom activity leads to greater engagement and greater learning (Boomer, Lester, Onore, & Cook, 1992). Ira Shor, advocating a relatively far-reaching version of power sharing, contrasts "dialogue" with "unilateral teacher authority" and states that with a dialogic approach, the teacher "opens the process to . . . more fertile contact with student thought and experience" (1992, p. 90). He writes of students coming to occupy the "enabling center of their educations, not the disabling margins" (1996, p. 200).

A third kind of negotiation is more informal, and partly implicit, and can be found in the ongoing relationships between teachers and students. Writing about such relationships, Nel Noddings (1984) assigns to student power both a constructive role and an inherently prominent one:

> The . . . teacher is not necessarily permissive. She does not abstain . . . from leading the student, or persuading him, or coaxing him toward an examination of school subjects. But she recognizes that, in the long run, he will learn what he pleases. We may force him to respond in specified ways, but what he will make his own and eventually apply effectively is that which he finds significant for his own life. This recognition does not reduce either the teacher's power or her responsibility. . . . [However], she realizes that the student, as ethical agent, will make his own selection from the presented possibilities and so, in a very important sense, she is prepared to put her motive energy in the service of his projects. (pp. 176–177)

This view highlights an informal power that students have over what they think about and how they think about it. By exercising this power, students develop standards, in their minds and in their work, that are more than replicas of teachers' or other adults' standards.

Noddings's statement also suggests that teachers' recognition of this sort of student influence and support of its results can lead to heightened student achievement. When a teacher puts "her motive energy in the service of his projects," she may very well be focusing her efforts in those areas where the greatest learning will take place. At the same time, teachers' "leading," "persuading," and "coaxing" are important parts of the negotiating relationship Noddings outlines.

Arising

The writings of Patricia Carini advance the theory of standards arising. Students' input, to her, is not a matter of their active role in learning, or even negotiating with, teachers' standards. Rather, she views students as the primary creators of standards.

To Carini, when students' "individual assertions of value and worth" (1988, p. 11) establish the meaning of their activities to them, standards are being formed. Furthermore, when a student places positive value on an activity, he or she is often led into new endeavors and new accomplishments, and standards then grow.

Carini emphasizes students' interests, as a form of valuing. She speaks of "standards that arise through students' active pursuit of interest" (1987, p. 20). She elaborates on this notion:

> It is my consistent observation that sheer delight in a medium, the love of it, exerts an enormous pull on persons. Like an absorbing idea or persisting question, it is often the "something" which . . . "leads us through ourselves beyond ourselves" and in doing so transforms both standards and values in the climate in which they exist. (1994, p. 48)

Carini's ideas focus on how students' *strong* interests lead to the development of *high* standards. However, the arising theory suggests that more moderate interests can also play a role in students' construction of standards.

Carini sees students' work—both "work" as activity, and "work" as products that result from activity—as the primary locus of the arising process. As students work, they discover and act on their interests. "The doing of work, the making of things and ideas, embodies worth and value and is, therefore, a context in which standards can be seen to arise," Carini writes (1988, p. 12). The products that students create, in turn, give standards concrete form.

The process of standards arising, as Carini describes it, is social as well as individual. When students are attracted to an idea, their work is often noticed by other students. Carini writes about how, in the elementary school where she worked, this led to the development of new standards: Classmates emulated one boy's large and complex block edifice, for instance; a trend of writing novels started once one child produced one; and prior to such large achievements there was an ongoing process of sharing more modest ones. She comments:

> Watching, listening, it was exciting to notice how the children struck imaginative sparks from each other and themselves. I placed high value on the frequency with which a child would say to herself, "I got a *good* idea" and the frequency with which that was said by one child of another: "That's cool. How'd you do that?" (1994, p. 47; emphasis in original)

Regarding teachers' role in her conception of standard setting, Carini suggests ways that teachers can foster the process of standards arising. For instance, she says, "Linking strength with activity and impulse toward worth requires an education and classroom in which children can be seen, '*looked at*,' as active and persistent in the making of meaning, order, knowledge and standards" (1987, p. 19; emphasis in original). She also states that there is a need for teachers to provide "an evaluation that makes [students' standard-creating] activity, the conditions that support it, and the standards that arise . . . *public* and *compelling*" (1987, pp. 19–20; emphasis in original). How, or whether, teachers' own standards or goals are to come into play is an issue that Carini does not address at any length.

This study depicts classroom standard setting as a process of negotiation. It considers negotiation as a reality of classroom life, rather than as a direct teacher strategy. Negotiation, as described in this book, is embedded in teacher–student interactions. It is also a cumulative result of the simultaneous operation of standards originating from teachers and standards originating from students.

Subsequent chapters show forms of student input that both Carini and Noddings suggest: students making their own meanings of the work they were doing, or asked to do, and making decisions about what, and what not, to focus on and pursue. Teachers, also, are shown pursuing their own standards in various ways, and influencing their students while also making adjustments in response to students. The construction of classroom standards is presented as involving the interaction of teachers' and students' meanings and purposes, through work they do together. This is a dynamic process, because teachers' and students' standards remain in tension and because those standards themselves are not fixed.

None of the other four theories encompasses the range of what enters into classroom standards to the extent that the negotiating theory does. However, within a framework of negotiation, there is room for demanding, informing, teaching, and arising to contribute to the formation of standards—and for teachers to make use of each in their repertoires of strategies. As teachers pursue their standards, they demand, inform, and teach. Recognizing students' inevitable influence on standards, teachers can also attempt to facilitate the arising process. This book discusses issues that accompany each approach.

SETTING OF THE STUDY

Classroom standards are examined here through a look at one educational effort: the use of "exhibitions" in humanities classes, during the 1993–1994 school year, at the Earl Powell High School.[1]

---

[1] Throughout this book, pseudonyms are used for the high school and all teachers, students, and administrators.

Powell is an alternative program, serving grades 9–12, in the public school system of a large eastern city. It was founded in 1983 as a "school within a school" at one of the city's district high schools; it moved to a separate location in 1990. The school is characterized by small size (approximately 180 students in 1993–1994) and an emphasis on teachers' and students' knowing each other well.

Since 1989, Powell has belonged to the Coalition of Essential Schools, the school reform organization based at Brown University. The school had, since its beginning, followed many of the broad pedagogical approaches favored by that organization: interdisciplinary classes, for instance, and a curriculum that prioritizes depth over breadth in its treatment of content knowledge. After joining the Coalition of Essential Schools, Powell gradually undertook to implement some additional strategies that the organization promotes. Exhibitions—student projects and presentations that serve as an alternative to conventional testing—are one such strategy.

Powell students in 1993–1994 represented the general pool of students who attended the city's district high schools. They were not admitted by selective criteria such as test scores. Students arrived at Powell via a variety of routes. Most, themselves or through their parents, identified Powell as a preferable option to the city's large high schools—either prior to entering high school, after moving to the city, after being out of school for a period of time, or after experiencing dissatisfaction or difficulties (academically or otherwise) at another school. One subset of Powell students were referred by schools from which they had been expelled. Another subset had attended one of the city's academically selective schools and not fared well in the highly structured routines there and/or not found those routines to their liking.

The racial composition of Powell's student body resembled that of the school district's total student population: Approximately 50% of the students were African American or African Caribbean, 25% were Latino, and 20% were European American. Approximately 60% of Powell's students were eligible for free lunches under federal income guidelines (Technical Development Corporation, 1993).

Of twelve full-time teachers in 1993–94, six were European American, three African American, and three Latino.

Three features of this school setting are especially significant as they relate to this study of standards. One is the educational histories of the students. Like many students in contemporary urban high schools, most Powell students had not acquired academic skills and competencies to the extent typical of students in more affluent settings. In addition, the students' general stances toward and commitments to school and schoolwork were a greater issue to teachers than they are in some schools. Thus, there was less a priori convergence between teacher and student standards than there might be in some high schools, in two important respects: in the degree to which teachers' visions of high-quality performances matched students' experiences of accomplishment, and in the degree to which students consented to work as teachers wanted them to. This book speaks to specific issues that accompany the development of standards in such a context. It suggests ways of understanding what might occur in the many schools where, for instance, student performances on state-mandated assessments indicate that the standards embodied in those assessments have not come to life in the school. At the same time, broad principles presented here, involving the negotiated nature of standards, apply to educational situations more universally.

A second feature of the setting is that students and teachers developed standards for exhibitions without regard to explicit standards formulated externally to the classrooms. The students did not take state or school district examinations in humanities—or in English and social studies, the two subjects combined in the interdisciplinary humanities course. Also, the Powell faculty, at this point in time, had not established schoolwide graduation requirements in terms of subject-area performance, or developed rubrics that spelled out detailed criteria for evaluating exhibitions. Such requirements or scoring devices could enter into the mix of factors affecting classroom standards. The nature and extent of their impact is an issue pertinent to current educational practice, on which this study cannot report. It is quite clear to me, though, that were these requirements or devices present, they would not have been the final word on classroom standards. This study shows the importance and operation of other forces.

Finally, the results of Powell exhibitions, in terms of the student achievement they brought forth, were mixed at best. Consequently, this study is not intended to present a model of how to establish high standards, or of how to employ exhibitions most effectively toward that end. Rather, it offers observations about what the process of building standards entails.

CULTURE AND STANDARDS

An additional feature of the setting that deserves discussion at the outset is the fact that, in the classrooms described in this book, the teachers were White and the students mostly Black and Latino, and the teachers were of more privileged socioeconomic status than most of the students. This is a common situation in contemporary urban schools (Fuller, 1994).

Students from diverse racial, ethnic, and socioeconomic groups often bring distinct, culturally nurtured attributes to their classrooms. These can include communication patterns, cognitive and affective strengths, learning styles, and values (Hale-Benson, 1982; Heath, 1983; Murrell, 1993). Since experiences and values are both central to the formation of standards, "cultural discontinuities" (Ogbu, 1982) between students' home and school environments are significant to processes of classroom standard setting that involve students. Nonetheless, in this particular study they are not my primary focus.

The standards that I discuss in this book pertain to aspects of student performance such as spending time on school projects, acquiring information, and developing understandings of humanities content. Teachers wanted students to achieve in these areas. At root, teachers' goals of this nature were considered worthy by students, as well as by students' families. Regarding the more specific differences among teachers' and students' standards, furthermore, racial, ethnic, and class differences were far from determinative. Students and teachers within as well as across cultural groups experience disagreements similar to those that existed at Powell.

The literature about "culturally relevant pedagogy" or "culturally responsive pedagogy" (Boykin, 1994; Ladson-Billings, 1994; Murrell, 1993; Nieto, 1999) generally does not call into question the appropriateness, for students of color, of academic goals such as those held by Powell teachers. Rather, it emphasizes how teachers can make the classroom context supportive for those students' achievement of such goals.

It would be wrong, though, to regard cultural responsiveness simply as a route to the attainment of academic standards and as having no bearing on the nature of the standards themselves. Culturally responsive teaching, as described by the authors cited above, involves recognizing strengths that students have and building on those strengths in instruction. It also involves recognizing how the political, economic, and historical realities surrounding students' lives make certain subject matter, questions about the world, and issues of identity development especially significant to those students. When teachers use knowledge of students' lives in these ways, it will affect what teachers value and validate as good work and what they consider important to work on. It will also affect standards as they reside in and develop through students' activity.

By the same token, the distance between Powell teachers' and students' ways of thinking about, talking about, and approaching schoolwork—and between the standards reflected therein—surely had some roots in the different cultural and material contexts of their lives. I wish to acknowledge, then, that racial, ethnic, and socioeconomic differences can add a significant layer to the process of negotiation, and also that they can make the understanding and empathy that support effective teaching more difficult to achieve. All the same, I do not use those differences to explain the negotiations that are shown in this book. Such cultural explanations would be extremely slippery and in some instances simply off target. They could misrepresent effects of the age and experience differences that characterize all secondary school teacher–student relationships. They would tend, furthermore, to erect false boundaries between cultures. Identifying certain standards with one group and not others, for instance, would mean viewing cultures as less multifaceted and less fluid than they in fact are (Nieto, 1999).

It is also important to note that the White teachers at Powell were, I believe, respectful of how their role as teachers involved the building of cross-cultural bridges. This did not eliminate cultural tension between them and their students. It did facilitate their participation in a multicultural environment.

DATA COLLECTION

I first worked at the Earl Powell High School, teaching a writing class, during the 1992–1993 school year. In September 1993, the director invited me to document the school's experience with humanities exhibitions over the upcoming year. My work was to be part of a larger staff development effort around the school's emerging alternative assessment practices.

As a way of carrying out this project, I co-taught a tenth- and eleventh-grade humanities class with Diane Jennifer, a veteran teacher who had taught at Powell since its inception. I also participated as a faculty member in humanities department meetings and retreats. My research focused most intensely on our class and extended to all the school's other humanities classes as well. It consisted of observations, conversations, the recording of student presentations on videotape, interviews with students and teachers, and my own experiences teaching.

The sets of data that these methods produced, and on which this book is based, are as follows. In daily field notes, I described events in Diane's and my class, with special focus on my interactions with students around their work. Also documented in these notes are department meetings; informal, out-of-class conversations with teachers and students; and exhibitions that I observed but was unable to videotape. I observed exhibitions in each of the school's seven humanities classes—a total of 176 exhibitions by 98 different students—and of these, I videotaped 105 by 71 students. I was present for all the exhibitions (48) in our class. There were six students in our class who attended throughout the year and presented each of the four times they were required to do so, and I video-taped each of them three times. I also saved copies of student written work from our class, including nine students' portfolios as submitted at the end of each marking term.

In addition, I audiotaped one interview apiece with 17 students who were in humanities classes other than the one I co-taught. Of these 17, I observed 10 perform at least one exhibition as well. I also taped one inter-view with Diane and two apiece with my other three humanities depart-ment colleagues. In all of the interviews, I posed questions, concerning how students and teachers viewed exhibition work and what they had experienced, that specifically related to standards.

OUTLINE OF THE BOOK

Part I follows, with Chapter 2 providing more background for the study. Chapters 3 through 6 consist of portraits of four individual students, in Diane's and my humanities class, preparing and performing ex-hibitions throughout the course of the school year. These chapters are intended to ground the discussions of standards in the subsequent chap-ters, by providing a detailed picture of a Powell classroom and the work that took place in it. These chapters also identify and illustrate some key principles concerning how standards are negotiated.

Part II then analyzes the standards in Powell humanities classrooms and the process of negotiation. It looks at the standards of both students and teachers, and it describes how standards developed in an interactive classroom environment. Each of Chapters 7 through 11 considers a partic-ular element of classroom standards and/or a particular way in which standards formed. Then, Chapter 12 revisits the five theories of standard setting discussed earlier in this chapter. Following that, a brief Epilogue revisits the four students portrayed in Part I, 5 years later.

PART I

Observing Standards in Context

The humanities classes and exhibitions at Earl Powell High School constituted a particular context for the negotiation of standards. Students approached their work with certain skills and inclinations, and teachers structured the work and interacted with students in certain ways. Detailed knowledge of such particulars makes possible a clearer understanding of how standards were negotiated.

What did students' exhibition performances look like? What actual contents underlay whatever general descriptors might be applied to those performances? How did the performances reflect traits of the students? How did they reflect teacher–student interactions? What classroom activity led to the performances? The student portraits in Chapters 3 through 6 address these matters.

In addition, these portraits offer an initial look at the process of negotiation. They show students being influenced by teachers, in terms of what they tried to achieve. At the same time, they show activity being shaped by student intentions, abilities, and interests. Within exhibition projects, decisions about what to focus on and how much work to do were students' as well as teachers'.

Chapter 2 provides background in terms of the theory and practice of exhibitions and the structure of the Powell humanities course. Then, Chapters 3 through 6 each portray one student, through condensed narratives of the four exhibitions that he or she produced over the course of the year. These narratives show oral presentations made by the student, along with his or her preparation for them. The portions of the presentations and prior activity selected for the narratives illustrate the characteristic features of the student's work, the purposes he or she expressed when doing the work, the teacher–student interactions that occurred around the work, and the interactions among peers that occurred during the presentations. Each chapter's set of narratives also shows some key aspects of the negotiation of standards.

2

Exhibitions and Humanities at Powell

As a preface to the portraits in the next four chapters, this chapter first provides background regarding the pedagogical practice—exhibitions—shown in this book: how key theorists have conceived of exhibitions and how exhibitions evolved at the Earl Powell High School. Then it describes the humanities course at Powell, the exhibition assignments that students were given in 1993–1994, and the assessment practices used by teachers. Finally, it comments on the ways in which the four students portrayed in Part I represent their classmates.

EXHIBITIONS IN THEORY

By having their students perform exhibitions, Powell humanities teachers were putting into practice an idea given prominence by the Coalition of Essential Schools within that organization's approach to school reform. The Coalition of Essential Schools' rationales and visions for exhibitions provide a conceptual context for the efforts at Powell.

As promoted by the Coalition of Essential Schools, exhibitions are intended to be a more meaningful form of assessment than the conventional tests they supplant: a way for teachers and students to gain a better view of what students are learning and accomplishing. They are also intended to foster greater student learning, by involving work that is more engaging and by placing greater emphasis on certain skills of inquiry, reflection, and presentation. They are therefore an attempt to raise classroom standards.

Through their contact with the Coalition of Essential Schools, Powell teachers and administrators encountered a general set of ideas pertaining to exhibitions, rather than exact procedures to follow. This is in part because the Coalition of Essential Schools, as a matter of policy, does not supply its member schools with detailed curricular and instructional blueprints, believing it is important for schools to shape their own practices. It is also because, in the case of exhibitions, the Coalition of Essential Schools began with a broad concept, which needed to be put into concrete form through the experiences of schools.

In its "Nine Common Principles," the Coalition of Essential Schools refers to exhibitions as "the students' demonstration that they can do important things" (Sizer, 1984, p. 226). Exhibitions have taken different shapes in different schools. In general, though, exhibitions are characterized by students working on projects over periods of time, being expected to show their own understandings and/or applications of what they have learned, presenting the results of their work to live audiences, and fielding questions from adults and/or peers.

The Coalition of Essential Schools also proposes that a high school diploma be contingent on a successful final exhibition. Such culminating exhibitions would build on practices established in earlier grades.

Exhibitions, as described in Coalition of Essential Schools literature, are typically integrated with instruction and involve work that students and teachers do together. Grant Wiggins (1989), who served as assessment consultant to the Coalition of Essential Schools during its formative years (in the 1980s), states, "The exhibition of mastery is as much a process as a final product, if not more so" (p. 43). According to Joseph McDonald (1991a), another key person in the Coalition of Essential Schools' early efforts around exhibitions, it is appropriate for teachers, when assessing an exhibition, to consider a student's research efforts and written work along with his or her oral presentation or other public performance.

Like precise models of exhibitions, precise targets for student performance are not disseminated by the Coalition of Essential Schools to its member schools. However, in the minds of those who conceived and have promoted them, exhibitions are clearly intended to provide an occasion and a stimulus for particular kinds of student work.

Theodore Sizer (1992), founding director of the Coalition of Essential Schools, summarizes his vision of exhibition work when he writes that through exhibitions, students are "to practice the art of using their minds well." That art, to him, involves "using" knowledge rather that simply acquiring it. It also involves displaying certain "habits": centrally, "the habit of thoughtfulness, of having an informed, balanced, and responsibly skeptical approach to life" (p. 69). McDonald (1991a), similarly, invokes the idea of students "using" their knowledge when he writes that exhibitions call for students to "have more than textbook knowledge of the major subjects they have studied, [and be able to] apply 'content' to investigations of the important issues of their time" (p. 1).

Wiggins (1989) speaks of student work, as it takes on these qualities, coming to resemble "expert" performance:

> The final exit-level exhibition reveals whether a would-be graduate can demonstrate control over the skills of inquiry and expression and control over an intellectual topic that approximates the expert's ability to use knowledge effectively and imaginatively. (p. 43)

Another concept integral to Sizer's, McDonald's, and Wiggins's visions of exhibition performances is put forth in the Coalition of Essential Schools' "Nine Common Principles": "The governing practical metaphor of the school should be student-as-worker" (Sizer, 1984, p. 226). McDonald calls the "student-as-worker" notion a "focus on student production" (1991a, p. 1). A publication from Central Park East Secondary School in New York City, the Coalition of Essential Schools' most renowned member school, explains "student-as-worker" in a way that emphasizes a certain kind of student involvement: "Learning is not an observer sport. Students must be active participants and active citizens, discovering answers and solutions, and learning by doing rather than by simply repeating what texts or teachers say" (quoted in Darling-Hammond et al., 1995, p. 25).

Wiggins and McDonald both elaborate further on the kinds of student exhibition work they envision. Such work is notable for the extent and nature of the student effort involved, as well as for the depth and scope of thought it contains. Wiggins (1989) writes:

> An exhibition challenges students to show off not merely their knowledge but their initiative; not merely their problem solving but their problem posing; not just their learning on cue, but their ability to judge how to learn on an open-ended problem, often of their own design. (p. 43)

McDonald (1991b) mentions similar skills, along with the integration of knowledge from different disciplines:

> To address the question "How pure is Baltimore's water?" (as one exhibitor . . . recently did), one may reasonably explore chemistry, engineering, biology, geology, politics, public health, public policy in general, and even history, literature, philosophy, and the arts. And to address the question well, one will have to know how to do some things that are the province of none of these subjects alone—for example, how to use a question like a search-

light and like a knife, how to keep track of emerging insight, . . . and so on. (pp. 6–7)

The goals expressed by Coalition of Essential Schools personnel contain principles that could form the basis of standards for student work. These goals were not, however, sufficiently grounded in the actual work in Powell classrooms to represent the standards there. They were, rather, the ideas of theorists external to those classrooms. Also, if these goals were to function as classroom standards, the attributes of the student work envisioned would have to become more specifically defined.

It is nonetheless relevant to consider these goals in the context of this study. Not only do they bear a historical relationship to exhibitions, but in addition Powell teachers were aware of them and embraced their general thrust. These goals entered into the teachers' thinking about what they were doing and why they were doing it. They loom in the background, so to speak, as what the classroom standards might have become were it not necessary for negotiations to take place.

Another factor distancing the above goals from the 1993–1994 Powell humanities exhibitions is the nature of the projects assigned to students. The "expert" and multidisciplinary performances Wiggins and McDonald outline are imagined in the context of final senior exhibitions—as signifying the completion of high school and involving as much as a year's work on a particular project. The Powell exhibitions described in this study were smaller-scale events at earlier stages of students' high school careers, and students were not expected to produce the fully elaborated performances Wiggins and McDonald suggest. Still, those performances represent a direction toward which Powell teachers hoped to be moving with the exhibitions in their classrooms.

HISTORY OF POWELL EXHIBITIONS

The 1993–1994 school year, when the research for this book took place, represents one point in the evolution of the practice of exhibitions at the Earl Powell High School.

During the previous 3 years, teachers had experimented with various forms of exhibitions. In 1991, for instance, each graduating senior was required to present and defend, in a formal exit interview, pieces of work done during the year. From this and other early experiences, teachers and administrators saw ways that exhibitions might benefit the ongoing work in their classes. Students appeared quite motivated for their presentations, and teachers could view aspects of students' knowledge and understanding that were less visible on pencil-and-paper assessments. Students' opportunities to choose the content of their exhibitions also coincided with the director's interest in project-based pedagogy.

By 1992–1993, Powell teachers had begun holding exhibitions in their classes at intervals throughout the year. As this practice was being implemented, the director spoke often of the eventual goal of having students "graduate by exhibition," as in the Coalition of Essential Schools' scenario—rather than graduating according to points accumulated for courses passed, the method that was followed throughout the city school system. He saw the smaller-scale and smaller-stakes exhibitions being staged in Powell classes as both valuable in their own right, and useful toward the longer-term objective by helping to build teacher and student understandings of what exhibitions are and how they might be done well.

In 1995–1996, Powell established a "Senior Institute," modeled after that at Central Park East Secondary School. Students were required to present and defend portfolios of work in different subject areas, before graduation committees, in order to graduate. The structure of a system of "graduation by exhibition" was in place. Adjustments in the form and frequency of in-class exhibitions continued to be made, during that year and subsequently.

It is important to point out that the word *exhibition* can be used to denote both an event when students present before a live audience and the overall project that includes that event. As the word was most frequently used among Powell students and teachers, it meant the former. However, it was used in the latter sense as well, and in some instances the boundary between the two meanings was blurred. Readers are alerted to note the context in which the word appears in this book.

HUMANITIES CURRICULUM AND EXHIBITION ASSIGNMENTS

Powell's humanities course combines the content and skills conventionally taught in separate English and history/social studies classes. All Powell students must take humanities each year. In 1993–1994, most of the students, excepting the ninth graders, did so in classes that included students from more than one grade.

The humanities teachers in 1993–1994 engaged in curriculum planning as a department. As a result, the large topics of study and major assignments—including the exhibitions—were the same in all humanities classes. The curriculum would change for each of the next 3 years, with the 4-year cycle of topics then to be repeated.

There were five terms in all in 1993–1994, each lasting approximately

8 weeks. At the beginning of each term, the students would be presented with a unit guide: a single sheet of paper with information printed on both sides. Included in the unit guide would be the essential questions for the term (see below), a listing of the (five to ten) written assignments that would constitute the term's portfolio, and the main requirements for the term's exhibition. The department tried different formats for exhibitions in the different terms. There was no exhibition in the fifth term.

For the entire first term and half of the second, humanities classes used the Facing History and Ourselves curriculum, which focuses on Nazi Germany and the Jewish Holocaust (Strom & Parsons, 1982). During this time, students were presented with information, and/or asked to explore ideas, through a variety of means: novels, shorter readings, class discussions, guest speakers, videos, writing assignments, and analytic exercises. For their first-term exhibitions, students presented "propaganda campaigns" to their classes. This assignment used one aspect of the history of Nazi Germany—Hitler's use of propaganda—as a point of entry, rather than attempting to encompass the unit topic more comprehensively. Each student was asked to promote a position on a controversial issue. Students' campaigns had four required elements: a poster or video; a slogan; a logo; and a poem, song, or rap. This was a shorter-term project than the other exhibitions. During the week before the exhibitions were held, in-class activities focused on helping students identify topics and prepare for their presentations. Students presented their campaigns to their classmates during the last week of October. In Diane's and my class, these presentations lasted 3 to 5 minutes apiece.

In the second term, the Facing History curriculum was concluded shortly before Thanksgiving. The remainder of the term, which ended at Christmas break, was devoted to the production of student research papers. All class time was designated for work on this project: for periodic structured activities and for students to use the school library, read, compose, confer with teachers, and type in the school's computer lab. Teachers were concerned with teaching the skills of doing a research paper rather than with a particular area of content. We circulated lists of potential topics, which were grouped under "People," "Events/Issues," and "Other Ethnic Conflicts or Civil Wars"; most students chose from this list, although they were not required to do so. Rather than have the students give oral presentations of their completed research during the last week of the term, teachers called for 5- to 10-minute "research-in-progress" reports during the second week of December, so that the questions and feedback students received might benefit them as they prepared their final written products. Compared to the other terms' oral presentations, these were conducted more informally and affected term grades less.

Teachers referred to these oral presentations as "exhibitions" and at the same time viewed the papers as the central student products—as the "exhibitions" in that sense.

In the third term, the humanities classes studied the history of slavery and the U.S. Civil War. For his or her exhibition, each student was directed to pick a topic related to what we were studying and teach a lesson to the class about it. Diane and I first elaborated on the instructions to this assignment, in class, during the third week of the term. Throughout the remainder of the term, we continued having whole-class activities through which students might gain a base of knowledge about slavery and the Civil War. As in the earlier terms, some of these activities provided occasion for the teaching of reading and writing skills as well. One or two days per week, we spent some time on exercises specifically related to the exhibition or conferred with students individually as they worked on their exhibitions and other portfolio assignments. In our class, regular sessions with a visiting artist occupied a significant amount of class time during this term; as a consequence, the students did not present their slavery/Civil War lessons until the second and third weeks of March, shortly after the fourth term had begun. These presentations were around 25 minutes in length.

During the fourth term, the classes studied the U.S. civil rights movement. The texts we used most prominently were the *Eyes on the Prize* video series (Hampton, 1986) and Anne Moody's novel *Coming of Age in Mississippi* (1968). Students' major project for the term was to conduct an interview with an older person who remembered, or perhaps had participated in, this movement. Students wrote "oral history reports," and their exhibitions took the form of panel discussions. In panels of four to seven, students briefly summarized what they had learned from their interviews and then fielded questions. Over the last month of the term, teachers devoted some class time to this project while proceeding with other work as well. The panel discussions took place during the first week of May. They were around 50 minutes long.

In the fifth and final term, the classes studied the Vietnam War. Instead of working on new exhibition projects, students prepared final portfolios, which included work from throughout the year.

In planning each unit, the department framed a set of "essential questions." Essential questions are a curricular feature advocated by the Coalition of Essential Schools, which envisions them as focal points for student inquiry. Essential questions are "larger questions that can go to the heart of a discipline" (Coalition of Essential Schools, 1989, p. 3), and they are questions that suggest exploration. Powell humanities teachers listed five to eight essential questions on each term's unit guide. Examples included: How do leaders get power? How do people face and fight destructive beliefs, powers, and prejudices? How can you judge the "rightness" of a belief? What civil rights are worth fighting for? Some questions, such as the first three, were used in more than one term. Teachers referred to these questions in various activities and in various interactions with students over the course of a term.

ASSESSMENT PROCEDURES

For the 1993–1994 school year, the humanities department did not develop formal procedures or tools for scoring exhibitions. Reflecting the locus of our concerns, teachers' conversation was much less likely to focus on issues of evaluation than on how exhibitions might be designed and conducted so as to have the greatest instructional value. Only in the third term did Diane and I assign letter grades, or any formal ratings, to our students' oral presentations.

Students did receive grades on each term's report card, though, and exhibitions did figure into the grading process. First of all, to pass terms one through four a student had to complete all the written assignments required for the term's portfolio, and present an exhibition. Teachers then considered the exhibition alongside the portfolio to determine students' report card grades. We graded the entire portfolios holistically—putting comments, and sometimes checks, check-plusses, and check-minuses, on the individual pieces. We then decided whether the exhibition should raise, lower, or maintain the grade of the portfolio. The exhibitions did not count for an exact percentage of students' term grades, but they were weighted more heavily than the average portfolio assignment. This process was somewhat different in the second term, when the research papers were students' final "exhibition" products and their major written assignment. We graded those papers separately, and then considered students' other portfolio work alongside them.

While formal assessment of exhibitions was not a major focus of teachers' efforts, informal assessment was occurring constantly. Teachers' observations and thoughts about the strengths and weaknesses of student work are an important part of the story presented in this book.

FOUR PORTRAITS AND A LARGER PICTURE

Every individual student is unique. Thus no set of four students can be fully representative of a broader student body. Nonetheless, the portraits of Wayne Gallaton, Gloria Ruiz, Pierre Cyrille, and Anwar Martin are intended to be illustrative as well as distinct. Qualities of these students' performances—the content knowledge they displayed, the analyses they offered, the reading and writing skills they demonstrated, their responses to the task of presenting before their peers, how they planned and executed research projects—resembled what appeared in other students' work throughout the school. Issues that these students and their teachers confronted while preparing for exhibition presentations arose with other students. Furthermore, these four students illustrate diversity that existed among the student performances in our class: different levels of effort, competence, commitment to a project, and comfort before an audience; and various reading, writing, and speaking skills, including those associated with learning English as a non-native language.

One way in which Wayne, Gloria, Pierre, and Anwar were not a representative subset of the students in our class is that they each completed all four of the year's exhibition assignments. Our class roll fluctuated around a mean of 17, with 12 students attending consistently throughout the year while others attended sporadically and/or transferred into or out of the school or class. Of the 12, only 6 completed all four exhibitions. Nonparticipation is not represented in these portraits, though, because the focus of the study is on how standards were negotiated when the work was being done. Furthermore, issues of student commitment to the work, and their relation to standards, still appear in these portraits, as they would if nonparticipants were portrayed.

In fitting with the human complexity of the four students, each of the next four chapters shows performances and interactions with a variety of characteristics, and illustrates multiple points related to the formation and operation of standards. Nonetheless, there are central themes in each chapter, which are highlighted in the opening and closing sections.

3

Wayne

Wayne Gallaton was in the tenth grade in 1993–1994. He was on the whole the strongest student in Diane's and my class, given the combination of regularity and quality with which he did his assignments. This account of Wayne's exhibitions shows a student meeting some of his teachers' goals for exhibition performances. It also shows how Wayne, by meeting those goals in particular ways and by framing some of his own goals as well, participated in the negotiation of classroom standards.

WAYNE'S EXHIBITIONS

First Term

On the day of Wayne's propaganda presentation, as on most days, four long tables were arranged in the center of room M-101 so that they formed the perimeter of a square. As Wayne assumed his position in front of the room, seven students sat around the outside of the square, at the three tables from which they could face him. Three more students filled seats in the space inside the square. Diane and I sat among the students, at different tables from one another. An adult visitor sat along one side wall, and Paul, a student from another class, sat against the wall opposite her, tilting back on his chair's rear legs.

Wayne's poster was taped to the room's front wall. A drawing of an 80-ounce bottle of beer occupied the center of the poster, and there was writing above, below, and along both sides of the drawing. Wayne stood next to the poster and faced the class.

"All right," he said. "Yeah, mine's is on beer, and it's promoting it—it's more like an advertisement. I'll read you what it says." He turned sideways and tilted his head slightly upward to read the poster. "It says, 'What comes to your mind when Gallaton beer is mentioned? Pure, genuine taste, gratifying, commendable, worthy, excellent, precious, real, valuable, satisfactory, fine, big, enormous, gigantic, huge, extra large, glorious, grand, mm mm good.' And then it says down here, 'For a real good time, for a good time.' It says, 'Gallaton, fine American export, 80-ounce challenge.'" Several students laughed. Wayne explained, "And I was trying to, y'know, point out to young people that—show everybody that this is a good time if you drink beer." He then pointed to two smaller posterboards that were also mounted on the wall. On one, he explained, was a rap he had made by substituting his own lyrics into an existing beer commercial. The other listed some benefits of drinking beer. "'One sip of a good time won't hurt,'" he read from the latter poster. "'Alcoholic beverages taste good, helps you adjust in parties, puts hair on your chest, loosens up, relaxes you, puts you in a problem-free world, makes you forget about your problems.'" He concluded, "And so I didn't, I didn't mention anything, y'know, bad about it. I was just saying all the good things."

Diane asked him if he would read the rap.

Wayne's voice became softer. "No, that won't sound right."

"You don't have to read it like a rap; just read it regular."

"All right," Wayne said. "All right." He proceeded to read the words. The chorus was, "Here's something that's sweeping the nation by surprise. / So if you want some look for those happy guys." After he spoke the last line, he pointed to two smiling faces he had drawn beneath the lyrics and added, "And that's the logo."

Several classmates laughed. Celia said, "That is so cute!" Wayne smiled.

"Okay," Diane said. "It's pretty effective propaganda for a lot of reasons I think." Turning toward the students in the audience, she said, "Can I, can I do this—does anybody else want to say anything?" A few voices indicated for her to continue. Addressing Wayne again, she said, "A lot of reasons. Nice, nice um, sound reasons, like you use a lot of repetition of first letters, and just the word choice on your poster's real nice, I thought. By the end of it you were goin', 'Gigantic, glamorous, good'; I was goin' like, 'Yeah, that sounds nice.'"

"Yeah because um—oh, it's um, it's not like a regular beer like a 40 ounce. It's a 80 ounce," Wayne said.

"No, a regular beer's like a 16 ounce, a big beer," Diane said.

Paul spoke up. "Well, a regular beer that's known to us . . ."

"This is 80," Wayne said.

" . . . a regular beer that's known to some of the boys in here is 40."

"This is 80," Wayne repeated.

"Okay, listen," Diane said. "Y'know what he neglects to say on his poster?"

"What?" said Wayne, momentarily lowering his brows.

"And this is good propaganda, too. It doesn't say, 'And you'll be dead by the time you finish drinking this.' 'Cause it's so much."

Wayne smiled.

The previous week, when we showed the class examples of Hitler's and other propaganda, Diane had pointed out how an important characteristic of propaganda is that it only presents one side of a story. On Friday, when Wayne told me of the idea for his project, he had said, "I'm just going to present the good side of it and not anything bad." Wayne had apparently made note of Diane's explanation of propaganda and pursued a standard that stemmed from what his teacher had told him. At the same time, his and Paul's comments show that the size of the beer bottle carried a significance to them that it did not carry to Diane; in this sense, the students were applying standards of their own to Wayne's project.

Second Term

The second-term exhibition project was a different kind of task from the previous one, in that it revolved around research and writing. On the Monday before Thanksgiving, Diane and I introduced the project to the students and gave them a list of potential topics. Wayne picked "U.S.– Native American Conflict" from this list.

The next day, I brought to class Dee Brown's *Bury My Heart at Wounded Knee* (1970), a one-time bestselling account of several tribes' loss of lands, with the intent of helping Wayne get started. "You want me to read this whole book?" he asked apprehensively. I told him that it contained different stories, about different groups of Native Americans, that he could look at. When he asked the question again, Diane suggested he read the first chapter, at least to begin with. Sampling sections of a 418-page book to discover possible foci within a broad topic, as I had intimated he might do, appeared not to be a strategy to which he was accustomed. He did, later in the period, thumb through a section of pictures and captions in the center of the book.

Over Thanksgiving weekend, Wayne read Chapter 1 of the book and filled an index card and half a sheet of notebook paper with notes. The notes were mostly about Christopher Columbus's early encounters with Native Americans, which are described in the first two pages of the chapter. Wayne also read an encyclopedia article about Native Americans and took another card and a half of notes, mostly about their initial arrival on the American continents.

When he shared his notes with me, I raised the question of how he might narrow his topic from "U.S.–Native American Conflict." Wayne said he had not thought about this. I suggested that one way would be to pick one tribe. He said that his grandmother was part Cherokee, adding that he had looked up "Cherokee" in the index of *Bury My Heart at Wounded Knee* and found them mentioned only on one page. When I mentioned the phrase "Trail of Tears" to him, he said he remembered seeing it on that page. He responded favorably to my suggestion that he find out more about the Cherokees' forced move from the Southeast.

The following day, while sitting at a library table with two classmates and me, he read an encyclopedia article about the Cherokees. "Hey!" he whispered more than once, upon reading a particular sentence. At one such point, he remarked to me about how the Cherokees had been made to move all the way from North Carolina to Oklahoma.

On the next day, he asked me whether, if he wrote four pages that "really went into detail," we would accept a paper of that length (our stated requirement was five pages). I told him we would not, and that he should look in the library for a book in which he could read further.

Research-in-progress exhibitions took place at the end of the following week. By this time, Wayne had also read a chapter, titled "Trail of Tears," from a book about the Cherokees' relocation. From this source and the encyclopedia article, he had assembled some information about the tribe before they moved (he noted, for instance, that they were one of the few Native American tribes to have a written language) and about their trip west. The day before these exhibitions, a class activity directed students to list the points they would make in their presentations. I met with Wayne as he worked on this task, and together we narrowed his subtopics to what the trip was like and why it happened. "But I don't have my information organized on that," he then told me. I responded that this was what he needed to work on. He spent the remainder of the period looking at his notes and writing. At the end of class he said, "We got a lot accomplished today."

For his exhibition, Wayne presented to Diane and five other students. Each listener filled out a sheet that had two headings: "I'd like to know more about" and "I recommend that you." On her sheet, Diane wrote in the first space, "Protest vs. the Trail of Tears; what happened to the children." In the second space, she wrote, "Make a connection to the cattle cars during the Holocaust."

In the remaining 2 weeks of the term, Wayne's efforts were focused on the production aspect of the paper. During class time, all of which we allotted for students to work individually on their projects, he was consistently on-task. He spent several class periods in the school's computer lab, first typing from a handwritten draft and then returning to the word processor after Diane edited the typed draft with him. He typed in as many as 15 rewordings or corrections on a page, following what both Diane and he had written on the draft.

Once he began preparing his final product in this manner, Wayne did not collect more information. The paper included practically all that he had written in his notes, from all four of his sources. It totaled five pages. The first two pages talked about Native Americans in general, and the remainder was about the Cherokees.

An in-class assignment during the first week after Thanksgiving had directed students to compile lists of 10 questions about their topics. These lists were to be submitted in students' portfolios along with the papers. Wayne's questions included, "Why were the Cherokee pushed off of eastern land?" "Why did some Cherokee agree to leave?" "What kind of experience did the Cherokee go through on this journey?" "Did they do anything about it?" and "Did some Cherokee escape 'The Trail of Tears'?"[1] These questions provided a potential focus for his research efforts. Some of them, also, were the sort that could lead to explorations of issues as well as recording of facts.

In his paper, Wayne said most about the third question, concerning the experience of the journey: His last two pages gave details about how the Cherokees traveled, hardships they faced, and deaths that occurred. The issues of what led to the move and how Cherokees reacted received much less attention. The first question, about why the Cherokees were pushed off the land, was answered incidentally in this sentence: "During the 1800s Caucasian settlers demanded that the U.S. government move all southeastern U.S. Indians to areas west of the Mississippi River." The second question, about why Cherokees agreed to leave, was not addressed. Wayne's description of Cherokees "doing anything about it" was a statement that 1,000 people escaped—also an answer to the last question.

I was mindful of the limits in the extent of Wayne's research and analysis as I regarded his work. Wayne showed me another angle from which to view it. While he was working on the paper, he remarked more than once how he was glad to have learned about the Trail of Tears. He had acquired knowledge that he valued because of a connection to his own life. "I'm going to show this to my grandmother," he told me.

---

[1] Throughout this book, students' grammar and spelling are reproduced exactly as they appeared in students' papers, drafts, and notes.

Third Term

Students' third-term exhibition assignment, to prepare a lesson and teach it to the class, entailed another research project. As in the second term, the shaping of this project for Wayne was an interactive process, involving his teachers.

Diane and I explained the parameters of the assignment to the students during the third week of the term. Over the next 3 weeks, we periodically raised the issue of topic selection in class, discussing possibilities with the students and instructing them to turn in sheets of paper with their ideas written on them. During this time, Wayne, like most of his classmates, did not settle on a topic. In mid-February, I met a college student who was working at the city's Museum of Afro-American History, where he gave talks about the local abolitionist movement. He said he would be willing to meet with students from my class. I mentioned this topic and resource to some students as a possible exhibition project, and Wayne took the suggestion.

Wayne and a classmate, Ronald, decided to do the project together. It proved to be a collaborative effort in that the two students jointly interviewed the young historian, watched their videotape of the interview, planned the presentation, and presented to the class. Wayne took the lead, though, in preparing and organizing the information for the presentation and in conducting the exhibition itself. Ronald's input notwithstanding, much of what happened during the course of the project can be understood as Wayne's work.

I had a series of short conversations with the two students, before they did their interview, about preparing for it. I advocated learning something about the subject ahead of time, and gave them a pamphlet from the museum that described several important people and places. In the last of these conversations, I asked them to name some questions they would ask. Wayne suggested, "Who were some of the people involved?" After they had offered no others, he said, "I'll just ask a couple of questions, and then I'll think of more based on what he says."

After Wayne and Ronald did the interview, I asked them what was most interesting about it. Ronald said, "The different incidents," such as one where anti-abolitionists had William Lloyd Garrison dragged through town by a horse. Wayne added how he and Ronald had been shown an alleyway where fugitive slaves used to hide. I asked what else, besides describing these items, they could do in their exhibition. "Give names," Wayne offered.

At this point I wanted to find a way to push them further—and was having difficulty doing so. What could be a good focusing question? The topic did not have clear boundaries within which to dig deeply, nor did it lead to an obvious question to discuss. I wanted them to do more, but what should they do?

When Wayne and I conferred a few days later, he had worked at organizing their information on a sheet of paper. He had written a few names and listed a few incidents. I raised questions, such as What can you say about how the abolitionists functioned as a movement? What can you learn from them about how to fight injustice? What kinds of relationships existed within the movement? These questions brought little response. I then suggested he go into more detail about some of the people. "I don't want to talk all about who William Lloyd Garrison was; that would get boring," Wayne responded, thinking of the lesson he would be teaching. I replied that it was up to him to make it interesting. Then Wayne said, "I don't like to go back and do more research once I've already done it and written it down." I told him that good research required this, and that this would be expected of him later in his educational career. "To go back and do more research?" he asked earnestly. "Yes," I told him.

The next day Wayne came in with a longer list of names from the interview, with a sentence or two of explanation after each one. I read it, and said, "This still looks like a list."

"Aw, c'mon," Wayne said.

"But didn't you say yesterday you didn't want to just give a list?" (He had, at one point, when I was suggesting he get more information for his presentation.)

He allowed that he had.

I groped again for a question that would resonate with him, and ended by telling him his exhibition should show that he had done some thinking about his topic.

Two days later he brought in a paragraph he had written, which contained a few general statements about the abolitionist movement. He mentioned the Fugitive Slave Law, for instance, as an issue that abolitionists faced.

Ronald started their oral presentation by asking the class to write down what they knew about abolitionists in the city. The most common response was "Nothing."

Wayne said, "Alright" and began reading from a four-page, typed script, of which he and Ronald each held a copy. He briefly described how they had researched the topic.

Ronald followed. "And next we're gonna talk about the people." He then read three sentences about Louis Hayden and gave the names of seven other "people included in our exhibition."

Wayne took the next part. He read, "Robert Gould Shaw was commander of the Fifty-fourth Regiment." Then he asked, "Anybody know what that is?"

"The what?" asked Estella.

"Fifty-fourth Regiment. He was commander of the Fifty-fourth Regiment," Wayne said.

Jorge said, "First African, first African regiment in the army."

"Yeah, it's like a military-type thing," Wayne said. He read from his paper again. "Which is the first comprised, comprised of only Blacks. He lived in the Beacon Hill, Beacon Street area at age 25. Eventually being in the Fifty-fourth Regiment he fought in the Civil War." He looked up and said in a more conversational tone, "And uh, that led to his death, which he was killed by a southern military, or the army that represented the South." He returned to his text. "George Middleton led an all-Black company called the Bucks of America. The Bucks of America flag was donated by John Hancock, one of the richest men in the city. He was White. John Hancock," Wayne looked up, "he wasn't an abolitionist but he was a patriot."

Diane interjected. "Was he around the Revolutionary War period?"

"No, about the Civil War period." Wayne resumed reading. "And then there was John J. Smith. John Smith was a small-time businessman that owned a barber shop. He was later a part of the Fifth Calgary and the House of Representatives. And he was Black, so," he gestured to the class with the hand holding the paper, and added a point that was not in the script, "so Blacks did have a little power in that time." He glanced at his page and then looked back to his audience. "In that barber shop he often held community meetings so, in the African Meeting House, that wasn't the only place that community meetings were held. Sometimes they were held at small businesses like John J. Smith's barbershop."

After Ronald took a turn, Wayne read a paragraph that gave a more general overview of their topic: "The struggle against slavery or the abol–, abolishment move–, abolitionist movement, started sometime after the Revolutionary War. This probably because attention was now set off the problem of the United States not being independent and shifted to the next biggest problem which was slavery. Shortly after the, the independence of the, of the country, in 1883, slavery was abolished here but still existed in the South. Blacks here were mostly escaped slaves in 1850, the Fu–, in 1850, the Fugitive Slave Law was enforced. This made it dangerous for escaped slaves to roam around, because they would be——." He explained, "Um, the Fugitive Slave Law said that um, that escaped slaves

that went to the North had to be returned to the South, stuff like that."
He looked back at his script. "Let me see. Uh, to prove that free Blacks
were free they had something called, a card called the freeman's pass. Uh,
that they had to show." He added, looking at his audience, "And it would
actually state that they were um, that they were free. Say if you, if you
were Black and you had a free card, that means that you are free." From
the script, he concluded, "All of this went on until, until the Civil War,
ending in 1865, which was when slavery was abolished throughout the
country."

As part of their third-term exhibitions, presenters were required to
collect from the audience something in writing that represented learning
on the audience's part. Accordingly, Wayne and Ronald asked the class a
series of questions. Wayne read the first one: "Which abolitionist or
people stuck out the most to you in our exhibition?"

"What was that name, the guy that was dragged by the horse?"
asked Estella. Ronald had read a sentence about the incident involving
William Lloyd Garrison. He answered Estella by giving Garrison's name.

All the students present wrote a name down. During the talk they
had been taking notes, per the instructions of our student teacher,
Nancy.[2]

Ronald read the next question: "Do you think having power makes
a lot of difference being an abolitionist, or being a person for slavery?"

"Anybody want to comment on that?" Wayne added. "Do you think,
like, having power makes a difference, or not having power—being like,
in the U.S. Senate like Charles Sumner, or just like starting from scratch
like, like John J. Smith but before he became a Representative? Do you
think there's a difference between power and no power?"

"Yeah, because they could do more," said Danilo.

Wayne nodded.

"Can I offer an opposite view to that?" I asked, hoping to provoke
further examination of the issue Wayne had raised.

"Go ahead," said Wayne.

"I think that like, in order to get in power, a guy like Charles Sumner
might have had to make some deals with people so that maybe, when
push came to shove, he might not've supported the slaves as strongly as
somebody else."

---

[2] Nancy Flannery worked with our class for most of the third term and all
of the fourth. Diane and I remained in the room throughout this time. Nancy
often led class activities; Diane and I continued to work with students on their
individual projects.

"Yeah, he was White and he was an abolitionist. No, wait a second, he was a lawyer, also," Wayne said.

Diane entered. "See, the thing about Sumner, though, that we know is he's the one who pushed all those amendments through. Thirteenth, Fourteenth, Fifteenth Amendment; Sumner was the one who was pushing them. So it's interesting that you should say that John, 'cause he was making those deals"—Wayne began to nod—"but he was making the deals and winning in Congress."

"Yep, y'know, his vote counted," said Wayne.

I resumed. "But I guess the—it's like, okay, the slave, himself or herself, still has another kind of power."

"What do you mean?" Wayne asked.

"Well, if they don't go along with slavery—I mean, if they resist it, eventually it can't happen. Y'know. If they refuse to cooperate, eventually it would cost the slave owners so much time and effort and money, to try to keep them under control, that it wouldn't, it wouldn't work on their part either. So—"

Wayne broke in. "I think that's kind of easy controllin' 'em. 'Cause you can—just like in the Holocaust you can shoot one, one person and make everybody else scared and make 'em do what you want 'em to do, 'cause they don't want to be, y'know, the next example."

I continued. "I guess, I guess though but, like if you're talking about a movement of people, like it seems like the common people—this is an opinion, you can argue back with me—but I think the strength of a movement is in the masses. I mean, the civil rights movement eventually became what it was because you had many people just down there marching, ordinary people."

Wayne brought me back to the question as he had originally formulated it. "But do you think that um, that being like, being a U.S. Senator, or lawyer or something like that, do you think that—is that helpful?"

I granted that it was.

Wayne's next question—about John Coburn, a man who ran a gaming house and donated money to abolitionists—pulled classmates into the conversation. "What did you all think about that dude that was doing stuff illegally?" he asked.

A number of students spoke simultaneously. "Huh?" "How did he get—" "What did he do?" "Was he Black or White?"

"He was Black." Wayne faced a group of male students on one side of the room and explained. "And he owned a gaming house, and y'know everybody, the mayor and all them—and they came chillin' up in there, y'know, gettin' the prostitutes and the drugs and everything."

Estella asked, "But he made—did he make his money just to give it to the abolitionists?"

"No," Wayne said. "He would support himself, his, like his little illegal business, and then he gave stuff to um, the abolitionists."

"So when you look at it," Bruce said, "he was doin' somethin' bad, but he was still doin' somethin' good."

"Yeah," Wayne said. "And that's just like, do you see this like um, being like a drug dealer? You have to support your family and, but you, you know you're doing something illegal, but still you gotta support yourself and your family."

"Yeah," said Estella.

Wayne's and Ronald's next question referred to an incident they had mentioned earlier, in which anti-abolitionists had interrupted a speech by Frederick Douglass and pushed him down the stairs of a church. "What would you have done if you was pushed down the stairs by a group of people, while you was giving a speech?" Wayne asked. This led to another discussion, involving both teachers and students.

I wanted to ask Wayne and Ronald some questions that required them to draw some generalizations about the abolitionist movement. However, the class period, and the 25 minutes we had allotted to the exhibition, expired before I had a chance to do so. It occurred to me that by being confident enough to proceed smoothly with their program, and then by raising some issues for discussion that engaged both teachers and students, Wayne and Ronald had determined what was talked about.

Fourth Term

For his civil rights oral history project, Wayne interviewed his godmother's husband, who had participated in sit-ins in Nashville, Tennessee. He presented on the first of our two panel discussion days.

When asked to give a brief opening statement, Wayne explained whom he had interviewed and added, "And, things that he had to say were like, that the civil rights movement didn't have so much of an effect on uh, on Whites being racist. Or any racism. Only um, only civil rights. It didn't have any—he thinks it didn't have anything to do with oppression. And that, and that it moved in a slow pace."

As the session proceeded, Wayne was questioned directly by teachers on a few occasions, and his responses revealed more of what he had learned.

An open-ended question from Nancy gave Wayne an occasion to share some fairly detailed information. She asked him what the most intriguing part of his interview was; Wayne answered that his godmother (who had been present at the interview) had told him she had known Emmett Till in Chicago. Wayne went on to describe Emmett Till's wake, as his godmother had recalled it: "She said there was grown men passin' out in the street. Uh, she also said the body was like, it wasn't even embalmed. And um. She said that it was the first time she saw her, her father turn colors, like really be affected by anything. So it really, like touched people."

Nancy followed up. "What um, did she say what [Emmett Till] was like at all?"

"What he was like. Uh, she said, well she said that, according to her that he was, he was kind of slow. He um, talked weird, y'know like a whisper and stuttering, like that. And that he didn't, he didn't bother anybody. He wouldn't seem the type that would be so, um, heroic. Or— no, uh, bold enough to say something to a White woman."

At another point, I asked Wayne to tell more about his interviewee's civil rights activities. In his response, Wayne mentioned that the protests had not always been violent. Diane, having seen a draft of his written report, recalled an insight he had articulated there and saw an opportunity to elicit it.

"Say that thing about the um, the protest being peaceful," she said. "You were starting to talk about that."

"Oh, not always that um—not every time they um, protested would the Whites act violent. That's what I was saying. Not all the time they acted violent."

"Right," Diane said. She then referred to his written report. "And you had talked a little bit about how *Eyes on the Prize* [Hampton, 1986], it just makes it look like it was just one big fight."

"Uh, yeah I mention that uh, that if I didn't know anything about the civil rights movement and I looked at a videotape I would think it was, all of it was, like exciting. And it always got to the news, and stuff like, things like that. And no attention was brought off of it. But, um, but hearing what he was saying, it wasn't always um, so violent and exciting."

I then brought up an issue that Wayne, apparently, had not focused on in his interview or subsequent reflections. I asked him if Whites had given in to what his godmother's husband was "asking for"; if he and his fellow protesters had gotten "what they wanted."

"Yes," Wayne answered.

"How did that happen, how did that—"

"What are you talk–"

"Okay, you said, well you said there was a sit-in, for instance, right? So, their goal was to get the lunch counter to desegregate."

"Uh huh."

"Did the lunch counter desegregate, and how did, how did it go down that they actually decided to do that?"

Wayne's answer was unclear to me, as my question apparently was to him. "Well he didn't describe how they go, go down or somethin', but it did. But it did. He said, he had mentioned that it did. That, that y'know he had felt proud that he, of what he was doing even if it didn't. He felt proud of like fighting for himself."

The next day Wayne was in the audience while six other students presented, and a question he asked catalyzed a discussion that involved the whole panel. His question approached the topic of the civil rights movement in a way that connected to his own interests and his class-mates' as well. As panelists spoke, they used information they had ac-quired during the term and also reflected on their personal perspectives.

"I'd like to ask all of y'all," Wayne said, "would you choose nonvio-lent, or violent, when it came down to defending yourself when, like when crowds would be around you?"

Jorge, who was seated at one end of the panel, answered first: "It depends." Both Wayne and Diane questioned him further, and Jorge said that if someone hit him, he would probably hit back.

Gloria then joined the discussion. She spoke about the 1960s protest-ers and their nonviolent approach: "Like if they've trained for it, I mean then it's cool but like, we, the way we think now, today? You can't just let somebody hit you and not react—that's like in your nature to react vio-lently no matter what."

Diane asked Danilo, who was seated next to Jorge, to take a turn with the question. Danilo described an incident in which he had been attacked by a group of people and fought back.

"That's a street fight," Diane observed. "But [we're] talking about a fight about a political issue."

"I'm talkin' about in the movement," Wayne added.

"I would fight," said Danilo.

Pierre, seated next to Danilo, had the next turn. "I'd probably choose nonviolent because, if I react back—. If I'm by myself, right? Like—if I'm by myself, I can't do nothin' about it. So."

Wayne said, "No, I'm talking about period—like if, if you wasn't with a group, a group or nothin', but like a racist White was tryin' to get you from the sit-in and they come up there, and they hit you. They just hit you real hard and loud."

"I'd fight back," said Pierre.

"'Real hard and loud.' This is funny," said Gloria. Others laughed with her.

"Yeah, everything gets silent before and after," said Wayne.

"Yeah, I'd fight back," said Pierre.

"Okay, would the people organizing that protest want you at that counter?" Diane asked.

"No," said Pierre.

"Yeah, because he's with a violent now," said Wayne.

"They don't want you messin' up the protest," said Gloria.

"Just personally, it's personally," Wayne said. "Not with them being under King's supervision. I'm talking about personally."

"Mm," Diane said.

"It's like, that sit-in was like, nonviolent, you had to control yourself," said Danilo. "I wouldn't even put myself in that type of situation, to let myself get, y'know, beat up and everything. I couldn't do that."

A seventh student, Fred, arrived and joined the panel while this discussion was going on. Diane eventually turned to him and said, "How about you?" He asked for clarification of the scenario being discussed, which Wayne provided.

Fred continued, "I mean back then, back in the civil rights movement?"

"Yeah," said Wayne.

"I wouldn't hit him back."

"No, I'm not talking about with a group of, of White people just surround you, surround you like, 'What you gonna do?' like that. Like if somebody just, came by and they saw you protestin', and hit you," Wayne said.

"Y'know like throwin' rocks," added Danilo.

"I'd keep goin'," Fred said.

"You wouldn't hit him?" Wayne pursued.

"No."

"Why not?" Wayne asked.

"Because, I mean if I was in the same state of mind they was in, y'know back in those days, I probably wouldn't know how to react. Because there wouldn't have been no threat to my life anyway, because, y'know, I'm doing what I believe in. So therefore it's like um—I wouldn't know how, I mean I wouldn't know how to react on a violent level. Y'know what I'm saying, I could handle it more in a better way, just by, y'know what I'm saying, protestin' what I believe in, than fight back and get myself in trouble."

Danilo addressed Fred. "What about in *Eyes on the Prize* [Hampton, 1986], remember when that dude got hit with the brick behind the head, by the White dude when he was walking? What would you do in that situation, would you just keep on walking?"

"In the state of mind today, today," Jorge added.

"See now, I thought that's what you're talking about: now," said Gloria.

Wayne said, "But there was people, there was people that thought like us now though. Like people that were down with the Black Panthers."

Gloria then turned to Fred. "If it was now do you think you would react violently to—nowadays?"

"No," Fred answered.

"No?" said Gloria. "You would just go for what you believe in and just keep walking?"

"Yes I would, let me stop lyin'," Fred said with a laugh. "Yeah I would, yes I would."

The discussion lasted more than 14 minutes, and was the most animated part of a class period that Diane and I both felt was, in its entirety, unusual for the degree and spirit of participation. Wayne established standards in the sense that he identified what about the topic the panel would find most engaging to talk about. In addition, the discussion he sparked demonstrated possibilities for collective inquiry in our class, and represented standards in that sense as well.

CLOSING THOUGHTS

In the context of exhibitions, Wayne met the responsibility for completing tasks, and took the assignments, and his own ideas, seriously in a public way. He became more practiced at habits such as identifying questions, producing schoolwork that integrated his own thoughts with content knowledge, and leading discussions. In these respects, he showed the kinds of achievements that teachers intended for exhibitions to encourage.

Through exhibitions—even short-term, small-stakes exhibitions such as ours—students might have done more research, become more knowledgeable, and done more extensive synthesis and analysis of their material than Wayne did. Yet the meaning of concepts such as "student-as-worker" and "thoughtful habits," *as those concepts were brought to life in our classroom,* was defined not by what students might have done, or by what students elsewhere have done, but by work such as Wayne's.

4

Gloria

Gloria Ruiz was in the tenth grade. In her exhibitions, she demonstrated some of the same strengths that Wayne did. She spoke, at times, to the meaning of her material, and "thought on her feet" to generate responses to questions. She was less consistent as a worker than Wayne, though. While to some extent the standards realized in her performances concerned skills she displayed regardless of how much work she had done, they also pertained to the products that she took the time to produce. Her decisions about whether and how to expend her energy were of central importance.

GLORIA'S EXHIBITIONS

First Term

On the day before exhibitions were scheduled to begin, students, in class, were working on their projects in various ways. Some were designing logos or decorating posters; others were composing raps or speeches. Gloria and four other young women formed a group for most of the period, creating and practicing songs for three of the students' presentations. As Gloria, whose exhibition was scheduled for 3 days hence, prepared to leave the room, she told me she did not have a topic yet. I asked her if she had considered any. She mentioned abortion, but said she did not want to do her exhibition on that topic because she did not want people in the class attacking her position and because she did not want to come off as a community moralist, so to speak. I asked if there was something she saw every day that was not fair. Age discrimination, she answered: 14-year-olds can't get a job. I said that could make a good topic. She was doubtful. "I'd have to have a slogan," she said.

By the day of her presentation, Gloria had chosen a topic and devised a campaign.

Gloria stood in front of the class with a sheet of paper in her left hand and a poster in her right. On her poster she had pasted three pictures cut out from a magazine. On the left side of the poster was a photo featuring a woman. The woman was leaning back, from a standing position, with one leg suggestively draped around a man; the man, partially hidden, was leaning forward and kissing her neck while supporting her with a hand around her waist. The other two photos, on the right side of the poster, were of men. In one, the man was shirtless, with well outlined chest muscles. The other, as Gloria later explained, showed "a man with his little butt sticking out. You don't see the front; you just see the back."

Gloria waved the poster in front of her and announced, "Equality in televised sex."

"What's that?" asked Anwar.

She turned to face him. "That's like, y'know, they always showin' the female parts and—you always see females be put down, like that, and you don't see the men."

She then read from her paper: "Do you notice that every time there is an intimate scene in a movie, the only ones being exploited are women? Why is that? In my organization that will be a problem of the past. We are living in the nineties, and still women are not being treated as equals. What kind of society do we live in? Women are not being treated fairly, and only being used as sex objects. I think it's time that females be treated with respect. It's time to make a change. And my organization will help us females accomplish our goal of equality in every way possible. I guarantee you will have a feeling of satisfaction once you join my organization. You will gladly see that together we can make a difference." She then pointed to the lower left corner of her poster, where she had drawn, within a small circle, the male and female symbols and an "S" attached to an "E." "And that's my logo, 'Sexual Equality.' Any questions?"

Anwar said, "Um. Yeah I got a question, let me think." He paused for a couple of seconds. "Nah, you can—." His voice trailed off: "I don't . . . ."

I asked Gloria what her organization would do. The assignment had not required her to conceive such a plan. I raised the question as germane to thinking about one's position and campaign.

Gloria turned her head briefly to one side and said, "I don't know," with a small smile. She added, "I guess," and paused for a second. "Try not to have like the networks show the movies, y'know, and if it's too graphic, like if it shows—I mean they don't really show that on TV but on cable, y'know you be seein'—"

"Good porno flicks," Anwar broke in.

"No, no, the regular movies. You see women with their titties stickin' out in the air, and you don't see no guy, all you see is their little butt. And that's not right." Female classmates laughed.

"Why ain't it?" said Anwar. "If she choose to do that scene, that's on her."

"Yeah but, if a man was to choose to do that, they wouldn't let him," Gloria replied. "I don't think they would. If a guy was to say, 'I wanna show my—,' y'know whatever, they wouldn't let him. So."

Diane began another line of questioning. "From what you wrote up," she said, "I would think you would want there to be less sex in general. Fewer women getting exposed, and fewer men getting exposed, and if they're exposed they're equal."

"Yeah," said Gloria.

"But from the poster it looks like you want men to show their stuff more."

"Exactly," Gloria said.

"So which one?"

"If women are showin' it too, why can't men?" Gloria explained.

"But which one do you want?" Diane asked. "Do you want TV that has more sex . . . "

"I don't think—"

" . . . or do you want TV that has less graphic sex, less open sex."

"I think it should be less graphic," Gloria answered. "And if they're gonna show, y'know if they're gonna be graphic they should show both of them. Not just one."

"She says she's tired of looking at the women," said Patrice.

Diane then asked, "What's the name of your organization?"

"Sexual Equality," Gloria answered.

"Okay. Great. Explain your logo so people who don't really see—"

"Oh. That's an S and an E and a, a female and a male," Gloria said.

Diane then asked Gloria, "How'd you get that idea?"

"I don't know, I just—"

"You were watching TV and—" Diane offered.

"No, I wanted to do somethin' about, sex, and I didn't know what to do. So I just cut out pictures and, 'Oh, shit,' y'know, I just thought of that." She put her hand over her mouth in an "oops" gesture. "I mean, I just thought of that, I don't know, it just came up."

When there were no more questions, Diane said, "That was a great job, Gloria." Indeed, there was an originality to Gloria's idea, and clarity to her presentation, that made her exhibition one of the strongest in our class. The class applauded, as was the Powell custom at the end of an exhibition. Gloria smiled as she returned to her seat.

Second Term

Gloria received a failing report card grade for the first term, because she had not turned in a complete portfolio. During the second term, she was anxious to achieve a better result. While working on various assignments, she often asked what she needed to do to get a good grade. In her research project, she was more task-oriented, for a longer period of time, than at any other point in the year.

As in the first term, Gloria was searching for a topic after several of her classmates had begun work on their exhibition projects. The Monday after Thanksgiving, in class, she perused the list of possible research paper topics Diane and I had distributed, and asked me about "Nuremburg Trials." I explained what they were and said they would be an interesting topic. No, she preferred a person, she decided. By the middle of the week she had settled on Billie Holiday.

Gloria read about Billie Holiday in four different sources: two biographical dictionaries, a chapter from a collection of essays about jazz, and a biography. She took notes in her own shorthand: for example, "attempted rape when she was 10—sent to reformatory. She was locked up with a dead corpse. 1927—released"; or, "1950 decline drug-alcohol." Most of her classmates' notes, by contrast, consisted of entire sentences that they reproduced or paraphrased from their sources.

Among the ten questions that students listed for their research, one was required to be an "essential question," as selected from the list on the second-term unit guide. Teachers saw the essential questions, in the research projects, as vehicles for encouraging students to connect their immediate topics to larger issues. Gloria chose "How do people face and fight destructive beliefs, powers, and prejudice?"—a question we had first presented in the context of the Facing History curriculum. During in-class conversations with Gloria, Diane and I directed attention toward this question by asking how racial issues were reflected and addressed in Billie Holiday's life and art.

When Gloria presented to a small group for her research-in-progress exhibition, my questioning focused on these matters, and Gloria thought of points to make in response. Having listened to a tape of Billie Holiday that I had given her, for instance, she generalized about the tone and lyrics of several of the songs and connected these to conditions under which Holiday lived.

In writing the paper, Gloria interwove information from all four of her sources to produce a five-page chronological narrative. She expanded on and reworded the phrases that were in her notes. Diane felt, afterward, that because of the flow of the writing, and how clearly it traced the course of Billie Holiday's life from beginning to end, Gloria had written one of the best papers in any of Diane's three classes. A typical passage read as follows:

> Drugs and alcohol made her health and career decline for a while, but soon enough she was back on her feet. In 1954 she participated in a jazz festival. Among those that were there were Dizzy Gillespie and Erroll Garner.
>   1954 was a good year for Billie Holiday. This was the year Billie won the Down Beat Award. Also this was the year she went on tour to Europe, which was a long awaited dream for Billie. Her tour took her to places like France, Germany, Belgium, Switzerland, England and Holland.

As Gloria moved steadily through the steps of reading, note taking, drafting, and typing, her commitment to the project was evident. At the same time, there were differences between her framing of the project and Diane's and mine. This was apparent to me on the day she submitted the paper.

We were in the computer lab. Gloria finished typing changes to her paper, printed out a copy, and asked me to read it. "I don't want to have anything wrong that you'll mark me down for," she said. I noticed a few mechanical errors (six—at least four of which were typographical—remained in the whole paper; Diane and I had both edited earlier drafts with her). More glaring to me was the fact that a section at the end addressing the essential question, which she had drafted earlier (per teachers' suggestion), was missing. Gloria had overlooked it when preparing the final version of her paper on the computer. I brought this to her attention.

Gloria then went to a terminal and typed two paragraphs, which were essentially the same as what had been in her previous draft. It was close to dismissal time, and she did not labor over the writing, nor pause and consider when I suggested that she could say some other things. It was also 2 days before Christmas vacation, and we had encouraged the students to have all their work turned in before the final days of pre-Christmas week. Gloria had already said, earlier in the class period, that she thought she deserved an "A" on the paper because she had "done everything" and "worked hard at it."

Gloria's paper did not present the range of ideas about her essential question—how Billie Holiday "faced and fought" racism—that she had touched on during her oral exhibition. Her narrative made a couple of references to racial issues: one sentence about restricted accommodations for Black artists and another about how one White audience did not like Billie Holiday. In the section addressing the essential question, Gloria focused mostly on a point I had shared with her one day about how the movie *Lady Sings the Blues* emphasized Holiday's drug use over her musicianship. She wrote, "This could easily have been done because of prejudice," and may or may not have realized that the movie was posthumous.

Developing and articulating her ideas around this essential question were not Gloria's main focus as she worked on the paper. She appeared to regard assembling her information into a coherent story, and creating a product that was mechanically polished, as worthy and sufficient tasks.

Third Term

The urge to perform well that Gloria displayed during the second term was hardly apparent after Christmas. By mid-January she seemed to be moping around school. She was absent for two or three days during each of several weeks in February and March. She did little work for humanities, in or out of class, during the term. While we did not discuss specifics, I suspected that issues outside school were affecting Gloria's state of mind.

When Diane and I told the class, at the beginning of the third term, that we would be studying the Civil War and slavery, Gloria said that she did not like this topic. She reiterated this position on other occasions during the term. While a larger malaise may have been coloring her feelings, it also seemed that this topic did not resonate for her as others might.

In the morning on March 4, the due date for the third-term portfolios and 1 week before students were scheduled to begin their third-term exhibitions, Gloria saw me in the teachers' office and told me she had done a couple of her portfolio assignments the previous day. When I asked about her exhibition, she asked, "When's it due?" She said she had forgotten what her topic was. Then she said, "Oh yeah, the Fifty-fourth Regiment. But I don't want to do that; I'd rather do a person." I asked her what kind of person; she thought for a few seconds, and said perhaps a leader of slave revolts. I offered Toussaint l'Ouverture as a suggestion: a slave revolt that won. No. I mentioned William Lloyd Garrison and told her what he had led. She said, "There'd probably be a lot on him," and appeared to make a mental note.

When I saw her in the computer lab later that same day, I pulled a book called *North of Slavery* out of my bag and showed her a chapter called "Abolitionism: White and Black." The book, by historian Leon Litwack (1961), was one I had read for a college class. Gloria's brief encounter with it resembled several other students' experiences with scholarly texts, which for certain topics were among the most readily available sources. The first paragraph of the chapter briefly describes the founding of the New England Anti-Slavery Society and quotes William Lloyd Garrison at the organization's first meeting. The second paragraph begins in prose typical of the book:

> Although the antislavery movement eventually divided into several factions, abolitionists generally agreed that slaves and free Negroes shared a similar plight. Consistency demanded that they move against both northern and southern abuses of the Negro population. (pp. 214–215)

Gloria read from these two paragraphs, and then gave the book back to me. "I don't know what it's talking about," she said. She then said she would like to read about slaves who escaped.

The next day I shared with Gloria another book from my personal library, which had a less daunting writing style: a collection of slave narratives, as recorded by Federal Writers' Project members in the 1930s. She kept it, and returned it to me a week and a half later, unmoved to use it in a project.

Gloria did not have an exhibition prepared to present during the time period when we held third-term exhibitions in class. Because these exhibitions took place after the third term officially ended, they counted toward students' fourth-term report card grades. When a few weeks remained in the fourth term, Diane and I began reminding Gloria that she still needed to do a Civil War/slavery exhibition in order to pass for the term, and that she needed to arrange with us a time outside of class to present it. She said more than once that she understood and that she would do one; she had failed for the third term, and expressed a desire to pass this time. She did not show us any work she had done to prepare for this exhibition, though, or say when she would be ready to do it. Finally, 4 days before the end of the fourth term, Diane and I sat down with Gloria and Estella (who also had yet to present a third-term exhibition) and told them that the next morning, an hour before school, was their last chance to do the exhibition. They both nodded and said they could do it. "Okay, repeat after me," Diane said. "'If I don't come and do my exhibition tomorrow morning, I will fail the term.'"

"If I don't come and do my exhibition tomorrow morning, I will fail the term," they said in unison.

Gloria and Estella arrived at 7:30 A.M., and presented to each other and to Diane and me. For her topic, Gloria had chosen Harriet Jacobs, a woman who escaped slavery and whose autobiography, *Incidents in the Life of a Slave Girl* (1861/1988), remains one of the most widely read slave narratives.

As we took seats around a table, Gloria told about the sources she had consulted: *Within the Plantation Household: Black and White Women of the Old South* by Elizabeth Fox-Genovese (1988), a book which Gloria said was "difficult to understand" but from which, I later discovered, she obtained most of the information she used in her talk (see Chapter 8); a book of Harriet Jacobs's "letters" (perhaps Mary E. Lyons's fictional *Letters from a Slave Girl* [1992]), of which she said, "It was much easier; I mean, I read like a few"; and a radio-drama script about Harriet Jacobs that she and a few classmates had read with our visiting artist. When conversation about these sources began to evolve into a discussion of what Gloria had learned, I cut it off. "You're going to make a presentation, right?" I said.

"Barely," she said with a small laugh.

"Okay," she began, without looking at her notes. "Well, like, the book said, I mean she was a slave who fled from the North and um—hold on—oh yeah, to protect her friends she wrote under the name, when she wrote letters or whatever, she wrote under the name Linda Brent. . . . And then like, people didn't hardly, they didn't really believe when she published the book—whatever, her autobiography—people wouldn't really believe that, y'know, that it could be true. They thought she was kind of lying because they figured, y'know, how could a slave write under those horrible conditions, and they thought she was kind of lying. But, y'know, I guess they understood afterwards and they knew that she wasn't lying. Um." She paused for a few seconds. "Oh yeah, and it also said that she strongly believed in like, um, racial oppression like, well, oppression of a slave woman—she thought that slavery was like against woman's nature. I mean she thought women shouldn't have to go through all that." She consulted her notes, and read a sentence: "She wanted the readers in the North to be aware of the conditions that the slave womans would be under." She added, "Like in South." She then explained, "Y'know that's kind of like why she wrote, y'know, her book and all that. And then, they kinda didn't believe it. Then I guess they became aware."

Gloria then began glancing frequently at her notes, and presented a chronological narrative. "Her parents they were like, they were real light—called them mulatto, they were like, brownish yellow. And then, y'know, when she was little she describes how she had a nice childhood. And then, like, at the age of 6 her mother died, so she had to stay with, y'know, her mother's mistress—whatever, the lady, y'know—well, mistress.[1] And then, she was real nice to her, and, y'know, she loved her a lot because she, the mistress was the one who taught her how to read and how to spell. So she kind of appreciated that. And then she got sick. So she raised her like when she was like, 6 to 12. Y'know, she was around 12 her m–, the lady died. And um, she kinda felt strong towards her but, y'know, well she died. And, like—hold on—oh yeah. Kinda hard for me to do, um. So in the will um, the mistress told her to take care of her sister's kid, so it was kind of, her niece or whatever, so she had to do that, and um—oh [sigh] my goodness. So like—."

Gloria paused for a few seconds and studied her notes, before continuing. "Oh. Okay. She describes how her mistress was a, I mean, she would not give her hard duties to do, she was just—I mean she was nice toward her compared to, like, the way other slaves were treated. And then after she died, she had to stay with um, Dr. Elliot or some, some person and, um, she kinda describes when she went to him she kinda, things started to change and um, she—I mean she started to feel like, she really, that's when she started to feel the cruelties y'know, that slaves can, y'know have upon them. And um, kinda skip all that, and then like—I don't know, it's like, I only know like bits and pieces of her life. I don't know all together."

Gloria continued for almost another minute and then said, "So, I mean, that's, I don't know too much—that's like how much I know."

After Gloria finished speaking, I began the questioning by asking her what themes about slavery she had learned from reading about this person. In her response, Gloria shared reflections about Harriet Jacobs's story.

"I learned that, I mean, it was difficult like under certain circumstances—I mean, some slaves were kinda afraid to get away. She managed to do it, 'cause she had the will—and there's a quote that she said where, um, 'My master had power and law on his side. I had determination and will.' [Gloria had written this quote at the top of her sheet of notes.] I think that's kinda, that's nice for her to say because it was kinda, I think it was kinda hard for slaves back then to, like, to y'know—damn, how to explain. I guess they was kinda afraid to just do what they had to do, y'know, and if they had to die and—just like, generations kept being born

---

[1] In an earlier class session, some students had discussed how they did not like using the word *master*. I believe this sensibility led Gloria to hesitate over *mistress*.

into that, but, I guess, she escaped, so I mean it was, I guess it was different for her. But like, I don't, I don't know if there are—I mean there's a lot of people who escaped too but like, mostly, I guess they kinda lost hope. And like that's a theme you kinda keep seeing—it's like, they talk about how people kept doing this and this and this to them and they really didn't have the strength to go out and do for themselves. So um, she did. I mean, that's one thing that I thought was nice about her."

Diane asked how Harriet Jacobs's book was published. Gloria said "it talked about the lady" who helped her, and reiterated how "people didn't believe" she had written the book. I followed by asking how Harriet Jacobs became connected with the people who helped her publish it. "I don't know, it didn't really describe all that. I don't know," Gloria said with a small laugh.

Gloria and Diane had an exchange about how a young child might not understand she was a slave. I followed by asking if it was after her mother's mistress died and she went to the harsher master, that Harriet Jacobs realized that she was a slave.

"No," Gloria answered, "that's when she realized the cruelty of being a slave, but she knew when she was like 6 to 12, she was a slave, because the lady who she was with, I mean she would tell her to do this for her and that—but it wasn't like cruel. It was like, like if you're staying in somebody's house and you're just cleaning for them, like that—it wasn't bad."

"So do you think if she'd never been sold to the crueler guy, that she would've developed the same kind of opposition to slavery?" I asked. This question asked Gloria to construct an alternative scenario, using what she knew.

"Well I mean eventually yeah because, maybe the slave owner'll treat her, treated her like that because she was young. But after she got older I think she probably would've realized it, y'know. I mean, I guess when she was younger she didn't think bad of it, but like as she was growing up, even if she was with the same woman she still would've thought, y'know, 'This is not right for me, I shouldn't be a slave at all.' So maybe she would've still ended up leaving."

After her presentation, we asked Gloria to write what she thought she had done well and what she thought she could have done better. What she did well, she wrote, was that "I kind of understood the concept in general about slavery." Echoing a feeling she had expressed at a couple of points during the presentation, she wrote that her exhibition would have been better "if I had more information on Harriet Jacobs' life." Continuing, she wrote, "I can't really relate to what she felt, so if I would have had more information, then I would have a better understanding on how she felt."

As we discussed this self-assessment, Gloria spoke about not having spent more time researching. She indicated that the long-term and open-ended nature of the assignment had presented a challenge to her. "It's hard when you have so much time," she said. "It's like you think, y'know, you've got the rest of the time, so you don't do it. But like, the other day I stayed in the library for 2 hours, and I found so much that, like, if I would have stayed up there, y'know goin' a little bit each week? Like when you really know that's what you have to do, you come out doin' better—instead of just if you have a whole bunch of time, and kinda keep it all until the last minute, which I have been known to do."

Gloria also said, "Yeah like when you said yesterday, 'If I do not have this in, I will fail.' I mean that kinda got to me—I was home thinking, 'Damn. Let me do this.' Y'know."

During this conversation, Gloria also discussed the evolution of her interest in the subject matter of the course over the preceding few months. "I don't know," she said, "it's like, when we first started doing slavery, I kind of really didn't put my mind to it, but after a while, when we started doing the civil rights I kind of understood the importance of it, and it's different now. If I would've known all that back when we was doing the exhibitions on slavery, then I would've paid more attention [to classmates' presentations]. 'Cause now when you're talking about civil rights, you kinda know that it goes back to way back in the days and that's important. But I didn't realize that when we was doing slavery—it kinda seemed just boring to me, and now it seems different."

This conversation indicated that Gloria had standards in her mind, concerning the quality of an exhibition, to which her performance had not measured up. It also indicated that she saw her own motivation to work as a central issue. Her feedback, in addition, suggested that Diane's dramatic warning had been an effective means of spurring her to prepare her presentation. Both the timing and the novelty of that tactic, however, had made its impact greater than it might have been if used on other occasions.

At another point in this conversation, Gloria's remarks suggested standards in her mind that diverged from Diane's. Diane told Gloria it seemed to her that the presentation, in essence, amounted to "giving a report." Gloria's reply stressed the distinction, as she saw it, between what she had just done and what she had known, in previous school experience, as "giving a report." She said that in those other situations, "It kind of seems like you know what you're talking about but like, well maybe if you answer questions afterward you can explain your opinions, but it just seems that you're just reading off somebody else's opinion." Indeed, during her exhibition Gloria had articulated her own understandings about Harriet Jacobs in ways that students in many high school classes are not asked to do.

With a stronger investigative or analytic focus, Gloria's project might have further transcended "giving a report" in Diane's or my view; she might have done more in her presentation than share and discuss the contents of a set of notes. The notions of quality work that Gloria expressed when assessing her exhibition did not include such elements. They did, by contrast, include being better informed about her topic.

Fourth Term

Teachers gave the students a more specific schedule to follow for preparing their fourth-term oral history projects than we had provided during the third term. Nancy, our student teacher, emphasized this schedule to the students and called for intermediate products at specific points. Students' interviews were to be conducted 3 weeks before the panel discussions. Nonetheless, Gloria conducted hers 2 days before she presented.

Seated among fellow panelists, Gloria gave her opening summary. "Well, I interviewed Ms. Ramirez [a Powell teacher]. And um, my interview was about—she was tellin' us about how, when she was around like, 8 or 10, when, y'know back when the civil rights was started, she wasn't really too old to get involved. So, her brother was, um, involved in this group called the Young Lords, and they would protest against, for um, for rights for minorities, um, to have more access to, to school and like—to, y'know, have better funding for s–, for them to go to school. And when she got older, before she started college she was in the um, this protest, and they took over a building, and they didn't eat for a week. And then, um, she stayed in there and, it kinda worked because, after that they kinda, that allowed her to go to, like, college and have more, minority students going to school. So, her focus was really on having education accessible to all races. Y'know, that's basically what she was talkin' about."

This summary relayed the main points from the first page of Gloria's two-page written narrative of her interview. The second page of that narrative included a brief description of another demonstration in which Ms. Ramirez had participated, and some comments Ms. Ramirez had made about the role of leaders and the degree of change since the civil rights movement.

The bulk of this exhibition was spent with the whole panel addressing issues such as those about nonviolence that Wayne raised (see Chapter 3), rather than individuals talking about the specific subjects of their interviews. As the conversation spurred by Wayne's question illustrates, Gloria was an active participant, offering opinions, asking questions of others, and following the threads of the discussion.

There were three more instances, after the opening summary, when Gloria was asked to refer directly to her interview with Ms. Ramirez. At one such point, Diane said, "I want to ask either Danilo or Gloria whether there's any connection between the Young Lords and the Latin Kings." (Danilo had referred to the Latin Kings in his summary.)

"The Young Lords, that was a group of, um, Puerto Ricans who protested, like, the civil rights of the minorities, but I don't know about no Latin Kings," said Gloria.

After Danilo shared what he knew about the Latin Kings, Diane said to Gloria that she would like to know more about the Young Lords.

"I think that's in there, somewhere," Gloria said, looking at the top page of the papers in front of her. "They was a, they were a militant group. Yeah."

"Were they like the Black Panthers? Were they like a Puerto Rican version of the Black Panthers?" Diane asked.

Gloria answered, "Yeah and then, Ms. Ramirez was talkin' about how they got together, and—but like the, the Black Panthers was like violent protesters, they believed that, y'know you had to do things, goin' out and gettin' guns. But then, the Young Lords weren't like that, they were mostly y'know—"

"Did they have guns?" Wayne asked.

"I don't know. Well, that's what she said, I mean, they were the, more like, like the type—they were followin' like Malcolm X's philosophy, like that."

Gloria's knowledge base about the Young Lords was restricted to what Ms. Ramirez had told her. Perhaps, also, she had not recorded or retained all that Ms. Ramirez had said about this subject. The assignment had not required students to further investigate topics that arose in the interviews. In addition, follow-up inquiries, even if led by teachers, would have depended on the interviews being conducted earlier in the term than Gloria's was.

In the final section of her written report, which, in accordance with our guidelines, was her "reflection" on the interview, Gloria indicated some lasting meanings she took from the project. She wrote, "I never knew their was another side to [Ms. Ramirez] other than a school teacher. I never imagined her as being young and participating in things I had only heard of." She also wrote, "I never really thought about Latinos and Asians being discriminated against because it is seldom discussed. By doing this interview, I have a better understanding of not only Black discrimination but also Latinos as well." As Wayne had when doing his research paper, she placed value on historical information that had personal significance to her.

CLOSING THOUGHTS

The question "Is it worth doing?" assumes considerable importance in Gloria's account. It underlay the creation of standards for the quality of her performances.

On one level, this question pertained to whether Gloria believed a particular topic merited investing in a project. In each term, she was quite selective in arriving at an exhibition topic, declining those that teachers suggested before eventually identifying one—each time, a female life or perspective—on her own. In the third term, also, a feeling of disinterest toward our unit topic in general made it harder for her to become motivated to work. By contrast, her efforts near the end of the fourth term (in addition to preparing two exhibitions, she wrote the two required essays about *Coming of Age in Mississippi* and submitted a complete portfolio) coincided with her seeing the subject matter in our class as relevant.

"Is it worth doing?" pertained to school achievement as well as to the study of particular topics. During the second term, when Gloria made her most concerted effort, she appeared to be motivated largely by a general desire to do well: to meet our requirements and have a good report card. In the following term, this desire became much less prominent, and procrastination prevailed.

Gloria's ad-libbed responses to questions during exhibitions displayed her ability to reflect on and analyze her material. Beyond a certain point, though, her demonstration of those skills was constrained by the amount and kind of work she had done on her projects. The extent of her analysis depended in part on how much knowledge she had acquired. Developing an analysis can also entail sifting through one's information to connect various pieces and generalize among them, while preparing an oral or written presentation. More thoroughly addressing the essential question in her research paper could have involved an undertaking of this sort—one that might have strained her academic skills while presenting an opportunity to expand them. Again, the question "Is it worth doing?" arises. Such an undertaking would follow a student's judgments regarding its significance to the quality of a project, and her consideration of the added time and struggle it would entail.

5

Pierre

Pierre Cyrille was in the tenth grade. In a sense, he was the opposite of Gloria: His strongest attribute as a student was his commitment to working, while his skills were such that the tasks we assigned tended to be more difficult for him than for most of his classmates. A factor that made the work challenging for him was that he was in the process of acquiring English as a third language (he also speaks French and Haitian Creole). Because Pierre's learning issues were different from Wayne's or Gloria's, the account of his exhibitions shows how the standards that are negotiated can differ among individual students in a classroom.

PIERRE'S EXHIBITIONS

First Term

Especially at the beginning of the year, Pierre solicited teacher coaching more frequently, and welcomed it more readily, than any of his classmates. The day before his propaganda exhibition was one occasion when he endeavored to complete a task with my assistance.

Pierre came to class with a poster. Using a thin black marker and a white posterboard, he had made a line drawing that depicted a Jewish man killing Hitler with a machete. He had colored in the Jewish man's clothing and beard with the black marker, and added two red pools of blood by the fallen Führer. He explained to me the idea behind his poster: "The only way to get rid of Hitler is to kill him."

Pierre had not prepared the "poem, song, or rap" part of the exhibition. He told me he was sure that he could not do any of these. I felt it was best to find another option and suggested that he could give a speech. He assented, and asked me to help him write it.

I asked Pierre what would be a convincing reason why people should follow his plan. Pierre hesitated and asked to hear the question again. After I repeated the question, Pierre said this was a way for Jewish people to be free. I said, "Good, write that down." He asked me to say his words back to him. I could not remember them exactly, and neither could he. I asked him the question once more. Working with me in this fashion, he constructed a paragraph.

The next day, Pierre stood in front of the class and unrolled his poster. Anwar, assisting him, held the poster so that it faced the class. Pierre had a sheet of notebook paper in his left hand.

"What's your slogan?" asked Celia.

"It's right here." He pointed to four words written along the bottom of the poster. "Make Germany . . ." His voice became inaudible for the remaining two words.

Pierre then pointed to other parts of the poster. "Um, this is Hitler right there. That's a Jewish man, who want freedom. That's the only way that he think, that he want, um, to make Germany better, right? So that's the only way he think he can get rid of Hitler. So, he try to kill him. This is my slogan"—he pointed again to the words at the bottom of the poster—"and this is my speech." He turned the sheet of paper so that the audience could see the writing, and then back so that he could read it.

As a rule, Pierre spoke softly and accented words and syllables somewhat differently than a native English speaker would. When he was presenting to the whole class, especially if I was sitting across the room from him, I would often have to strain to catch his words, and I was not always successful. Classmates would be quiet and make an effort to hear him, although some would appear to make diminishing efforts if he continued at much length.

Pierre read from the paper: "The only way out of this trouble is to get rid of Hitler, so we can have our freedom. Because Hitler is the Führer of Germany, even if we had an election nobody can compete with Hitler. No matter what we do, he's gonna keep fighting back, he's, he's not gonna give up. So my plan is, you people gonna try to help me, how we can get to, how we can get to Hitler. The way I think, how we can, how we can get to him by, is, by one of us join the Party, and try to get to, and try to get to his office and kill him, and then, make a suicide."

"And then—what's the last thing?" asked Diane.

"Suicide," said Pierre.

"That ain't a bad idea yo. Kamikaze," said Paul, the student visitor who also spoke during Wayne's exhibition.

"Suicide, 'cause, we, we gonna get caught anyway, so, we might as well kill ourself," said Pierre.

"Okay, so you're accepting that that person is gonna get murdered by Hitler's guys," Diane said.

"Yeah."

Diane then asked, "Is that effective as propaganda? The poster?"

Wayne answered, "Yeah. It might influence people to fight back."

Paul said, "But the only thing that would be kinda ill yo, is that his whole thing could turn backwards on him though."

"Explain," said Diane.

"Because, yo, say you're, if—I ain't tryin' to put down your whole thing or nothin' yo, I'm just tryin' to say. It's like, say if old man goes in there and carves him up yo, right? Carves up Hitler? And then he goes and kills himself? When the Nazi soldier discovers this, he be like, 'Oh, Hitler must've been tryin' to defend himself against the bad Jews,' and all this and that, and that stuff would still be goin' on right now yo."

"But you know what—" said Diane.

"'Cause they killed Hitler yo."

Diane directed the conversation back to Pierre as she continued. "I want to ask Pierre this, too. Could it go on without the figurehead of Hitler? Was he so powerful that he got, he persuaded people to go along with him in a way that someone under him couldn't?"

"Yep," said Celia.

Pierre stood expressionless for 5 seconds and then turned his head toward Paul.

"What do you think, Pierre?" Diane asked. "Do you think if he was out of the way, that that would make a huge difference in Germany?"

"Yes," Pierre answered.

"Okay, can you explain why?"

"Because, he was like, he didn't like Jewish at all. So."

"So, a lot of other people didn't like Jewish people either," Diane said.

"Yeah but he made 'em, like, he made the Party, y'know, go against the Jewish," Pierre replied.

"So what was it about him, that was different from any other person who didn't like Jewish people?" Diane asked.

Pierre was still. Then he gave a faint smile.

"Your poster's powerful because it says, 'Look! This guy's so dangerous we gotta kill him.' Why is he so dangerous?"

"He's powerful," Pierre answered.

"Say a little more about why he's so powerful."

Pierre said, "'Cause," and then paused.

There was silence for almost half a minute.

"Does it make sense that it, that that guy would want to kill him?" Diane asked.

"Yeah," said Pierre.

"Yes, it does, doesn't it." Diane then continued, "And we were in the computer lab the other day with—I don't know who, what class was in there—somebody said, 'Gee, if I was there I would've killed him.' And we all went, 'Oh, no, you couldn't do that,' and then somebody was there and said there was something—I don't know the statistic, we'll have to find out—there was something like thirty attempts on his life."

"On whose life, Hitler?" asked Claudia.

"Hitler's life, right. He was so well guarded that none of them succeeded."

"Throw a grenade at him," said Anwar.

"Okay," Diane said. "Would that, would that poster ever be able to be published in Germany?"

"No," said Anwar.

"No way," said Diane. "But it would be kinda nice to, to think that somebody probably did do something like that and put it up secretly. Okay, I thought that was a pretty interesting idea that Pierre came up with." The class applauded as Pierre returned to his seat.

Diane was unable to pose a question that engaged Pierre in a dialogue about the issue his campaign and Paul's comments brought to her mind: whether Hitler's presence would be crucial to the ongoing persecution of Jews. She made a judgment as to when she had persisted far enough with this line of questioning, before continuing the conversation with remarks of her own. Neither she nor I knew enough French to repeat the questions in his native language, and discover if and how his responses differed.

Second Term

Compared to the propaganda assignment, the second-term assignment asked Pierre to create a more extensive product. This in itself posed a challenge for him. Particular elements of the writing task, also, commanded his, and Diane's and my, attention.

Having played baseball for a team called the Babe Ruth Yankees, Pierre chose Babe Ruth from our list of research paper topics. When we returned from Thanksgiving vacation, Pierre had been to his neighborhood library and checked out a book on Babe Ruth. He said he could not read the whole book in the time we had. Diane suggested the first and last chapters. In the next week and a half, he read the first one, about

Babe Ruth's childhood, and found information about Babe Ruth's career in baseball encyclopedias. He made notes on index cards.

When it was time to present his research-in-progress exhibition, Pierre had written, with some coaching from Diane, two full pages in his notebook. There, he had reorganized, and in some cases reworded, what was on his note cards.

For his presentation, Pierre read portions of what he had written in the notebook. Gloria, three other students, and I were seated in a small circle with him. We did not have to strain to hear him. When he finished reading, one classmate brought up a detail Pierre had mentioned: that all but one of Babe Ruth's brothers and sisters had died during childhood. How? she wondered—as did others in the group. Pierre did not know, but as the group discussed why this might have happened, he supplied some more related information: that Babe Ruth was one of eight children and that his family was poor.

"Good," I said to Pierre when he finished. Unlike two of the five students in his group, he had brought an organized set of notes and presented a comprehensible body of information. He appeared to be on his way to completing and fulfilling the assignment.

On a number of occasions during the next 2 weeks, Diane and I worked with Pierre on the writing of his paper. Sometimes at his instigation and sometimes at ours, we addressed issues of organization, grammar, spelling, and what to add to his two pages.

One day, for instance, I was seated at a word processor with Pierre when I noticed one paragraph in which the sequence of the sentences was clearly a problem:

> In 1927 Babe Ruth was with his second wife Claire and daughter Julia. An official of the baseball Hall of Fame in Coopestown, New York proudly places Babe's uniforms in a display case for all to admire. in 1925 it was the Yankees worst season after felling third place in there division. Babe Ruth led the Yankees to seven championships including four world series titles. . . .

I pointed out to Pierre that 1925 was after 1927, and said this should be rearranged. He expressed concern that this would mean retyping the whole paragraph—typing was a slow and laborious process for him at this point in the year. I then showed him a way to move blocks of text on the word processor. Pierre observed, brightened, and proceeded to reorganize the paragraph.

In Pierre's final draft, the paragraph began as follows:

> In 1925 it was the Yankees' worst season after falling to third place in their division. In 1927 Babe Ruth was with his second wife claire and Daughter Julia. Babe Ruth led the Yankees to seven championships including four world series titles.

Needing to prioritize our use of the remaining conference time, Diane and I had chosen not to discuss with Pierre the flow of ideas between these sentences. (In most of Pierre's other paragraphs, the sentences were more closely related to one another.) We had focused instead on expanding the paper and reducing its large number of mechanical problems—tasks that we had established as aspects of completing the assignment and that aligned well with what Pierre was learning to do. Diane had emphasized to the class that final drafts should be of "portfolio quality"—that is, presentable in terms of neatness and minimal errors.

While our coaching focused largely on these sorts of writing issues, Diane and I also called some attention to the analytic content of the paper. We addressed this largely through the essential question.

Pierre chose, from our list of essential questions, "Does the person make the times or do the times make the person?" One day in class, I worked with him on adding a paragraph about this question. Pierre had written a sentence stating that the times make the person and that if Babe Ruth had lived in the 1600s he would not have played baseball. I read this, and asked what if Babe Ruth lived today. Pierre said that he did not think Babe Ruth would be as good today, because he did not work as hard to get to the major leagues as today's players do. After further discussion, he added this point to what he had written. In his final version of the paper, he used some information from his research and elaborated as follows:

> If you compare the players from the past and the players today I think today's players would be better because they work hard to get where they are and I don't think Babe Ruth did all that to get to where he was. Babe Ruth played baseball for fun. If he didn't go to St. Mary's [boarding school] I don't think he could've been to the pros. Babe Ruth didn't go to college. He went to the pros after he played for the Baltimore Orioles [then a minor league team] and from there his step father sold him to the Boston Red Sox. So that's how he got to the pros.

Using most of the class time available to him, and staying in the computer lab after school on a few occasions, Pierre made numerous mechanical corrections and expanded the paper from two to three and a half pages. When grading the paper, Diane and I did not penalize him for having fewer than five pages, because we felt he had applied himself well to the task and because, by comparison with his previous term's portfolio work, his producing a paper of this length seemed to be a worthy achievement.

Third Term

Pierre chose Nat Turner as his exhibition topic on a day in mid-February when I was offering suggestions to students. I explained briefly why Nat Turner was famous. Pierre expressed gratitude for the suggestion, as he had not come up with a topic on his own.

Two days later, we asked the students to write what they already knew about their exhibition topics. Pierre said he could not think of anything. Eventually he stated that Nat Turner was Black.

Pierre began his research by finding a young-adult biography (Bisson, 1988) at a library. Taking notes from this source, he filled four index cards: one about Turner's childhood, one about Turner's adult life before the revolt he led, and two about the revolt.

I then decided to advise Pierre to look further at one slice of Turner's story: the uprising itself. I thought that Pierre might get to know this set of information in a way that would enable him to demonstrate command in an exhibition. I brought to school a photocopy of Turner's confessions, as recorded in 1831 (Turner, 1831/1975; see also Greenberg, 1996). After class one day, Pierre and I sat together and took turns reading aloud from the five-page section in which Turner gives a detailed narrative of his insurrection. We discussed each passage as we read it. I noticed that Pierre was remembering facts he had learned from the biography and connecting them to what we were now reading.

Pierre went home, with the photocopy, and made four more note cards describing details of the revolt—mostly, what happened at particular houses Turner and his men visited. While these notes contained phrases from the confessions (e.g., "spill the first blood") and followed that source's order of telling, they were mostly in Pierre's own words. They included generalizations he had remembered from our discussion (e.g., "Each house that they go to the group got bigger, it got bigger because in every White house their were slaves"). He inserted these new note cards between the two previous ones he had made about Turner's revolt and numbered his whole set, now totaling eight. There was a small overlap between the information on his first new card and the information on the card preceding it.

The third-term project asked students, in addition to researching their topics, to plan how they would teach a lesson. One of our requirements was that each student use some form of visual aid. Diane and I also encouraged the students to use teaching strategies other than simply talking to the class. Pierre decided that eight drawings from the biography could be his visual. I suggested photocopying and distributing them, and building the lesson by having the class discuss each picture. Our conference time, however, was not spent discussing step-by-step how he would conduct such a lesson.

I realized, afterward, that Pierre would have needed considerable guidance in order to teach in this manner—and that conferences were a limited tool for preparing him. Building his lesson primarily off the pictures—generating dialogue, and sharing his information about Nat Turner in the context of that dialogue—would have entailed much new learning on Pierre's part, in terms of both how he used content knowledge and how he spoke, in English, to the class. Pierre did select, photocopy, and distribute the pictures, but for the most part he relied on presentation techniques with which he was more familiar.

Pierre stood before the class and said, "My name is Pierre Cyrille, and my top–, my s–, my paper is on Nat Turner. I'm gonna talk about Nat Turner's childhood, and while he was youngsters, and while he was an adult."

He then commenced reading from his cards. "Nat Turner was born in South Hampton, Virginia in 1800. Nat Turner, Nat Turner's mother didn't want Nat Turner to—." Pierre looked up and explained. "Like, when she was pregnant she didn't want Nat Turner to go through the things, through, through slavery. So what, what she was about to do was, as soon Nat Turner was born, she was gonna kill him. Um, the masters, didn't want that to happen so they, they held her and tied her to her bed and all that, until she got calm." These three sentences conveyed what was written on his card, the first two practically verbatim.

Pierre looked back at his note cards and read for seven and a half more minutes, glancing up briefly three times. As he read, his voice varied little in pitch and emphasis. He concluded: "On August twenty-two Turner was attacked by, by the masters. August twenty-three, twenty-three, at the, at the home of Dr. Blunt, their group was, was repulsed and, several men in Turner's f–, in Turner's force were killed. By midday, Turner was, Turner was alone. The mem–, the members of his group were dead, captured, or hiding. Turners himself was hiding, in, and around the South Ham–, Virginia, but he was captured on October thirtieth, eighteen thirty-one. Turner's confession was, was dic–, was dictated to Thomas Gray on

N– November one and three. On No–, on November fifth, Turner's found guilty. He was hanged. He was hanged on November eleventh."

After he finished reading, Pierre distributed copies of the eight drawings to each student. He called the class's attention to each one and provided commentary, referring to and expanding on notes he had written on his own copies. "The next page," he said, for instance, "um it shows, when the, um, slaves were, when the masters came out and when they heard about the, the slaves killing the people, killing the White people. They went out and tried to capture all of them. The slaves and the masters were fighting. It shows right here, uh, one of, one of the group had, had a gun. It means that they, they got, the guns from the other houses." With some pictures his comments were shorter: for example, "This shows Mr. Travis house. When they went to Mr. Travis house and killed all the member of the family."

During this portion of the exhibition, Pierre had a few exchanges with his classmates. Twice, Patrice indicated that she was uncertain what he had just said, and Pierre clarified with a simple statement ("It's a church"; "That's Mr. Travis house"). Claudia asked two questions about what she saw in the pictures. Regarding the drawing of the scene at the Travis house, she asked which person was Nat Turner. Pierre looked at the drawing, which showed four men wielding weapons, and said he did not know. In reference to another drawing, Claudia asked what Nat Turner had in his hand. Patrice and Danilo said that Turner was holding onto a branch, and Pierre echoed them.

After Pierre finished with the last picture, I asked, "Who in the class has some questions for Pierre?"

Wayne responded by asking when and where Nat Turner was born. He wrote down Pierre's answer. Nancy had instructed the audience members to write, in their notes, at least three facts and one question (as she did before each third-term exhibition).

Patrice followed Wayne's question with, "What year did he die?"

"He died in eighteen thirty-one," said Pierre.

Claudia asked him to repeat. "Eighteen thirty-what?"

"Eighteen thirty-one."

"I thought—," Claudia said. "So when was he caught then?"

"The same year," Pierre answered.

"And they killed him a couple of days after they catch him," said Patrice. "Duh."

"I thought he said eighteen thirty-nine," Claudia explained to Patrice.

I initiated the next exchange, with the intent of eliciting knowledge that I believed Pierre had, and that he had not shared in his talk. "You told us how many people he had with him when he started."

"He had four," Pierre said.

"He had, he had four people with him when he started. What was the, most nu–, how many people did he have with him, later on in the—"

"He had a lot of people because, in each house that he goes to, um, had slaves, so, the slaves that were in the house helped him doin' this."

"Do you remember how big his army got?" I asked.

"It got up to sixty."

Shortly after this, I asked Pierre and the rest of the class to consider alternative ways Nat Turner's uprising might have proceeded and resulted. Was there anything Turner and his men could have done differently so that they would not have been defeated? The ensuing discussion was the segment of the exhibition during which students in the audience spoke, and displayed their understandings of Pierre's subject, the most.

Danilo started, and focused on Turner's method of attacking one house at a time, which Pierre had recounted in some detail. "He should've organized it," Danilo said. "Like, if he got, if he knew that he had so many people, he should've sent like some out to like, this person's house and everything like that, and then just rush 'em all at one time so then they can't get no arms or whatever, 'cause it would be like a surprise attack."

"No, they only started with four," said Claudia.

"I know but after he got all those people, I'm sayin'," said Danilo.

"He didn't get all these people until after he killed the masters," said Claudia.

"He didn't do—," Pierre started.

Danilo reentered, "I know but I'm sayin' after he got all them people, then after he did all that—,"

"To go kill more people?" Claudia asked.

"Yeah, like that," Danilo said.

"But he was caught before he could," Claudia said.

There was a short silence, and Pierre stood still. I turned to Wayne, whose hand had been raised, and said, "What were you gonna say, Wayne?"

"That just shows that he was, he should've been more organized," Wayne said.

Pierre then said, "If the group didn't, um, didn't split, I think that they could've gone, far, than they did. Like when Nat Turner said they gotta split, if he didn't said that. They got scared when the masters came after them. Nat Turner got scared."

"Nat Turner got scared or the other, or the people with him got scared?" I asked, recalling that in his confessions Turner describes some of his men fleeing while he tried to persist and regroup.

"All of them," Pierre said.

Ronald then suggested that Turner might have exerted stronger leadership in a personal sense: "He could've persuaded the people that was under him. He could've like, gave 'em more heart. 'Cause everybody got scared. He could've, talked to them differently, so they would like, almost give their life away, just about."

Diane and I asked a few follow-up questions that continued this discussion. When the point about Turner beginning with four people resurfaced, Pierre remarked that Turner began only with the men he was sure he could trust.

Diane then raised a new question. During this exhibition, she and I were in different positions: I had worked more closely with Pierre while he was preparing for it and thus knew more about what information he did and did not have. Her question was about a part of Nat Turner's story that she thought Pierre might have encountered: "how he decided what day to do it on and stuff like that." Pierre had no answer when she asked if he could "say a little about that." She followed, "Do you, did you come across that at all, Pierre, that he used like this spiritualist thing, and like, looked at the sun, and—did you come across that?" Pierre said that he had not. His two sources contained this information, but in sections on which he had not focused.

To conclude the exhibition, Pierre presented some questions to his classmates. Pierre functioned as discussion leader as the class navigated the task.

"I have some questions, some four questions," Pierre said. "You're gonna write 'em down, on a piece of paper."

"What'd you say? How many?" asked Claudia.

"Four," Pierre said.

"Ain't your 15 minutes up?" said Patrice. (Our directions had described the task as to teach a "15-minute lesson.")

"You ought to say, 'Sure, no problem,'" Diane said to her.

"I didn't hear a word he said," remarked Anwar. During some of Pierre's presentation, Anwar had been looking at the notes for his own exhibition, which was scheduled to follow Pierre's.

After the students got papers and pens ready, Pierre read his first question from one of his cards. "Um. The first question. Uh, what kind of person was Nat Turner?"

After writing the question, Anwar asked, "What's the second one?" He added, "Just give the whole questions and then answer 'em."

Pierre read his second question. "If, if you were in, if you were in his place, what would, what would you do?" After his classmates wrote this question, he continued to the third one. "Um, what motivate Nat Turner to make that move?"

"What move?" asked Claudia.

"That he did, fighting against the White people." Pierre then repeated, "What motivate Nat Turner to make that move?"

Patrice laughed and said, "Was I not listening." Then she asked, "Did he escape?"

Pierre said, "When he went at, at his master's house, shot Joseph Travis." He paused. When Anwar said, "Four," Pierre went on to the fourth question: "What do, what do you think of Nat Turner?"

"Didn't you ask that for number one?" asked Anwar.

"I said, 'What kind of person?'" said Pierre.

"What kind of person," said Patrice.

"Same thing," Anwar said.

"'What do you think of him'?" Claudia asked.

"Yeah," Pierre confirmed.

Pierre's classmates wrote answers to his questions and gave him their papers, for him to include in his portfolio. Answers to his first question (What kind of person?) included "He was a strong willed person," "A confused strong person," "A leader with a grudge against whites," and "What I understand was that Nat Turner was a slave, and he tried to kill all the white people in order for him to survive and not be a slave any more. I guess he would fit in a violent category."

Answers to the second question (What would you do in his place?) included "I wouldn't have surrendered to the whites so easily," "I would make my followers mentaly stronger," "I would do the same exact thing," and "I would of had everything more organized and waited for a better time."

Answers to the third question (What motivated Nat Turner?) included "He wanted to take over the town," "All the slavery and hardship that went on," "His hate against whites made him rebell," and "I forget what happened."

Answers to the last question (What do you think of him?) included "He was a average leader," "I think he was stupid because he didn't organize his plans right," "He was a killer and prejudice person in a way, he felt the same against whites as they did to him," and "He was a hero who set a tone for the next blacks to following in his foot steps except a lot better than him."

In completing this written exercise, Pierre and his classmates were responding to a teacher requirement—a means, in principle, for teachers to hold presenter and audience members accountable for exhibition content. Because the students carried out this task among themselves, though, it was they who determined the more particular standards that were represented in the activity.

Pierre's questions asked for classmates' thoughts, rather than simple facts, and his classmates responded with some ideas about Nat Turner, at least some of which appeared to have been gained from the exhibition. The students' conduct of this exercise also reflected limits in the extent to which they had engaged each other in analysis. In part these limits can be attributed to Pierre's abilities as a public speaker, but written responses of similar extent and specificity were the norm for exhibitions in our class. A student stance toward writing at length, which was expressed on other occasions as well, also entered into the prevailing standards for this exercise.

Fourth Term

By obtaining information for his third-term exhibition and spending time with that information, Pierre was able to assume a more authoritative role in front of the class than he had in the first term. Pierre's appreciation of the value of preparing for an exhibition in this way was quite evident in the fourth term. In his oral history project, he also experienced further success as a researcher. At the same time, this project showed how exercising command over his information in an oral or written presentation continued to challenge him.

Pierre interviewed Thomas Slocomb, the interim director at Powell. Thomas had a variety of experiences from the civil rights era to share. In addition, he was renowned in the school as a loquacious storyteller. As Pierre would say in his written report, "He's the kind of person who talks a lot so I figure if i interview him I would get a lot of information."

Pierre had to persist in seeking a time when Thomas was available to be interviewed. Eventually, he rode with Thomas across town on an errand, during the school talent show. Pierre transcribed his entire interview—he was the only student in the class to do so—and the transcript came to 10 handwritten pages.

Later, when writing his report, Pierre would indicate how he had framed his purposes in the project. The success he identified—acquiring information—corresponded to a goal on which he had focused.

> I think that i did a pleasant job on the interview. I got the information that i wanted, I even got information that i didn't even expected. I really think if you put your mind into something and you say to your self i am gonna get it than. I really think that you can.

In order for you to do something you have to set your mind to it.
That's what i did to got my interview than. The interview went
well. I ask him about four or five questions and he gave me like
six or seven [typed] pages. now this what i called an interview.

During his panel presentation, Pierre sat with his complete transcript
in front of him. Before the exhibition started, his set of papers attracted
his classmates' attention. "Look at him, shuffling all those papers," Gloria
remarked. Later, Wayne asked, "How long did the interview take?" Other
students suggested answers: "Five hours?" "Three days?"

Pierre was the fourth student to give an opening statement. He did
not have a speech written out for this task; he therefore had to compose
a summary extemporaneously or deliver one from memory.

"I interviewed Mr. Slocomb," he began. "Who was tellin' me about
the, how he was involved in the, in the civil rights movement. Um, he
was involved in the civil rights movement when he was like 19 years old."
Pierre then paused for almost half a minute. He shook his head slightly,
and then looked at Nancy, who was serving as moderator.

"What did he do?" Nancy asked.

"Um. It's like." He tucked his lower lip under his tongue for a few
seconds, before proceeding. "When he, when he was in college, he, he was
in this group for the civil rights movement, that calls, that was, I think it
was some Meth– Methodist something, something that he was involved
in. Like, they wanted him, those people from the Methodist church
wanted him to, to help them, like, give them advice. Give them advice,
why he thought about the, bus boycott, or, the Blacks and Whites in segre-
gated schools and stuff." He was silent for a few seconds. "What else.
And he, he said a lot of things but I just can't—I'm kind of nervous so."

"Why don't you say a little bit about [another high school in the city],
desegregation," Diane said.

"Um. He said [that school] was desegregated in 1974. He was, he
was in the school, he was the, he was the principal. When the riot happened, he," Pierre stopped. "Um, mm." He pursed his lips.

Pierre was silent, head tilted down, lips moving slightly, for another
40 seconds before Wayne suggested he look in his notes. Pierre then
looked through different pages for another minute and a half. The room
remained quiet as he did this. Wayne and Jorge then suggested we move
on and give him a chance to relax. He continued to read his notes while
the two remaining panelists presented their summaries.

Several minutes after the last opening summary, I asked each panelist to answer, "What evidence did you see, in your interview, of people of different races working together in the civil rights movement?"

Pierre studied one page of his notes while the three students sitting to his right answered first. When I signaled that it was his turn, he began speaking. "Um. He, Mr. Slocomb [who is White], when there was boycott, that was on television in Miami, Florida. Like, from Kansas City him, him and his teammates, uh, was going to play football at Florida, so. He didn't know why was the boycott, like, why were, why were all Black people walking to work, were going, going to work, um, without buses. So he asked himself why. Then, then he went, he went out and marched."

Given Pierre's earlier trouble, I was delighted that he had accessed information from his notes and delivered an oral response that spoke to the question. Later, when reading his written report (most of which consisted of a complete reproduction of his transcript), I noticed details that clarified the story Pierre had told: The players' car had broken down in Montgomery, Alabama, in 1955, during the boycott initiated by Rosa Parks's actions, and they had stayed in Montgomery for at least two nights. There was no mention, though, of Thomas Slocomb actually marching with Black workers (indeed, the 1955 Montgomery boycott did not involve the sort of mass marches that characterized later phases of the civil rights movement). I also noticed another passage in the report that Pierre might have used to answer my question, since it described Thomas's advising a group of Black students who were demonstrating in a Kansas City high school where he had taught.

In the more freewheeling parts of the discussion, such as the dialogue triggered by Wayne's question about nonviolence, Pierre was mostly silent. He spoke when asked to, though (see Chapter 3). The last question of the exhibition, for each panelist to answer, was whether one's interviewee thought the civil rights movement had made a difference. Pierre said, "I think he, he thinks that the civil rights movement made a difference because, uh, there are, certain things that's happening today that Black people couldn't do back in the fifties and sixties. And, there are things happening today, that shouldn't happen."

Listening, I viewed his ability to articulate that answer as a success. It was, I thought, perhaps a sign of progress: a sign that he was gaining some facility discussing issues publicly. While listening to Gloria's answer to the same question, which was longer and contained more specific references to her interview, I had been thinking about its limitations.

A couple of days after the exhibition I told Pierre I was proud of what he had done in the exhibition—specifically, how he had recovered from his early difficulties and been able to answer questions. He shook his head. "I didn't say everything that I wanted to say." His standards pertained to how he handled the public performance, as well as how he gathered information. His standards also included an image of a better performance that he wanted to attain.

CLOSING THOUGHTS

Examples can be found above where Diane's and/or my assessment of Pierre's work differed from what our assessment of the same work, done by another student, might have been. These include a formal assessment (the grading of his research paper) as well as informal responses.

Pierre's account shows another way, as well, in which standards varied depending on the individual student—that is, were negotiated on an individual basis. By virtue of what his skills were and what challenges he found most immediate, Pierre helped to determine what endeavors he would focus on. When we coached him, Diane and I collaborated in setting this focus. We spent more time with him around the process of composing a paper, for instance, and around the mechanics of written English, than we did with other students. We also put aside issues that we might have pursued with other students—such as becoming more broadly knowledgeable about Nat Turner, or making smooth transitions, in his research paper, between sentences with disparate information.

Pierre's classroom activities, and Diane's and my work with him, often centered around his learning what might be termed basic skills of reading and writing. However, in negotiating this agenda, we did not restrict Pierre to the practice of such skills. Through exhibitions, he was exposed to processes such as formulating and defending positions, posing questions, pulling together extended projects on his own, and teaching his peers about what he had learned. He was able to engage in these aspects of schoolwork to some extent. Individual negotiations need not mean separate curricula, with only certain students having the opportunity to practice "higher-order" (Resnick, 1987) skills.

6

Anwar

Anwar Martin was in the eleventh grade. His academic skills enabled him to display a certain degree of competence in our class. He was usually able to carry out the instructions for written assignments, for instance, more fully and with less difficulty than most of his classmates. Insights about the meaning of his subject matter often appeared in his work as well. Anwar's account illustrates the complexity of the process of *raising* the standards a student pursues and attains.

Evident in Anwar's account, also, is the significance of social interactions among students in the development of standards. Exhibitions accentuated the role of these interactions, because they were public performances. Social considerations assumed heightened significance in Anwar's case, also, because he was very uncomfortable in the role of presenting before the class. How he appeared to his peers was a central issue in his thinking about exhibitions, and his discomfort constituted a hurdle to his achievement.

ANWAR'S EXHIBITIONS

First Term

During the week before exhibitions, Diane and I shared with the students a calendar for the upcoming presentations. The following Monday, Anwar reacted in a surprised manner when he saw a sign on our classroom door, affirming that exhibitions would be on Tuesday and Wednesday. "I thought it was Friday," he said. Anwar was slated to present on Tuesday. He did all his preparation on Monday night.

On Tuesday, when Diane scheduled the order of the day's presentations, Anwar agreed to be fifth, ahead of Pierre. When his turn came, Anwar lobbied for Pierre to precede him. "I'm going after Pierre. I changed my mind. No," he said. When it was clear that Pierre was more willing, Diane consented to the change.

"Okay, Anwar," Diane said after Pierre had finished and returned to his seat. Anwar then brought his poster and a sheet of notebook paper to the front of the room.

Anwar began speaking while turning the poster toward the audience. "My poster. My slogan. My logo. Can y'all see?" After holding the poster in front of him for 2 seconds, he began to set it on the teacher's desk behind him. He stopped and held it so that those to his right could see it.

"Okay, hold it up so we can really look at it," Diane said. Anwar brought the poster back in front of him. Paul, seated to his left, asked, "Can I see, man?" Anwar turned it toward Paul, and back again.

The poster was an antismoking message. An empty Newport box, around which Anwar had drawn a circle with a diagonal line through it, was taped to the center of a lavender posterboard. Flanking the circle were two single-line drawings made with a black marker. There were words written across the top of the poster.

"The slogan says—say what your slogan says," Diane said.

"Um." Anwar pulled a corner of the poster toward him and peered at the words he had written. "Oh. 'Cigarettes, the legal death sticks,'" he said.

"The legal what?" asked a classmate.

"Death sticks."

"Okay, explain your logo," Diane said. "I thought it was pretty good, and it's hard to figure it out." The line drawings were difficult to decipher at a distance.

Anwar frowned, laid the poster on the teacher's desk behind him, and looked at his sheet of notebook paper, saying, "Let me see, what I say about that." He studied the page for a few more seconds and then looked up. "Oh you wanna know why I s–, why I say it?"

"No," Diane said. Anwar looked at her inquiringly. Then she said, "Do what you were gonna do."

"Alright," Anwar said. He then began reading. "I feel that cigarettes can cause bad health problems. Such as cancer and death. Cigarettes are nothin' but slow death." He turned toward Paul, smiled and laughed.

"He's not into this," said Paul.

"I'm not into it," Anwar repeated with a shrug. He continued reading. "Some people smoke so much they stain their hands and teeth. If you smoke a pack of cigarettes a day, you'll spend between nine, to a thousand dollars a year. And you'll smoke between seven and eight thousand cigarettes a year." He added, "That's it," and turned, grinning, back toward Paul. Paul laughed.

Diane resumed her previous line of questioning. "Explain your logo then. Show people that one again."

Anwar picked up the poster, while saying under his breath to Paul, "I didn't have enough time yo. I didn't have enough time." He held the poster in front of him, so that it faced the class, and addressed Diane. "Well. Why I say that?"

"No, what's the picture. Explain what the picture is." Diane said to the class, "Does everybody get the picture?"

"No," said Celia.

"A broken coffin," said Paul.

"Which one, this one?" Anwar said, pointing to one of the line drawings.

"Is that your logo?" Diane asked.

"Yeah, that's it."

"Okay. Explain what that is."

"Oh that's um—that's a coffin with a cigarette in it."

"A what?" said Celia. "A coffin with a c– "

"With a cigarette in it, y'know what I'm sayin'," said Anwar.

"And what's on the other side?" Gloria asked, referring to the second drawing.

"Oh that's two cigarettes broken in half. Y'know." Anwar paused, and then said, "That's it?"

"Okay, questions?" Diane said as Anwar, smiling, set the poster on the desk.

"I have no questions, man," said Paul.

"No questions?" Anwar said.

"I got a question, I got a question," Diane said. "Okay, I'm a smoker. I used to be. I don't smoke any more but I, I'm like an alcoholic. I know I'd never be able to have another cigarette because I love cigarettes too much." Anwar looked at his page while she spoke. "Do you think that your, that you propagandize well enough for me to start thinking about—"

"No," Anwar said, with a firm shake of his head, before she finished the sentence.

"—whether I should quit smoking or not."

"No," he repeated, as Paul laughed. Anwar smiled, and explained to Diane, "I didn't have enough time, so, y'know, it would've been better."

"Okay," Diane said. "'Cause I think, like, your logo's pretty neat. The one, the coffin one with the cigarette as a person inside it." Anwar raised his eyebrows.

"Really original," added Celia.

"It is," Diane concurred.

Anwar said to himself, "Embarrassing."

"But it probably needs a little better execution," Diane added.

Anwar believed that his late effort had not produced a very strong exhibition, and this added to his unease before the class. He was also hesitant to own publicly those ideas that were present in his work. Joking with Paul was a more comfortable social stance for him. It enabled him to be "okay," by standards different from those which Diane and I were promoting with the assignment.

Second Term

The use Anwar made of extended and complex reading material would define possibilities for the quality of his research paper. The second-term project also posed challenges to his academic writing skills.

Anwar elected to do his project on Booker T. Washington. On the Thursday after Thanksgiving, a day when we held class in the school library, he spent a class period writing notes from the *Encyclopedia Americana*. He also told me that he had checked out a biography from his neighborhood library. The next day, I brought in W. E. B. Du Bois's *The Souls of Black Folk* (1903/1989) and asked him to read as well the chapter where Du Bois spells out his objections to Washington's strategies.

A few days later, in class, Anwar told me that he had read this chapter. I asked him what he thought about it, and he said that Du Bois says Booker T. Washington is "great." Hearing a misunderstanding, I asked Anwar to pull the book from his bag so that we could refer to it. After flipping through the chapter, I instructed Anwar to read the last paragraph. I stopped him after he read the following sentence:

> But so far as Mr. Washington apologizes for injustice, North or South, does not rightly value the privilege and duty of voting, belittles the emasculating effects of caste distinctions . . . we must unceasingly and fully oppose him. (p. 42)

I then asked Anwar what he thought about Washington not pushing for the right to vote. Anwar responded, "What difference does that make, voting? We wouldn't win." I engaged him in a brief debate, stating that there were enough Black votes in many towns to exert some power and that not voting meant letting Whites have total control of the government. Anwar held his ground, asserting that focusing on education is the best way to get ahead. "That's what my uncle tells me," he added. At the end of the exchange, I told him that what he had said should go at the end of his paper and would make it good. I felt he had entered the issues behind the Washington–Du Bois conflict, and framed them in terms that made sense to him.

The day before the research-in-progress exhibitions were to take place, Anwar fretted that his books "don't have anything." Although we had told him these presentations would be less formal than exhibitions usually were, the word *exhibition* still appeared to arouse anxiety on his part. In addition, his comment suggested a way in which he was relating to particular kinds of books. The comment seemed ironic, in that his biography had more than enough information for his project. That information, however, was not laid out in direct, compacted form—as in an encyclopedia article, for instance—so that a student could extract what he needed through concentrated note taking. I would come to suspect that working with a longer text, in which information was dispersed and summary statements not necessarily provided, would mean a change in Anwar's conception of research. (In the following term, after we found a book for his exhibition, Anwar asked me if he should "just read the whole book and not do research.")

Anwar presented his research-in-progress to Diane and five fellow students, by reading from a page he had written during the previous day's in-class exercise. He began by saying, "I chose to do my research on Booker T. Washington because I wanted to know what he was famous for, and also to understand his ways of life that he wanted for Afro-Americans." He then gave a few facts about Washington's childhood, and followed them with the sentence that began his notes from the *Encyclopedia Americana*: "He was an American Black educator and social reformer who believed that Blacks should work for advances in education and employment instead of trying to win racial equality with Whites." He then briefly described Washington's attending Hampton Institute and founding Tuskegee University, stated that Washington organized the National Negro Business League, and concluded by naming two of the books Washington wrote.

On their response sheets, where they were asked to write recommendations for the presenter, classmates suggested that Anwar "elaborate on what he accomplished," tell more about "his pholosiphy," and "give a little more information." Diane suggested Anwar "find out about his family."

Early in the week following the presentation, Anwar brought a draft of his paper to class. The draft consisted of two paragraphs, each of which filled two handwritten pages. The first was a reproduction, with minor adjustments, of his notes from the encyclopedia. This paragraph included some facts about Washington's childhood and slightly more detailed information about Washington's career than he had shared in his oral presentation. The second paragraph reproduced his notes from *The Souls of Black Folk*. It began as follows. I have italicized words that are Anwar's; the remainder are Du Bois's (pp. 30–32):

> *W. E. B. DuBois say Booker T. Washington thinking* of industrial education, conciliation of the South, and submission and silence as to civil and political rights, was not wholly original, *in fact* the free Negroes from 1830 up to our time had striven to build industrial schools, *but never accomplished because of so many set backs such as money, segregation, and just being poor. So they original said this but Booker T. Washington acreditted from it. All he did was* put enthusiasm, unlimited energy, and perfect faith into his programme, and changed it from a by path into a veritable way of life. *Mr. DuBois stresses that the* Atlanta Compromise is by all odds the most notable thing in Mr. Washington's career. *Washington said* at the Chicago celebration of the Spanish-American war he alluded to the color prejudice that is eating away the vitals of the South. When he dined with President Roosevelt, *he was in danger in many ways, such as* Southern *White people* criticism *has* been violent enough to threaten seriously his popularity.

The last two sentences in the above passage represent the themes of a Black leader speaking against racism and coming under attack. Very possibly, the phrases from Du Bois's writing that they contain had caught Anwar's eye because they resonated with his understanding of racial politics. Anwar appeared not to have perceived how Du Bois embeds these points in a larger argument. In the passage where these phrases appear, Du Bois mentions the kind of criticism Washington received and then goes on to say that, on the whole, Washington met acceptance, especially from Whites, because he pursued a limited program.

Diane and I both read the draft of Anwar's paper. In written as well as oral comments, we identified a number of ways for him to work on it: reorganizing, making the section about Du Bois more comprehensible, adding more information about Tuskegee, giving an example from a Washington speech, writing a paragraph about an essential question, and correcting some punctuation.

Anwar's final version of the paper contained a few additions to what was in the draft. In his first paragraph, he had inserted sentences that told the names of each of Washington's three wives, when and how the first two died, and the names of their children. The second paragraph, pertaining to *The Souls of Black Folk,* was unchanged. A third paragraph had been added. It contained a brief quote from a Washington speech—asserting the "dignity in tilling a field"—followed by a sentence of explanation: "He's saying in my eyes it's o.k. to be a janitor because it's a honest paying job. . . ." The new paragraph also contained statistics showing the increase in Black high school attendance during Washington's time, and this final sentence: "W. E. B. DuBois said he was a fake and credited from the free negroes in the 1830s who wanted to do the same thing but never succeeded."

Anwar acted on certain suggestions—adding information about Washington's family and providing a quote from a speech—and left alone others that involved work of greater difficulty. Tasks such as reorganizing the paper or clarifying the section on Du Bois called for more extensive efforts. In addition, they required him to work with teachers, given the stretching of his skills that they would entail. When I tried to initiate conversation around these more challenging aspects of the project, Anwar withheld his involvement. This stance, on his part, was to change in the third term, and a much different sort of collaborative pursuit developed.

Third Term

During the third term, Anwar engaged receptively and even eagerly with coaching around challenging aspects of an exhibition. His fear of performing before the whole class seemed to heighten his concern about the whole project and, in this case, contribute to a push toward higher standards.

Like most of his peers, Anwar did not identify his own topic of interest from our class activities concerning the Civil War and slavery. He ended up taking Diane's suggestion and preparing a lesson on David Walker, a free Black man whose *Walker's Appeal to the Colored People of the World* was one of the most militant pieces of antislavery writing published in the antebellum period.

As a topic, David Walker differed from Booker T. Washington in that there were not encyclopedia articles about him or biographies filled with information about his personal life and career. After Anwar had looked for information on David Walker, unsuccessfully, in the school library and his neighborhood library, I took him to a university library one afternoon after school. We found a book that included the full (85-page) text of *Walker's Appeal*, along with some background and analysis by social historian Herbert Aptheker (1965). As Anwar remarked, "There's nothing about him, only about his *Appeal.*"

One day during the next week Anwar brought in two pages of notes, which he had made from this source. One section read, in part:

> [Walker] says ignorance is the mother of treachery and deceit. . . . "He may see there, a son take his mother, who bore almost the pains of death to give him birth, and by the command of a tyrant strip her as naked as she came into the world, and apply the cowhide to her, until she falls a victim to death in the road! . . . To me the . . . quote means White people are so cruel and cold-hearted they would kill their own mother after she almost lost her life giving birth.

We sat together and discussed the passage. Anwar correctly identified the word *tyrant* as referring to the slave owner. He did not detect, though, that it is a slave "son" whose actions Walker is describing. I asked him to read from the book, sentence by sentence. The sentence preceding the one he quoted begins, "Any man who is curious to see the full force of ignorance developed among the coloured people of the United States of America, . . . " (Aptheker, 1965, p. 84). Once Anwar read that sentence, I asked him, "Who's he calling ignorant?" After he answered, I followed with, "So who would he be talking about in the example?" "Oh!" he said. We talked a little further, and I told him to keep reading at home.

As he had periodically since the day the assignment was given, Anwar, during this conference with me, expressed concern about how to deal with the "teach a lesson to the class" aspect of this exhibition. While we were discussing sections of the text, he asked occasional questions such as "What can I do, have everybody read part of it?"

Anwar's curiosity about issues associated with his topic also emerged during this conference. At one point, we were discussing a passage that described a scene with 3 Whites and 60 slaves, and Anwar said, "I don't understand how if there were more slaves than the master, they didn't take over." Here was an "essential question" that he generated. Ideally, from my point of view, a whole project could revolve around such a question. That, however, would require the student to develop his inquiry around the question in a way that would have constituted both a shift and an extension of the project on which Anwar had embarked. Anwar's question did, nonetheless, point toward a theme in Walker's writing—that of rebellion versus submission—that he might reflect on and highlight.

The following Monday, 3 days before the first scheduled exhibition in our class and 1 week before Anwar's was to take place, I was videotaping an exhibition in another class, and Anwar poked his head in the door and watched for a few minutes. Then he said, "Yo K., is that all I gotta do? That's easy." I nodded, and he added, "You'll help me?"

The next day we met, and Anwar asked for step-by-step guidance on how to do the presentation. I provided a rough outline, which he wrote down: First, give background; second, share excerpts from the *Appeal;* third, get feedback from the class. I then asked some questions to suggest the kind of information he could provide in the background section. He tried to write each of them down, but I did not pause for him to do so. I said that he did not have to answer all these particular questions, but that he needed to give an idea, in a way that made sense to him, of who Walker was.

One possibility I offered was to tell how other people reacted to Walker. To this Anwar responded, without a trace of irony in his voice, "I wanna know how the *class* will react to him."

Friday he approached me again. "How'm I gonna do it?" he asked. We met toward the end of class. When I began reviewing Tuesday's outline with him, Anwar asked what he could do after presenting background on David Walker and telling about the *Appeal.* I clarified the outline's suggestion: that he photocopy and distribute some excerpts from the *Appeal* and discuss them with the class. He then identified specific passages he could use for this purpose. Over the past week and a half, he had been continuing to read small segments of the *Appeal,* although my urgings that he read more by the next day had sometimes been unheeded.

On Monday, Anwar and Pierre were both scheduled to present. Pierre was willing to go first. During Pierre's exhibition, Anwar made statements such as "I'm not gonna go" and "I'm gonna look stupid." When Pierre finished, Anwar had his papers out on his desk but was saying "I don't know how to do it." We decided to let him wait another day, rationalizing that time in the class period was getting short anyway.

Anwar and I then went to a separate room for a run-through. First I asked him some questions, which Anwar answered easily with essential facts about Walker's life and work. "Can we do it like this?" he asked. I told him no, but that I was trying to help him get a sense of what he could say. Then we role-played the section of the lesson that used the excerpts from *Walker's Appeal,* with me, as a student, reading the passages Anwar had photocopied and asking him "What does that mean?" at different points. After giving a few explanations in response to these questions, he commented, "Oh, that's easy, I can do that." Then he added, "I just need to get started."

Anwar also said he might ask the class if they thought Walker was a hatemonger—"the word they're calling Farrakhan." I asked him what passage would help him raise that issue, and he showed me one he had marked:

> But the Whites having made us so wretched, by subjecting us to slavery, and having murdered so many millions of us, in order to make us work for them, and out of devilishness—and they ... strip and beat us one before the other—chain, hand-cuff, and drag us about like rattle-snakes—shoot us down like wild bears, before each other's faces, to make us submissive to, and work to support them and their families. (Aptheker, 1965, p. 127)

With this comment and reference, among others, Anwar indicated that he had made some meaning of the text and that he had some understanding of issues it raised. I wondered, now, how he would fare at sharing that understanding with his classmates.

Anwar seated himself at a table in the front of the room, facing the class. "Alright," he said. He looked at the page of notes in front of him; then his eyes darted around the room. After several seconds passed, Bruce asked him, "What'd you do it on?"

"David Walker."

"Who?"

"David Walker." He smiled at Fred, and scratched his brow.

After several more seconds, I asked, "Who was David Walker?"

Anwar lifted his hands slightly off the table, with palms facing each other, and looked back and forth. Nancy encouraged him to go ahead.

"He was a Black abolitionist who wrote a pamphlet, called *Walker's Appeal*. The *Appeal* talked to Blacks about Whites and how they were being treated in the South. Y'all want to know when he was born?"

"Yeah, I do," said Diane.

Anwar gave Walker's birthdate. He then continued, telling that Walker was born free because his mother was free, that his mother taught him to read and write, that he moved from North Carolina to Boston, and that he was a tailor.

Next, Anwar distributed to each audience member four photocopied excerpts from the *Appeal*, stapled together in a packet. He explained to the class, "What I passed out was, certain parts of his article, that I want the class to go over. Somebody wanna read, volunteer to read?"

Nancy volunteered, and read the passage Anwar and I had discussed in our first conference, about the son beating his mother. After Nancy finished, Anwar asked, "Do y'all, y'all understand what he said?" There was no response, save for a side comment by Patrice. Anwar tried again: "Do y'all have any questions about what he's sayin'?"

"Oh yeah, what is he, what is he talkin' about?" asked Patrice.

Anwar perceived a sarcastic tone and did not answer her.

A visiting student teacher spoke. "He's saying here that ignorance among Black people is a bad thing. My question is, why is he saying, well, that ignorance is a bad thing?"

"Because he wants—"

She added, "'Cause he wants Black people to get educated?"

"Yeah he wants them to get educated, and he wants them to be aware of how they're being treated. 'Cause he says they're being treated like animals, but they, they're men too. And he wants them to be aware of it." He paused. "No questions?"

Wanting more of the meaning of this first passage to come out before Anwar went on to the next one, I asked him, "Well, the last two sentences, what's he talking about?"

"Which part? Read it."

I obliged: "'He may see there a son take his mother, who bore almost the pains of death to give him birth, and by the command of a tyrant strip her as naked as she came into the world and apply a cowhide to her until she falls victim to a death in the road.'"

"You want to know what that means?" he asked.

"Yeah," I said.

"What do you think it means?"

Our "teacher" and "student" roles had become tangled. I did not want to be the one to supply the interpretation of the passage. "Well I think I kinda know, so, um, I think it would be good if, . . . "

"I have a idea," he interjected, "but I just want to see—"

" . . . if every–, maybe if somebody else in the class could study that sentence and, try to figure out what he's talking about as an example of ignorance."

"Volunteers?" said Anwar. He paused and repeated, "Volunteers?"

No one responded.

I turned to Wayne, usually the most willing in such a situation, and asked him if he had a copy of the text. He retrieved his packet from an adjacent desk and asked which sentence we were talking about. Thus informed, he read the sentence aloud. "It seems like, um, kinda, some-body turned on somebody else, I think," he added.

"They turned on their own mother," said Diane.

"Yeah," said Wayne. "That his mother did somethin' for, um, to the child who gave birth but the child didn't, didn't do anything to pay the mother back or, something like that."

"Yeah," Diane said. "I think it's a good illustration and I like Anwar's choice of that quote, because it illustrates some, y'know, extreme bru-tality."

"Anwar," I said, "maybe you could tell what the—I mean when

would that happen in slavery? What are the circumstances in slavery when a son might do that to his mother?"

"Like, if she did something wrong, and, like if she like, I don't know, did something wrong and the slave master told him to beat her, he would, he'd do it. He'd be stupid and do it."

"And what's David Walker saying about that?" I asked him.

"It's not good."

After a few quiet seconds, Anwar said, "Alright." He looked at his papers. "Alright. Somebody wanna volunteer to read, the um, the paragraph where it says, 'Affray and Murder'?"

Jorge volunteered, and read the section Anwar had indicated. It was a story that Walker had excerpted from a newspaper, about a group of 60 slaves who were being transported interstate. Some of the slaves had broken free of their handcuffs, beaten their new owner and his two colleagues, and left those three men for dead. One of the three remained alive, though, and after a woman slave helped him flee, he rallied the local White community to capture those who had revolted.

When Jorge finished, Anwar said, "Was that a good enough example of the ignorance that he's saying that Blacks had for themselves, back then?" The room was silent as Anwar looked toward each table of students.

"What was the ignorance?" I asked. "Who was ignorant?"

"Um, the um, the guy named Gordon. And his associate Allen. Because, they were Black and they bought Black slaves to be sold, and that's like their own brothers. They were only thinking about money." Gordon was the slave owner; Anwar had identified him and Allen as Black, most likely because Gordon is referred to in the text as a "negro driver."

"Black owning the Black," Jorge said softly.

"What about the woman?" Diane asked. In the paragraph beneath the passage Jorge read, Walker emphasizes her "ignorant and deceitful acts."

"The woman?" Anwar asked. He studied his copy of the text for 15 seconds.

"She was, she was ignorant too," he said, "because, he had um, he had held her as a slave, handcuffed and shackled, and when she got free, she just helped them back up, like it was okay. Because, bein' dumb, whatever."

Anwar answered one more question of mine about this passage, and then said, "Any other questions? Questions?"

Several students spoke, with a mixture of humor and seriousness:

"What is this about?"

"Say like, what's the whole point of your whole exhibition like?"

"I still don't know what this is about."

"I don't know neither, he's just tellin' everybody to read. Read what? Who is he, when did he die?" said Patrice.

Anwar pulled the hood of his sweatshirt over his head until it covered his eyes, and lowered his head close to the table.

"Patrice, he can answer that," I said. Anwar pushed the hood back from his head and looked up. "Give him a minute to answer that." I looked toward Anwar and said, "Who is he, and what's the point that he's trying to make?"

"Naw, man, why do I gotta go through that again?" Anwar said.

"Just sum it all up," said Wayne.

"Give a summary," echoed Claudia.

"Like wrap it up, baby, wrap it up," added Fred, laughing.

Anwar frowned, and then brought his notes back in front of him and read. "He was a Black abolitionist, who wrote the pamphlet *Walker's Appeal*, in four articles. It talked to the Blacks about Whites, and how they were being treated. Okay? He was born in Wilmington, North Carolina. That's good enough for you? Alright."

"Anwar, what is the main point that he's making in these two examples that you gave?" I asked, wanting him to somehow share what he knew in a way that would connect to the class.

"They're ignorant."

"What does he say they're doing that's ignorant?"

"A lot of things. Killing their mothers. Selling their own brothers and sisters. A lot of things."

There was not time to look at the remaining two passages that Anwar had photocopied. To conclude the exhibition, Anwar asked the class one question, to be answered in writing: "Do you feel that David Walker's *Appeal* today would help Blacks see what's going on in society?"

"Could you repeat the question?" Jorge asked.

Anwar rephrased the question, in a way that revealed a connection he had seen. "Do you feel that David Walker's *Appeal*, today, would help Blacks see what they are doing to themselves? Such as, Black-on-Black crimes?"

"What was this appeal, anyway?" asked Bruce.

"Forget it, man. I'm not going over it. No. I'm not going over it," Anwar said. Diane and I explained to Bruce that the *Appeal* was the text from which we had been reading.

Anwar repeated his question (in its second form) once more. Each student wrote a one-sentence answer. Wayne wrote, "Yes, because if you accept being treated less than and acting like a less than you will be, and this leads to ignorance." Jorge wrote, "I really can't say but I think if people would be more informed of other races out there especially their own there would not be any ignorance." Ronald wrote, "He really didn't make an impact on blacks today."

After the rest of the class had left the room, Anwar and I conversed briefly. He said that he could talk about the material better than he had, and that he could talk about it more easily if I or someone just asked him questions. Showing exasperation, he also commented, "I ask them do they have any questions and they just sit there and don't say anything." I told him my colleagues and I often have the same experience. "Yeah, but you're trained to put up with that," he replied.

Anwar had pursued some new achievements with this project. He had worked to understand a difficult text, publicly articulated his understanding of its meaning, and attempted to lead a class session. Still, he did not meet one of the central goals embedded in this exhibition format, in that he did not explain or otherwise present his material in a way that engaged his audience with it. This was in many ways a harder task than explaining the material to me, as he had done in our last rehearsal.

One obstacle to his success was that the text itself, as a class handout, was opaque to his classmates. In addition, Anwar's obvious unease made him a less compelling speaker than he might have been. Furthermore, in order to successfully explain material such as this, he would have needed to improvise elaborations when his initial statements fell flat. That would have strained both his public-speaking skill and his knowledge of the material. More fully meeting the general challenges he had taken on would have entailed a more extensive, longer-term endeavor and repeated attempts.

Fourth Term

Anwar's fourth-term exhibition represented a retreat in terms of his efforts at presenting to his classmates.

For his oral history project, Anwar interviewed his grandmother. Two weeks before his exhibition was scheduled, he told me he had done part of the interview but that his grandmother had stopped for the night and he did not think she would do it with him again. It was not finished, he said. He did not do a second interview with her.

At the beginning of the class period in which he was to take part in a panel discussion, Anwar remained in the audience as the other panelists took seats in the front of the room. While giving instructions to the panel, Nancy looked toward Anwar and told him, "You need to be sitting up here too." "For nothing?" he asked her. He pursued, "What if it's no good, messed up?" When she explained that even if students had not done their interviews, they needed to answer general questions that were addressed to everyone, Anwar joined the panel.

When it was his turn to give an opening summary, Anwar gave a one-sentence description of the interview and added, "She didn't say that much." Diane then asked him if his grandmother had told him about any incident or story. He replied, "I don't know, she said some story, when she went to the movie she wanted to sing, or something like that. Like, White kids, and they wouldn't let her 'cause she was Black, somethin' like that."

"She wanted to sing?" Diane asked.

"Yeah."

"Hmm," Diane said.

"Something like that," Anwar said.

After Nancy instructed the students in the audience each to pose a question, Claudia asked the panelists, "Out of the interview, what questions intrigued you the most, or what answers intrigued you the most?" Nancy called on Anwar to answer first.

"What questions intrigued me most? None."

"Or answers," Nancy said.

"None."

"Well, pick one."

"None."

"There's got to be one that intrigued you somewhat," Nancy said. "At least more than the others."

"Just when she said, at the movies that she couldn't sing, they wouldn't let her sing—that's about it."

"I don't understand that story," said Diane. "What was she—"

"I don't know, figure it out later, man," he said. "Damn," he added under his breath.

"I mean it sounds like an interesting story but I don't get it," said Diane.

Compared to his performance in the panel discussion, Anwar's written report conveyed an impression of a much stronger project. It contained a similar amount of information from his interview as Gloria's and Wayne's contained from theirs. He described a few incidents from his grandmother's childhood, some details of race relations in her Indiana community in the 1940s and 1950s, and some strong responses she expressed toward the unequal conditions of that time. He explained the movie theater story: Her father's girlfriend took her to the movies, she saw some White girls singing on a stage outside and said she wanted to do what they were doing, and her father's girlfriend told her "only the Whites can do it." He also told in some detail about a visit his grandmother had made to a White elementary school classmate's house, a story that showed economic differences as well as some of the emotions that could accompany crossing racial boundaries.

In his "reflection" section, Anwar wrote,

> Although with the very little information that I had I was able to conceive a big general concept of how life was back then. I feel very bad for her and her family because she had severe expressions of hurt about how her life was back then. Especially how Blacks today are wasting their time and not doing anything with their lives. If only she had a second chance she could better herself. Till this day she stresses very much how she resents White people but said there are some okay ones out there.

Very likely, the prospects of discussing sensitive racial matters and exposing his grandmother's experiences and emotions made him especially uncomfortable, concerned for her privacy, and unsure of how to proceed—compounding the ordeal of presenting to the point where he decided to avoid it.

Powell humanities teachers attempted to follow the assessment principle of providing diverse ways for students to demonstrate their learning. While we required oral presentations of students if they were to pass for a term, students were not graded solely on those presentations. When an exhibition included other elements (e.g., research, a written report), those elements were also considered when we evaluated the project. Anwar's experience illustrates how such a policy affords some protection for students who have particular problems with one medium.

CLOSING THOUGHTS

In comments about his first-, third-, and fourth-term projects, Anwar identified ways that he would have liked for his work to be better. His propaganda campaign was put together too quickly, he did not express what he knew and thought about David Walker as well as he might have, and his interview with his grandmother was incomplete. Embedded in these self-assessments were ideas that converged with teachers' about what constituted quality work. To some extent, he wanted to meet those standards.

Anwar's standards also included a regard for schooling in a broader sense. On several occasions, he remarked that he was planning on attending college. Family support had nurtured this aim: The previous spring, for instance, his uncle, a teacher at another high school in the city, had taken Anwar with some of his own students on a tour of historically Black colleges. Anwar also spoke of wanting to become a doctor. There were ambiguities, though. One day in early spring, for instance, he asked me, "Could I get into a real good school—like Miami—from here [Powell]?" When I told him, "Yeah, but you'd have to pull your work up a notch," he replied, "I know, but I don't like it to cut into my free time."

Standards that clashed with teachers' were also embedded in Anwar's views of more specific aspects of his work. Once, for instance, when we were conferring about his upcoming *Walker's Appeal* exhibition, he asked me, "Why should I read all this stuff when I'm only gonna have a little in my report?" He apparently did not share my ideas about how broad knowledge of one's topic would benefit an exhibition, or about the distinction between an exhibition and a "report." A student's ideas—like his teachers'—may ultimately change, of course; in the meantime, such teacher–student differences are a source of friction, with respect to the development of mutual purposes.

In addition to the value he placed on working in certain ways, Anwar's standards had to do with the kinds of work he understood how to do. In his exhibition projects, he encountered texts that were difficult for him to read and a kind of research (digesting extended texts before distilling main points and analyzing significant passages) with which he was unaccustomed. He also encountered presentation tasks with which he had little experience. He needed to learn new competencies in these areas in order to feel ready to pursue certain achievements and/or in order to pursue them successfully.

If one takes into account the nature of a student's acquired skills, what might appear to an observer as simply a lack of student effort becomes a more complex phenomenon. For instance, Anwar did not do all the reading in *Walker's Appeal* that I asked him to do. Given his tenuous understanding of what he had already read, and of how to present it, he would have been within reason, especially toward the end of the project, to have judged that reading more would do him little good.

In his third-term exhibition, Anwar made an attempt to perform in ways that he had not performed before. Such an attempt, in principle, constitutes the kind of activity through which classroom standards can be raised. The negotiation of standards among teachers and students can take the form of a search for such activity: for new challenges in which the student will agree to engage. The project on *Walker's Appeal* revolved around a text that was perhaps overly difficult for Anwar to read and therefore may not have been the optimum challenge for him. On the other hand, the unavailability of other sorts of reading material forced him to focus more on Walker's ideas than on biographical data. At any rate, he stretched himself further in response to this assignment than in response to anything else Diane and I asked of him during the year.

The work through which such stretching occurs is a joint undertaking, involving teachers and students. A student's levels of both motivation and comfort develop in part through the relationships with his teachers. Anwar's third-term project shows how, in addition, teachers collaborate in the performance itself when they coach a student. My consultations with Anwar helped him make sense of the text, for instance. I also shared some responsibility for his exhibition's shortcomings. Afterward, I questioned the wisdom of having advised him to distribute the excerpts from *Walker's Appeal,* which were barely comprehensible to his classmates. Perhaps if I had suggested a controversial question for him to pose—such as, Is it ignorance to beat your mother when the slave owner is threatening to kill you?—I would have given him a better vehicle for engaging his classmates. Still, the teacher's role recedes at some point. The standards Anwar realized through a discussion around this question would ultimately have depended on how he conducted it.

Understanding the Negotiation of Standards

Part I shows that students and teachers both had input into standards. Part II examines the process of negotiation in more detail.

A classroom is a dynamic system in which standards exist in various forms. Through the reflections, actions, and interactions of the people in the classroom, those standards take shape and evolve. Each chapter in Part II focuses on a particular aspect of classroom standards and/or their formation.

Chapter 7 looks at one set of standards: thoughts that students had about the work they did. It shows student purposes that accompanied exhibitions similar to those presented in Part I, and it shows ways that students regarded their work after they had done it.

Describing standards that existed in students' minds does not answer the question of how those standards were created—or who created them. Chapter 8 begins to address these questions by looking at students' perceptions of challenge and students' interests as sources of standards. It considers, also, how standards evolved through students' actions, as well as in their minds. Chapter 9 continues to discuss how students created standards, showing the role played by students' interactions with one another.

Principles put forth in these chapters, concerning how students possess and determine standards, are central to the concept of negotiated classroom standards—especially since alternatives to that concept tend to have students depending on the standards of teachers and other adults. Also, a central tenet of this book is that because students do the ultimate work of learning in a classroom, the standards *they* follow as they carry out this work are of prime importance.

Negotiation, however, is a situation in which both students and teachers influence standards. It is a situation in which students and teachers collaborate to produce certain standards, and also one in which student-created standards and teacher-established standards coexist. The last three chapters focus on aspects of classroom standards and standard setting that involve teachers.

Teachers, like students, have standards in their minds. Chapter 10 describes how Powell teachers thought about exhibition work. It also considers how these teachers' ideas were, to some extent, influenced by their experiences with students—one way in which standards were collaborative.

Chapter 11 examines expectations that teachers projected to students, and how students responded to these. It shows students and teachers interacting to create—and negotiate—standards.

Chapter 12 concludes the analysis by returning to the five theories of standard setting—demanding, informing, teaching, negotiating, and arising—presented in Chapter 1. It discusses each in terms of the influence of teacher practices on classroom standards, in light of the evidence presented in this study.

Some additional students and teachers appear in Part II along with those who appeared in Part I. A group of students whom I interviewed—16 in all—are quoted frequently in Chapters 7 through 9 and 11. These students were in different classes from the one I co-taught. Their interviews provide a closer look at students' thoughts about exhibitions than my conversations and observations in our class provide. In addition, these students broaden the diversity of exhibition experiences shown in the book. They expand the variety of skills, habits, and performances presented by the four students in Part I. At the same time, fundamental traits appear repeatedly among these students' work that are similar to what was shown in Part I.

Wayne, Gloria, Pierre, and Anwar appear in Part II, as well. They are mentioned in Chapter 7 alongside other students' comments about work that resembles theirs. In subsequent chapters, about standard-setting processes, some of the examples illustrating points are drawn from their performances and from classroom interactions involving them. Some incidents involving other students in the class I co-taught are also presented.

Two teachers in addition to Diane and myself—Barry Sheehy and Charles Touchstone—appear in Chapters 10 through 12, via comments they made during interviews. Barry and Charles taught tenth- through twelfth-grade humanities classes, as Diane and I did. Barry taught four of the students I interviewed, in a class he co-taught with Diane (the others were in a class Diane taught by herself). Teaching with exhibitions was a project that humanities department members embarked on and thought about together. Barry's and Charles's remarks provide added perspectives on the year's experience and added glimpses at teachers' standards and role.

7

Students' Standards: What Students Thought About Exhibition Work

In one sense, standards are ideas that people have about what they are doing. Notions of what are worthy ways of expending one's effort, and of what constitutes quality work, are standards. Standards also frame an activity or performance: They define what aspects of it are significant in one's view.

Negotiation of standards in classrooms means that such ideas exist among students as well as teachers. Part I shows students expressing these ideas, directly or indirectly, as they decided where to focus their energies and how to go about doing their work. It also shows students using their standards to evaluate their products.

This chapter looks further into how students thought about exhibitions. In their remarks, the students I interviewed indicated what aspects of their exhibition experiences stood out to them, what their purposes were as they prepared and presented exhibitions, and what they considered a good performance. Their comments addressed various components of the overall task of doing an exhibition: having information, thinking about that information, working to prepare, and presenting.

The standards in students' minds are especially important because of their connection to student work. The relationship between thought and action runs in both directions: Students' views of exhibition work can both guide their actions and emerge from their experiences with the work. This relationship is explored at various points in the chapter and is the subject of the chapter's concluding remarks.

HAVING INFORMATION

Having information was an aspect of exhibitions that several of the students I interviewed identified as significant, just as Pierre and Gloria did when commenting on their work. Deniece Hodge, for instance, when describing what she had achieved in her third-term exhibition, emphasized knowledge of the Middle Passage that she had acquired:

> I had a lot of notes and stuff about it [from class] . . . and I went and got more information about it in the library. And I put it together, and I presented a map of how—the trip from Africa to the Americas, and to the Caribbean, the slave ships. That was the Middle Passage.

Information equipped students to both present material and field questions. Brett Loughran recounted how, during his exhibition on the Battle of Gettysburg, he had felt successful in the latter regard:

> I was sayin' like Confederates, and the Union, and the Federals, and [the audience] had to go back and ask questions like who was who and stuff like that. And then when I gave the figures on how many people died they had to, just like, double check, and then they asked like where the most people died, what strategies were used. . . . Some of them [were asking] just to get it straight 'cause like they must've not understood me. But some of them weren't, like somebody asked me who were the major generals, and like I had only said a couple of the generals. So I actually had to go back and look in my notes, to see who the major generals were. 'Cause I had them written down.

"Having information" is a principle. As a standard, its concrete meaning depended not only on whether students thought it was important to have information, but also on how much and what kind of information they thought it was important to have. Although students' standards were not precisely defined, fixed, or uniform in these regards, they did tend to have certain general dimensions.

The degree to which the students portrayed in Part I became informed about their topics is reflective of what occurred in exhibitions throughout the school. Some of the students I interviewed shared thoughts that accompanied work of this nature. A number of students described no areas of potential improvement—in terms of how informed they were—for exhibitions in which they, like Wayne in the second and third terms or Pierre in the third, covered some facts about a topic yet could have, with more research, become considerably more knowledgeable. Brett, for instance, obtained his information on the Battle of Gettysburg mainly from one 45-minute video. He said, "I did a good job I thought. 'Cause I understood it." When he allowed that he "could have done better" in this exhibition, he focused on the techniques he used to present his information to the class: "Yeah, if I like had had a handout or somethin', I think I would have done better." Nadine Carson, similarly, said of her third-term exhibition on the Virginia Slave Codes, "That was good, 'cause I found out some information about that." She noted that with this research, she was able to answer questions successfully. The questions she described asked for details about slave codes: "They was askin' like, in what states was there laws passed—'cause it wasn't in all states, the law wasn't the same in all states. Just askin' what states, and, could I repeat what I said and, like—and the punishment they would get."

The goals students pursued, and the kinds of performances they described as good, varied somewhat from student to student. Eva Ineshin, for instance, said that for her third-term exhibition on Harriet Tubman, "I wanted to know more about her, more than anybody else would in the classroom. Y'know, I wouldn't want to be standin' there, and they're like, 'Well, what happened there?' and I'm like, 'I don't know.'" An avid reader, Eva proceeded to read four books about her subject.

All the same, there were apparent limits to the amount and kind of information that Eva thought were good to display in an exhibition. Her 7-and-a-half-minute talk was a biographical summary: It began with some childhood incidents, and described the evolution of Tubman's efforts to help slaves escape. Eva gave the most detail about the childhood incidents. What she told about the Underground Railroad and her subject's role in it consisted of a listing of some of Tubman's trips, a mention of two collaborators, an explanation of why slaves called Tubman "Moses," and a mention that there was a $40,000 reward for Tubman's capture. It is not clear how much more Eva knew beyond what she shared in her presentation, especially since questioning was aborted by the ending of the period. When I interviewed her, though, she said, "The talk . . . really, you couldn't make any better." Her consideration of her audience, which is discussed in Chapter 9, appeared to contribute to this assessment. When discussing how she thought she might have improved her performance in this exhibition, Eva, like Brett, focused on additional presentation techniques she might have used.

Gail Purse approached her third-term exhibition less ambitiously than Eva. Her knowledge about her topic, John Brown, was constrained by the fact that she did all her preparation on the night before her exhibition. She used two American history textbooks that she had in her house. These two sources, she said, had "the same exact thing on him. All they do is talk about how he killed five people and then he did the raid." Gail was somewhat disappointed they did not say more: "I just thought there wasn't enough. I mean, there was enough, but y'know how usually there's so much information." However, she took into account what information was available in these sources and made a favorable assessment of her work: "I read the pages about him over a few times, and I wrote note cards. . . . There wasn't that much to know so I thought I knew it pretty good. I knew what I was talkin' about."

Neither Eva's nor Gail's manner when speaking of her exhibition suggested that she considered it to be especially outstanding or inspiring work. During our interviews, though, I probed for their conceptions of what would characterize a better exhibition, in terms of content; when pressed in this way, both students spoke of having done a good job. They did not reveal visions of what better jobs would be like.

THINKING ABOUT ONE'S INFORMATION

As the third- and fourth-term exhibitions in Part I showed, talking about one's topic during an exhibition entailed more than simply having information. Students also needed to gain a certain command of that information. This involved a sort of thinking that several of the students I interviewed identified as important. Nadine termed it "understanding" her material. She described what she felt would make an exhibition good:

> A lot of good note takin's . . . and research—not just copying something down but research. And understanding what you write— don't just write something because you think it seems good. Understand it when you write it, so when you do and you are asked questions, you will understand what you read and you can answer without being like, "Oh I don't know," or going back looking through your papers.

Gail was referring to a similar form of understanding when she spoke of having reread her information on John Brown, so that "I knew what I was talkin' about."

Gail's remark illustrates how this criterion of "understanding" did not necessarily mean knowing about one's topic extensively or understanding all of one's material. In her exhibition, for instance, she had read a quote from Frederick Douglass ("A system of brute force must be met with its own weapons"), added "I don't know what that means," and gone on with her talk. "Knowing what I was talkin' about" meant, rather, that she felt confident about certain information that she would present.

Some students referred to judgments they needed to make about what information to include in their exhibitions. Deciding what to include meant assessing the value of various pieces of information. LaTanya Jackson described this thought process as "tryin' to figure out, okay is this the same, is this different, is this significant? Or is this just somethin' to fill up the space? Y'know, you have to pull out what's significant and what's not." Eva alluded to similar judgments when she compared preparing an exhibition to studying for a test:

> If you do an exhibition, . . . you have to actually create this visual thing and you have to create this paper, upon which you're gonna base a conversation. . . . You know, you think about it a lot more, about how you're gonna construct it so that other people would pay attention to it.

There were other kinds of thinking about one's topic, which teachers might view as signs of skillful humanities performance, that the students I interviewed either did not mention or appeared not to regard as especially important. One was the making of connections to other subject matter. Humanities topics tend to have elastic boundaries. Past the areas of knowledge where students have prepared, there are innumerable directions in which they can extend. When presenters received questions from the audience that went beyond the information they had covered, those questions could be viewed by the recipient as arbitrary requests rather than as representative of a kind of thinking that would be good to do. Paul Wade's propaganda campaign, for instance, urged people to arm themselves with handguns. He enthusiastically took on questions that pressed him to defend his position. In our interview, though, he also noted, "Someone asked something about another country—it was corny." Julia Contreras gave an exhibition in which she discussed why the South lost the Civil War. She recalled:

> They tryin' to, like, ask you what did that have to do with this, or— y'know with other subjects? But I couldn't answer because, at that point I only knew about what I was doing, so—. . . .
>
> There's too many terms, and issues, and things that happen in history, right? And, like, I don't know everything that happened

like in the U.S. history, so when I did why the South lost, what if they said, "Oh how did that affect the economy?" or whatever?

As Julia's comments ("I only knew about what I was doing") indicate, students were restricted in their ability to make connections within and among topics because of the limits in their overall knowledge base. This lessened the likelihood of connection making becoming a valued practice.

Another kind of thinking students could do about their topics involved what Deniece called "theories." Most of the students I interviewed appeared not to view working with "theories" as having the central importance that obtaining and "understanding" information did. Deniece reported, matter-of-factly, that in her exhibition on the Middle Passage neither her presentation nor her peers' questions offered theories:

> What I presented to the class was just strictly the facts that I had got from the library and stuff like that. . . . We all in the class really never knew too much about the Middle Passage, so no one really came up with any, knew any theories about what was goin' on in the Middle Passage. . . . I just basically went with the facts.

Her comment, like Julia's, points to the significance of her and her classmates' limited knowledge of the topic, which gave them less basis for developing interpretations or points of view.

The first-term assignment was different from the third-term assignment in that students were instructed to take a position on an issue, and in that most chose contemporary topics with which their peers were familiar. When speaking of her propaganda campaign against marijuana abuse, Deniece noted that "there's a lot of theories about marijuana." Yet when such ideas were brought up during her exhibition, Deniece was, her later remarks suggest, unsure how to go about addressing them:

> I read from a paper the information that I had, and after that [classmates] had some questions—not exactly, they didn't say they're facts, but this is what they heard about marijuana. . . . I couldn't really answer those questions because I only had the facts about marijuana. So they was like, "Well a friend of mine told me that marijuana's this for you, it's that for you," and I was like, "Well—"—I mean I guess that's how they perceive it, but the facts is here like I read it on the paper, about what type of chemicals was in marijuana, what side effects it had on you.

In this recounting of the exhibition, she accepted the different ideas presented to her as her classmates' differing perceptions, to which they were entitled, rather than addressing the relationships among different theories and evidence.

To say that students did not, in interviews, discuss making connections or working with theories is not to say that they never felt inclined to think in these ways. High school students, like adults, are not necessarily aware of all they are doing at the time they are doing it, or able to articulate all they have done. Julia, for instance, based her third-term exhibition around a theory: that the South could have won the Civil War had its leaders followed a proposed plan to raise money for weapons. In her work, then, she approached a standard involving the presence of theories, even though she did not describe her performance in such terms. Other students, like Wayne, also raised issues in their research-based third-term exhibitions. The majority of the third-term exhibitions, though, did not revolve around such themes or points of view, just as students did not mention this attribute as a criterion for a good exhibition.

WORKING TO PREPARE

Most of the students I interviewed indicated that they thought being "prepared" and doing "research" were important determinants of the success of an exhibition. When assessing classmates' exhibitions, a number of students made comments such as "It sounded like [Beth] knew exactly what she was talkin' about, and she was prepared and ready" or "Sean could have done better, but he wasn't really prepared for it."

As was the case with "having information" and "understanding," the standards represented by "prepared" and "research" depended on what students meant by these terms—what kinds of performances they considered to be good in these respects. Some common qualities appear in several students' characterizations of successful or satisfactory preparation and research.

One aspect of preparation was finding information. Some of the students I interviewed described efforts that yielded information they felt served them well in their exhibitions. Harlan Franco, for instance, discussing his exhibition about Harriet Tubman, mentioned some pieces of information he had told his class that "nobody knew." I asked him how he found these; he replied, "Encyclopedias and library and stuff. And I think it was this Black history book up in the library. I xeroxed a bunch of sheets on her. And then I just read all of it, and just took out the main details. And put it all in one." LaTanya described a similar process—searching through a source for relevant data—in more detail:

> Well, I had two books. And they were both on the Middle Passage. . . . I started reading about how the slave owners would con other Africans into turnin' their people in, and things of that nature. . . . And I asked myself, "Is this the Middle Passage?" I read on some more. No, it wasn't. . . . And, so, I read on, and they started explaining when they got on the ship and when they were traveling across the sea. And I said, "Is this the Middle Passage?" And my question was answered: Yes, it is. When they were travelin' on the sea, cooped up in the cubby holes, and how they had to lie in their own waste and stuff. And I just read a lot of different facts that I had never even knew.

LaTanya remarked that she "had enough information" for this exhibition, which raises the issue of how much research was "enough." In their research, both she and Harlan were mainly concerned with locating information they would include directly in their presentations. If researching toward a different standard of "enough," students might seek to become more broadly knowledgeable about their topics and use some of their knowledge more indirectly. Gloria indicated that she saw the value in the latter sort of effort when she said that she would have had a better understanding of how Harriet Jacobs felt if she had obtained more information. Such a view was rarely expressed by students, though, and even more rarely acted upon. Anwar's question, "Why should I read all this stuff when I'm only gonna have a little in my report?" suggested a principle for determining how much research was "enough" that many students appeared to follow.

In addition to obtaining information, "preparing" meant studying and organizing one's information so that one could show a command of it and present it effectively. Some students described steps of this nature that they felt had benefited their presentations. Renée Shackleford had watched a videotape more than once, to familiarize herself with its contents and select portions to show. Brett had done the same. Gail had re-read her pages and note cards. Luis Hernandez had recruited humanities teacher Barry Sheehy, who did not teach Luis's class, to watch a videotape of the Gettysburg Address with him and answer questions that Luis thought audience members might ask. LaTanya, by contrast, said of her third-term exhibition, "I really wasn't prepared . . . to get up in front of the class. . . . I had enough information. But I was partly reading from the book. . . . Sometimes I thought I wasn't prepared for the question." She felt she could have done a better exhibition "[if] I would have wrote down my information. I just did it from what I remember reading."

Some students' overriding concern, in some instances, was simply that they be in a position to present on the appointed day. Deniece expressed how this aspect of preparing was significant to her, when I asked her what, in general, distinguishes a good exhibition:

> What makes a good exhibition a good exhibition? Determination: you have to have—you have to be determined to get this done, on time. And present it, on time. So you have to set your mind to, to say, "Look, . . . I have to do this. Let me do it and get it out of the way but—not rush it, but get it done." A lot of people, kids I know just slip and they'll wait till the last minute to try to sum up an exhibition and they fail. So, you have to have that determination.

During the third term in Deniece's class, only a minority of students had exhibitions ready to present on the days they were scheduled. It was perhaps with this experience in mind that Beth Lowenstein looked back at the first-term exhibitions and made the following assessment: "I mean everybody got up and went, so that was pretty—actually, I thought that was very good. I mean, everybody did it. They brought in those big posters and people did songs and stuff."

A theme that runs through several students' descriptions of their preparation for exhibitions is the short time span in which that preparation occurred. The time frames of the assignments limited the duration of students' efforts, especially in the first term. How students approached the assignments was also a factor. In the second, third, and fourth terms, the assignments were given a month to 6 weeks before the presentations, yet many students did most or all of their preparation in the last week or two. Referring to the third term in particular, Beth explained, "I get the feeling that you guys think, all along we're thinking about our exhibitions, we're kind of planning them, we're finding out what's interesting while we're doing other things. And I don't think we're doing that. I know I'm not."

For Paul, preparing quickly appeared to be a goal and a matter of pride. When I asked him what he had to do to prepare for his propaganda presentation, he said:

> Nothin' really, 'cause it's real easy for me to prepare things, y'know. I catch on to things real fast. . . . I'm just a very quick person; it's just that I get all my ideas put together real quick. I know what I'm

doin'. . . . It was nothin'—just gettin' the poster together and makin' it look good.

Several others also spoke of working quickly, but attributed their doing so to procrastination or time pressures rather than prowess. Most of these students also referred to working in such a fashion as a factor limiting the quality of their exhibitions. During the second term, for instance, Nadine had met with an outside mentor, who suggested some books for her to read for her research paper:

> But I did it like at the last minute so I had a lotta short time. . . . That's why I say it wasn't a good exhibition. 'Cause I didn't really take my time. . . . I would have got it done but it—you know how a lot of people like to put things off to the last week.

Gail framed the issue in terms of constraints facing her. When I asked her how she thought teachers could implement exhibitions better, she replied that students should be given

> more time in the library, more time in the computer lab, like, less portfolio pieces. . . . 'Cause, well, what I see is I spend like all my time on the little ones, and then I throw my exhibition together. 'Cause I don't have time. 'Cause like, people do have lives outside of school. I mean, I work three other jobs.

Luis described how the results of a last-minute effort could be felt during one's presentation. To him, whether or not one worked in such a fashion was a major distinction:

> If you just do it, and just, y'know, you just have like two days, and you're about to do it, y'know, and you just do it real quick—go up to the library and spend an hour, two hours maybe—you know, just finding real quick, and writing it and then typing it, and then just presenting it? And y'know, you don't feel good about it and you're like, y'know, you don't convince the people or whatever. And you always think to yourself, "Aw, man, I could have spent this time doin' that and that." But if you really do, like, research and stuff? And you just really get into it, and you're—if you feel good when you go up there to present it, I think that's the thing. That's what makes it good.

Several of the students I interviewed expressed feelings that their preparation did not measure up to their ideas of quality. A number spoke of "rush jobs" they did as inadequate. Like Luis, these students thought that time spent made a difference. However, their standards also encompassed countervailing impulses, in terms of the amount of time they were willing to spend or the amount of work they would actually require of themselves. Nadine and Harlan laughed sheepishly when they told me that they had used encyclopedias for their research. This suggested that they felt, on some level, that good research involved working with more in-depth and time-consuming sources. They had not made it a priority to work in such a manner, though.

PRESENTATION

Most of the students I interviewed, when they thought about doing exhibitions, focused quite a bit on the live performance situation: appearing in front of the classroom and interacting with the audience.

"Getting up in front of tons of people," as Harlan described it, made several of the students quite nervous, and managing this nervousness was an aspect of presenting that some emphasized. LaTanya described how presenting successfully meant keeping anxieties from derailing her:

> If you're worryin' about what [the audience is] thinking, you're gonna mess up. 'Cause if you start sayin' while you're in the middle of your exhibition, "Oh, what are they thinking? What kind of questions are they gonna ask me? Oh, oh," you gonna get side-tracked. You got to focus straight on one thing.

When identifying elements of a good exhibition, several students referred to the presenter's general projection. Paul said it was important to "look professional," Gail to be "confident" and "strong," and Eva to "give out very laid back comfortable energy."

By contrast, an image of poor performance that stood out in a number of students' minds, from their experiences as audience members, was that of a classmate reading from a book or piece of paper. Eva's comments describe the impression made by students who presented in such a manner:

> Most of the people that got up there [during the third term] . . . just read right out of the book, and that was the exhibition. And most of the [students in the audience] were just like, "Yeah okay, what-

ever." Y'know. 'Cause those people that were up there, they didn't even know what the hell they were talkin' about.

Reading from a book or paper, in many students' view, indicated lack of preparation and limited understanding. It was also connected to ineffective communication. Harlan said, for instance, "I seen some kids— I'm not puttin' down other kids' things, but, they read right off the paper, didn't use their own words, didn't have a clear understandable voice, kind of mumbled."

A central concept that appeared in several students' discussions of exhibitions was *explaining*. Deniece happened unknowingly upon a play on words: "To be a good exhibitionist you have to explain things to the fullest." "Explaining" meant talking about one's topic in one's own words and, if necessary, elaborating on what one has said. LaTanya described how "explaining" distinguished exhibitions from the oral reports she had presented at her previous school:

> When I lived in California, I used to have to do oral presentations before . . . but it wasn't like this. 'Cause when you had to do an oral presentation, it was get up and read your book report. Or somethin' like that. It was similar, but it was different because, when I, back then, I may have got up and read my book report, I'd read straight from the paper, and I didn't really—I just read what I wrote down on the paper from a book. I didn't explain it. When you're doin' exhibitions you have to explain what you're talkin' about. An exhibition is an explanation.

Gloria made a similar distinction when discussing her third-term exhibition with Diane (see Chapter 4).

"Explaining" entailed knowing one's information well enough to talk about it freely. It also entailed being informative and comprehensible to one's audience. Harlan cited these latter qualities when discussing, from his perspective as an audience member, a classmate's exhibition about the slave trade:

> I liked Juan's because he went into detail explaining, and he didn't just read out of the pamphlet. . . . He was talkin' about how they came over on the ships, . . . how they laid flat out in the boats, how they bit the guys who came down to feed them. And he talked clear, understandable. Not all fast . . . he talked clear, you could understand it.

Julia suggested that the purpose of explaining was both to get ideas and information across and to make a personal impression on the audience. Here, she also noted that reading an excerpt from a book could be an effective tactic, if the presenter's own remarks framed the reading as part of a larger attempt to explain:

> If you're gonna read something, just make sure that it emphasizes the whole point you're tryin' to make. And then explain that point. Because if you just make the point, and, you know, give like a brief example—if you give an example they'll get into it more, and then they'll understand why you made that point. And then they'll just look at you and be like, "She know what she's talkin' about."

In the propaganda campaigns, some students understood their task as involving a particular sort of explaining: projecting a position to their peers. Julia took a position—for teaching the Bible in schools—that most of her classmates disagreed with. She did not expect to change the minds of those classmates—some of whom "went to Catholic schools, and . . . didn't like it." She felt she accomplished her purpose, though, by supporting and defending her position:

> They didn't think the way I thought, but I did a good job y'know trying to explain. . . . I thought that [the] Bible should be taught in school and, that way when kids grow, you know, to be teenagers, they won't be thinkin' much of violence. . . . I don't [know], I just tried to give it a different, a whole new way of thinkin' at it.

Renée's purpose in her propaganda campaign went further than Julia's, in that she made a concerted attempt to *convince* her audience to oppose abortions. She said that presenting propaganda had meant trying to "get them to believe what we were sayin'." In her exhibition, she took some specific steps with this goal in mind. She staged her presentation as a "seminar," because "if you notice that sometimes when you go into seminars you're goin' to learn, so your mind is open to what they have to say." Leading the seminar, she took on the role of a doctor who had performed abortions before becoming opposed to them. In addition to speaking, she showed some graphic videos of mutilated fetuses. Hers was the Powell exhibition where the presenter tried most intently to "get them to believe." It also had an apparent effect on the audience: The vocal opposition Renée anticipated never materialized, and some "people in the audience broke down" and cried.

Several of the students with whom I spoke mentioned an engaged response from the audience as an indicator of success for an exhibition. To Julia, the fact that students spoke up against her position meant that her propaganda campaign had "brought big issues." Carlita Bedford was disappointed she didn't get a somewhat comparable result in her campaign promoting school uniforms:

> Instead of askin' me, "Why do you think kids should wear uniforms?" they should've been like—I mean, I wanted them, not to argue back and forth but just, have their own opinions—and they just agreein' with me. Like I wanted something stronger than that, but they didn't do that.

Similarly, Anwar's lament, after his third-term exhibition, that his classmates "just sit there and don't say anything" showed that he had wanted a different audience response from what he had received.

In assessing why her audience responded as it did, Carlita appeared uncertain as to whether or not it was a result of what she did as a presenter. She said, "They might've agreed with me just to, y'know get it done over with. 'Cause they really wanted to get theirs done with." She encountered a phenomenon many people encounter when attempting to draw a response from an audience: Factors beyond one's control often impact on the situation, thereby complicating the understanding of one's own role. This occurs when presentations appear to be successful as well as unsuccessful.

In Gail's exhibition on John Brown, the audience became quite involved, but this occurred essentially by accident, in terms of what Gail did to bring it about. After Gail finished her talk, Diane asked what her opinion of John Brown was. Gail answered that she thought he was "boring." She explained, "He tried but he didn't do anything. He tried to do a raid but that's all." Beth and another classmate, Warren, vehemently objected, and a lively discussion ensued.

During my interview with Gail, when I asked her for an assessment of this exhibition, she offered, "The people, like got into it, and started talkin' about it. . . . Like when you argue it's usually, people are interested." Gail cited such an audience response as a criterion marking a successful exhibition; however, drawing such a response had not infused her purposes as she prepared and presented the exhibition. She gave her opinion on John Brown, and sparked the controversy, only after Diane asked the question. I asked Gail why she didn't go into her opinion on John Brown during her talk, and she said, "I don't know, I really didn't think about it. I was just trying to do [my] thing, and sit down. Basically. Present my work."

While the students I interviewed tended to agree that questions from peers reflected interest and were a good sign, Deniece and Luis also referred to the absence of questions as an indication of success. They both talked about how a good presentation could, in Luis's words, "knock out" questions, by preventing audience confusion or by "saying everything and answering all the questions that they were going to ask, in the presentation." Luis described his laying out six reasons for the legalization of marijuana as such a preemptive strike, and referred to the fact that nobody in the class challenged him during that exhibition as an accomplishment. Both he and Deniece, however, also described positive functions of questions during one's exhibition. Students' standards included multiple images of good work, and they could even include contrasting images.

Visual aids were another element that figured into several students' conceptions of successful presenting. Some students, when I interviewed them, described classmates' uses of videotapes and the chalkboard as distinguishing features of exhibitions they had observed. Eva, in her third-term exhibition, had made drawings of Harriet Tubman to go with her narrative, and some of her classmates cited these when speaking positively of her exhibition. Eva commented on visuals as a communication strategy:

> I think that you'd have to have a very strong visual. 'Cause, once you got people's attention directed to the visual, you can talk. You can talk and—once you get their attention, when you talk they can picture it. . . . They can picture it a lot more and their attention is right there.

Deniece's discussion of the use of handouts also suggested a growing awareness, on her and her classmates' part, of tactics for bringing the audience into a presentation:

> You have to involve [the class] in what you're doin'. . . . If you have any handouts, give them handouts, you know, let them be a part of the exhibition. . . . It's like a hands-on. Instead of them just sittin' back and watchin' you explainin' everything. . . . A lot of kids are just startin' to do that now. I guess they realize, you know—they started handin' out handouts and stuff to the class, gettin' them involved in their exhibitions.

There were significant limitations to the emerging standard Deniece suggested. She herself did not, in her third-term exhibition, demonstrate the kind of performance she described here; according to Carlita, "She didn't have any visual or anything like that—she just read out of the book." Furthermore, during the "hands-on" activities that other present-ers initiated, the audience remained relatively passive: They looked at copies of the Gettysburg Address that Luis had handed out, for instance, or at Pierre's pictures. Still, Deniece's statement, like Eva's, reflects how a number of students had come to believe that exhibitions were better if the presenter, in the attempt to communicate, did more than simply talk to the audience.

THE NATURE OF STUDENTS' STANDARDS

It is possible to speak in a general sense of the standards that exist within a given school or classroom, but when one considers standards that are embedded in students' thoughts, there will also be variation among individuals. As shown above, there were differences, among the students I interviewed, in the amounts of knowledge, the kinds of prepa-ration, and the ways of presenting that they valued and aimed for. At the same time, the discussion has outlined some commonalities.

While some officially designated standards take the form of fixed, precisely defined targets, the standards that developed in students' minds were not of that nature. Rather, they involved general attributes that students identified as important for their work to have, and some-what amorphous conceptions of levels of performance that were "good." Sometimes a general attribute that was valued, such as having "enough" information, was framed in terms of a more specific criterion, such as being able to answer the audience's questions. Such criteria, though, were still ambiguous and fluid.

The attributes in question were not, by nature, easy to measure. Terms such as "understand" or "research" also do not carry any universal meaning in terms of the level of performance that is considered good. To the students, those terms took on specific meanings that were grounded in the work being done in their classrooms.

The standards in Powell students' minds tended not to take the form of exemplars, or ideal performances toward which people aspire. The students sought a sense that they had displayed some degree of compe-tence. They were less concerned, in most cases, with doing work they or others would consider superlative or groundbreaking.

Students' achievements help to shape their concepts of good work, as well as being shaped (or potentially shaped) by those concepts. The work that students do, and perceive as successful and satisfactory, helps to define "successful" and "satisfactory." Students' accumulated achievements also come to define what they can expect of themselves: levels of performance that become accepted norms, and perhaps foundations from which further pursuits and learning will proceed. There were cases in which students were building the capacity to say "I know how to do this," whether "this" was digesting and explaining a body of information, or having material prepared for one's exhibition, or speaking to a class. These were kinds of performances that the students could conceive of themselves doing. Their standards tended to focus more on such performances than on more distant notions of what they might do.

The preceding pages contain several examples of students having an idea about what would make a good exhibition, but not putting much effort into making their own exhibitions good in that way. In such cases, the standard was represented in students' thoughts but not in their pursuits. The students had not adopted the standard as a habit. Perhaps, also, they had not yet learned how to meet it.

Ideas can lag behind actions, as well. Some student efforts—such as Julia's use of an overarching thesis in her third-term exhibition—reached into areas of performance that the student did not mention when articulating what he or she had done.

All the same, what students worked on followed to some extent from what they thought was worth working on. Several students said that obtaining information to present, knowing their material well enough to talk about it, maintaining their composure in front of the class, and/or communicating clearly to the audience were what characterized good exhibitions; and also pursued *these* goals, as opposed to other possibilities. Some students also worked to meet additional standards for successful exhibitions that developed in their minds, as Renée did when she attempted to convince her peers about abortions, or Luis when he discussed prospective exhibition questions with a teacher. Conversely, when a student viewed a certain goal—exploring the application of and evidence behind "theories," for instance—as not especially important, it often meant that he or she would not devote much energy toward pursuing it, either.

8

Students Creating Standards, Individually

The previous chapter shows students making meaning of their experiences with exhibitions. Students identified certain aspects of their work as significant and certain attributes of a performance as markers of success. They formulated ideas about what to pursue.

These were ways in which students were active in the creation of standards. The present chapter looks further into that process. It focuses on two factors—challenges and interests—that affected how students both regarded and approached their work.

Students arrived at Powell with certain acquired skills, which dictated what tasks they would find challenging. They also brought inclinations to be more interested in some things than in others. Students' perceived challenges shaped their ideas about what was worth working on and what was good work. Their interests, likewise, affected the value they placed on certain kinds of efforts and products.

The previous chapter focuses on standards as they exist in students' minds, and discusses how these are *related to* students' actions. Standards also *reside in* the activity which students do. That activity proceeds according to certain principles, which are standards in practice. The products of that activity, in turn, embody those standards. Students' generation of classroom standards thus occurs not only as their thoughts form but also as their activity evolves.

The relation of standards to challenges and interests is discussed in this chapter in terms of individual students' thoughts and actions. In the following chapter, students' interactions with one another, and the contribution of those to the creation of standards, are considered.

THE ROLE PLAYED BY PERCEIVED CHALLENGES

An exhibition was a multifaceted task that had many possible emphases. In the visions of exhibitions put forth by Theodore Sizer, Joseph McDonald, and Grant Wiggins (see Chapter 2), notions of students' "using knowledge" or "demonstrating control over an intellectual topic that approximates the expert's" are more central than they became in classroom life at Powell. To some extent, the teachers in these classrooms shared the theorists' visions. When students were faced with the overall task of doing an exhibition, though, certain aspects of that task stood out to *them* as most significant, according to the challenges they found most immediate. Those aspects of the task would constitute focal points for students' standards.

Two primary sets of challenges about which students spoke, when I interviewed them, had to do with presenting before one's classmates, and acquiring knowledge and understanding of a topic before one's presentation. Their comments about these challenges contain some similar descriptions of exhibition work as are included in the previous chapter. In addition, they illustrate ways in which standards were related to challenges.

Presenting to the Class

For many Powell students, giving oral presentations was a new or practically new experience. Some students I interviewed said they had never spoken in front of a class before. Speaking in front of a group, in itself, can make people of all ages anxious, especially if they are unaccustomed to being in that position. In this case, there was an added factor: The audience consisted of fellow adolescents. "It's a lot harder to get up in front of your peers, than it is to get up in front of anyone else," LaTanya said. Many students were especially concerned about how they might appear in their classmates' eyes. Harlan pointed to a switching of social roles that felt awkward to him: "It's harder because here you're with them every day laughin' and jokin' and talkin', and then you're up there, like as a teacher. And, you know, it's different from how you usually talk to 'em."

The anxiety associated with facing the class was a central issue in some students' minds as they thought about how to do exhibitions. Sean Dolan had more difficulty getting a basic command of his information than most of his classmates did, and this intensified the pressure he felt. He described "the hardest thing" about exhibitions as follows: "Just don't mess up. Y'know, stay focused. Don't lose concentration on it. 'Cause then you start messin' up. . . . When you have everybody in front of you."

Prior to his third-term exhibition, Anwar was very mindful of the challenge of facing the class, and this shaped his ideas about how to prepare. In my conferences with him, my efforts were initially aimed at helping him develop knowledge and understanding of his topic. Periodically, he let me know that he had other concerns. At one point, for instance, I suggested to him and a fellow student that they could practice their exhibitions during advisory period. (All Powell students met with an advisory group for 1 hour a day, 4 days a week.) He responded that he did not think that would be useful. "We wouldn't be nervous, 'cause it would be our friends there," he explained. He believed that practicing during advisory would not be a worthwhile simulation of the exhibition, because it omitted an essential part of the task: dealing with the pressure that his audience would present.

Meeting the challenge of facing the class could lead students to an acquired sense of competence. For instance, Marcus Walton, when discussing what was hardest about doing an exhibition, said:

> For other people it's the presentation, it's gettin' up in front of people. . . . It used to [bother me]. It used to but, no. It was like, I could get nervous before, I could get real real nervous, then as soon as I get up there and I look out it's just like, it just stops—like I get butterflies before and then as soon as I'm up there, about to present, they just go down. And once I start talking I get into it.

Having met a challenge, repeatedly, meant that Marcus was expanding the standards embedded in his performances. It also meant an evolution in his thinking about exhibitions, for he could now expect himself to "get into" a presentation.

Sometimes perceived challenges defined areas where students would not work. This occurred when a challenge was regarded as too great. In the third term, for instance, Peter Connolly decided that facing the class made him nervous enough that he would (unsuccessfully) test teachers' resolve that students must present in order to pass for a term. He explained:

> I try to get away with just doing my work and handin' it in. Instead of . . . getting up in front of all those people, just wondering what they're thinking about you while you're doing it, if they like it, if they don't like it, if you're explaining yourself right, or well enough, so they can understand you.

Similarly, most students put aside the challenge of establishing and leading interactive class activities. Some students, when discussing the third-term exhibitions, talked about how interactive class activities would enhance a "teaching" presentation. However, Beth, who was in fact one of the most self-assured presenters ("I've been acting since I was in second grade, so that kind of cuts down on the fear aspect"), also said, "It's hard to do an activity with the whole class . . . to put yourself out there and do something." Leading activities would involve a range of teaching and planning skills that students were not likely to have developed. In addition, it would involve "putting yourself out there" in a way that pushed against the boundaries of even Beth's self-assurance. Like her peers, Beth stayed with other techniques for her third-term exhibition: giving a talk with a visual aid and giving her audience a question to answer on paper at the end.

Acquiring Information

For many students in earlier grades, "research" entails finding an encyclopedia article and paraphrasing its contents in a written report. Exhibitions involved looking more widely for information, and getting ready to present and discuss one's information orally. Various student concerns arose in these regards.

Nadine, for instance, described how exhibitions had challenged her:

When I first came here [midway through the previous year] I was confused. . . . And I had no ideas of what I was doin', you know. I seen exhibitions but still felt as if I couldn't do it. But then this year it's better, you know. 'Cause I got the idea. . . . [At first] I thought it was just a report—I thought an exhibition was just a report. You know, you look up and you write about—but it's not really, it's mostly notes of what you learnt. It's a report, but it's mainly got to deal with notes.

Learning to prepare notes and talk about their contents had commanded Nadine's attention. Accordingly, she placed importance on the kind of "understanding" that would enable her to present without reading a report.

While many students, as noted in Chapter 7, thought poorly of reading directly from one's source as a method of presentation, oral reading contained challenges that seemed significant to some. Some of the less skilled readers found themselves in the embarrassing position of mispronouncing words and reading sentences in a halting fashion while presenting exhibitions before the class. The day before Fred's third-term exhibition on slave music, I overheard him telling a classmate that he wanted to read without making any mistakes. In his presentation the next day, he read a paragraph-long passage in which he stumbled over only one word. Judging by how Fred read aloud on other occasions, he evidently had rehearsed this passage. The command of his material that he sought included being able to read fluently.

Marcus described how topics with large amounts of available information posed a challenge for him:

> Sometimes it's hard gettin' the information—or when you do get the information, if there's a lot of it, how to arrange it, put it together, so it like, suits yours the best. . . . Like when I was doin' W. E. B. Du Bois, it's like there was a lot of information on him, and I was, just like, had this stuff and I was like, "Where do I begin?" . . . There's other people who just have limited information and then you could just write, and then just go from top to bottom. But he had—there was like so many different books out there, like his life, what he did, and all this other stuff. So probably the information part about it, that's probably the hardest.

Marcus's remarks suggest that on previous occasions he had been able to find his information in one place and "just write." When he was preparing for his research paper on W. E. B. Du Bois, the challenge of digesting longer texts before deciding what information to present seemed daunting to him, and he did not read the full-length biography he had obtained. The task he addressed, rather, was locating and selecting smaller amounts of material that he could use more directly.

When students set out to do the latter sort of research, it was not certain whether they would come upon helpful sources. Accordingly, Luis's preparation for his third-term exhibition was distinguished, in his view, by his success at finding usable information:

> I found a lot of books actually—they got some [in the school library]. I don't know what it's called, there's this one, just about the Gettysburg Address, it's just full of pictures and quotes and everything. That kind of helped me out a lot—I didn't expect to find a thing like that, y'know. So that helped me out.

By contrast, Sean said that he "wasn't really prepared" for his third-term exhibition, in part because the book he obtained was "too hard." He had not experienced the kind of success that Luis described.

Part of the challenge of acquiring information was that it required an investment of time on students' part. Some students, when discussing exhibitions they had done, spoke of how there were sources available that they would have liked to use—if only they had devoted the time. Nadine said that her second-term project "wasn't a good exhibition" because, while her outside mentor had listed for her some books to read, Nadine "did it like at the last minute" and only used what was in the encyclopedia. Similarly, Gloria, after her exhibition on Harriet Jacobs, remarked that she "found so much" in the library and alluded to what she might have learned "if I would have stayed up there, y'know, doin' a little bit each week."

LaTanya noted, also, that once she began working with a source, locating the specific information she was after and determining the significance of the information she encountered were not so quickly—or easily—accomplished:

> It was actually harder than I thought, because when I looked up the information, it took a lot of time to find what the Middle Passage was and the in-depth knowledge of it. I mean, you couldn't get deep down into what you were reading, unless you took the time to do it. And it's a lot—it's hard to find every little detail between the lines.

Scholarly texts presented challenges that many students avoided. When the content and language seemed too remote and opaque, students often decided that they were not worth taking on. On some occasions, this meant that a given book was rejected. On others, students worked with a text selectively. Gloria, for instance, derived an essential chronology of Harriet Jacobs's early life from a six-page section of Elizabeth Fox-Genovese's study of women's lives in the antebellum South, *Within the Plantation Household* (1988). In these pages, there are passages that summarize parts of Jacobs's story in narrative fashion. Interspersed among those passages, also, is a discussion of how Jacobs presented to a White northern audience a slave *woman's* opposition to slavery; this discussion explores gender conceptions of Jacobs's time and their implications. Of the latter portions of the text, Gloria said, "Half of the sentences I don't even understand. . . . Like the words are too long—I don't know, it's like, the way they described it." Gloria chose essentially to ignore these passages when preparing her talk.

These several challenges that went with obtaining information helped to shape students' standards for what was a good research effort. There were obstacles, from difficult texts to students' own inclinations to procrastinate, that stood between the students and the acquisition of knowledge. In some instances, the students did not overcome them, and they accordingly saw their achievements as limited. In some instances, challenges were put aside as too vast and set boundaries on rather than giving content to students' standards. When, on the other hand, students did surmount or circumvent these obstacles to some extent, they valued the accomplishment—whether or not they "used" the knowledge they acquired as Sizer, McDonald, and Wiggins suggest.

THE ROLE PLAYED BY STUDENT INTEREST

Another way in which students generate standards is through their interest. Interest is a way of placing value on what one is doing, placements of value themselves being a form of standards. In addition, when students find their work interesting, they may apply more energy to that work and build standards for its quality through their actions.

As noted in Chapter 1, Patricia Carini's (1987, 1988, 1994) theories assign a primary role to students' interest in the process of standards arising. Carini emphasizes how students' interests can lead to the development of *high* standards in a classroom. When this occurs, there is *strong* interest on students' part and students become highly engaged in their work. In the process, collective as well as individual possibilities for achievement expand. This phenomenon could be observed in Powell humanities classes, but only to a limited extent. However, even in cases where the interest and activity were more moderate, students' interests affected their decisions about what was worth doing and their judgments about what was good to have done.

The outstanding instance of passionate interest described in my interviews with students was Renée's propaganda campaign against abortion (described in Chapter 7). Renée's purpose clearly extended beyond completing the assignment and receiving academic credit.

The issue of abortion aroused personal feelings in Renée. She had come to her anti-abortion position through an experience with a relative:

> Two weeks before I had did my presentation, I had went with my cousin so that she can have an abortion. And when we got there, like we was readin' over the procedure and things like that, and I was readin' it and it was sayin' all these side effects and things that can happen to her, and I was just—it was terrible. And as I was readin' it I was like, "Melanie, I know you don't want to go through

this"—I was like, "You know this isn't right." . . . And I talked to her, and she ended up not getting an abortion. She's still pregnant now. Her parents want her to get an abortion, but she won't.

Renée added, "It was weird to see how all the people were—who were sittin' in the clinic about to go through the, you know the little, the process. It was just, I don't know, my heart was so burdened. I felt so bad." She reflected, furthermore, on how "it's like I have nephews who could've been—you know, my sisters were contemplating whether to have an abortion or not."

Renée's interest pertained not only to the issue itself but also to the idea of making a presentation to her class about it:

> I chose abortion because, y'know myself I wanted to research more about it. And I could've done that on my own time, but I wanted to be able to present, and to see if I could change people's mind, you know. That was . . . one of my goals really, on the inside, to see if I can get people to not have an abortion. Y'know, if I can help somebody to understand that—you know, what the babies are goin' through or whatever. I don't know, maybe I was wrong, but that's what I wanted to do.

The short time frame of the assignment placed limits on how much work Renée's interest could spur her to do. Her preparation, however, exceeded that which most Powell students did for the propaganda exhibitions. She obtained pamphlets from hospital clinics that had "different statistics about people who have abortions and why, and stuff like that." She also recalled a presentation someone from a pro-life organization had made at her church, called one of her mentors from the church to get the phone number of the organization, and called the organization and arranged to have videotapes sent to her. She studied four different tapes to select two excerpts to show. Renée's apparent skill at using community resources made her more likely to undertake such a research effort than some Powell students were. She was also highly motivated in this instance.

No other exhibition I saw or heard about matched Renée's for the intense and serious nature of her purpose. Indeed, hers was hard to replicate in these regards. Paul's presentation on handguns, however, approached Renée's in terms of his interest, judging by the enthusiasm he demonstrated when discussing it with me and by his teachers' reports. When I brought up that exhibition in our interview, he responded, "The gun one. Oh, that's phat,[1] yeah." He added, "Yeah it was good, 'cause I think that all Americans should have one, have a piece, y'know. We all need one. . . . I convinced a couple people too."

Paul described in detail the poster he had conceived and made:

> I used women—like I used a picture of a woman who have a gun, who was attacked before. . . . It was a big poster; it had a picture of a gun over on the left side, my official logo of my company—it was called the Protect Yourself Campaign. It had what we're endorsed by, had a picture of the woman right there and a little clip-out article on her, that I made up myself. It was real good. It was like, "Mary Kay of St. Petersburg, Florida, is in favor of guns. She sa–," no, "'Protect Yourself!' is what Mary Kay of St. Petersburg, Florida says." And it was like she said that she was attacked outside of a mall one day, and, no thanks to the cops who couldn't hear her cries for help, she had to use her gun. Y'know. It cuts down on a lot of violent crimes nowadays, guns.

As noted in Chapter 7, Paul, in our interview, deemphasized the effort it had taken him to prepare this presentation. He recounted at some length, though, how he had strategized about how to affect classmates' opinions. He had thought specifically of female and male perspectives, and decided to aim his campaign toward women:

> You gotta have your own little opinion, but the thing is . . . you gotta have other people's views intertwined with your views, so people will know what you're talkin' about and where you're coming from. . . . A lot of women feel that they're not being protected by the law, y'know, because all this—domestic violence cases and all that. Y'know, the law's not doin' enough to help 'em out, y'know. The restraining order is not really working. . . . And women are arming themselves in America, 'cause it was in *Newsweek* magazine my mother has at home—women are arming themselves. And, if I brought that to the attention of a lot of people they'd wind up sayin' like, "Hey," y'know. "This could have happened to me," y'know. . . .
>
> Now I know what the dudes think, y'know: "Oh it's awright, I want a strap," y'know [laugh]. "He's all right."

---

[1] "Phat": a preferred spelling, among 1990s adolescents, of "fat." Possible synonyms: great, cool, hip, dope, bad.

Whereas Renée had pursued what was to her a very weighty matter, Paul spoke of his project more as if it had been fun. The topic of gun ownership interested him, and this had helped make his enjoyment possible. What had engaged him as well were the social dynamics he anticipated: male students thinking, "He's all right," for instance. "I think of [an exhibition] as a performance, yo," he said. "It's a showcase of your talent and who you are."

Paul's and Renée's interest propelled them into work that carried new standards, for themselves and for their classes. They developed specific, original ideas about how to do a presentation. They also created exemplars, within the Powell community, for the overall quality of an exhibition, by combining knowledge of a topic with spirited and skillful delivery.

In Paul's case, the standards-enhancing function of his interest began to extend past his own project. The day after he presented, he visited Diane's and my class on his own initiative. As shown in Part I, he actively participated in Wayne's, Pierre's, and Anwar's exhibitions, sharing his enthusiasm for propaganda presentations as a social activity. But this spreading of engagement ended there. One reason was that after that week, there were no more propaganda campaigns. Paul would have needed to transfer this level of interest to other kinds of activities, which he did not do. He also appeared to become less committed to schoolwork in general as the year wore on, quite possibly for reasons that extended beyond the nature of that work.

Most of the interest that students demonstrated was more moderate, in both degree and impact, than that in the two cases discussed above. Nonetheless, it played a role in how students thought about their work, in what they felt motivated to do, and in what they achieved.

When Brett, for instance, talked with me about his exhibition on the Battle of Gettysburg, he said, "I think I did a good job. 'Cause, like, I showed Pickett's charge as my visual, and I had watched that, and I found it really interesting, so I did a good job I thought. 'Cause I understood it." Brett did not display the level of passion that Renée or Paul did. He did not indicate that the topic had great personal meaning to him—a significant although not necessary component of such passion. But he indicated that he placed some value on this topic, in comparison to others he had worked with.

In our interview, Brett connected this interest to both his effort and his understanding. To prepare for this exhibition, Brett "went back and I looked at my video again, and I took four pages of notes just off of that, like, 45-minute video." He had done this only after receiving extra time to work on his project; still, he emphasized that he did become engaged in studying the video. When I asked him if he had been able to answer all the questions asked of him during the exhibition, his reply was, "Yeah, 'cause I was interested in it, 'cause I picked it." His interest did not lead him to extend the boundaries of his research and knowledge especially far. However, it helped him to experience competence, and to value his work.

In two of his exhibition projects, Bruce displayed interest similar in scope to Brett's. Over the course of the year, Bruce completed his portfolio assignments sporadically. In these two exhibitions, though, Bruce found the subject matter to merit his investment of energy. He worked toward higher standards than at any other time, and his exhibitions were relatively successful among those in Diane's and my class.

For his research paper, Bruce told me he wanted to do something on Hitler from a personal angle. I had noticed a book in the school library called *The Psychopathic God* (Waite, 1977), and I recommended it to him; he found the book, made a point of thanking me, and said he would read it "because it interests me." He read only portions of the book. Still, he wrote a paper that Diane and I felt intertwined the student's own ideas with information from research as well as any in our class.

The second instance was Bruce's third-term exhibition. During this presentation, he explained why he had chosen Crispus Attucks as his topic: "I wanted to do him 'cause I walk across that thing [a memorial to Crispus Attucks in the city's downtown] every day, so, y'know, I'm saying, 'Oh Crispus Attucks, I've heard of him before,' and I just wanted to do it." Bruce looked no further than an encyclopedia for his information, but he talked to the class about the Boston Massacre and Crispus Attucks' role in it in a way that made for one of the more engaging and informative third-term presentations.

Students' interest in topics also led them to assign value, afterward, to what they had learned. Wayne's telling me that he would show his grandmother his research paper on the Cherokees' relocation was one example. In some instances, students pointed to specific pieces of information that they had found and relayed. Harlan remarked that he thought classmates would remember, from his third-term exhibition, that Harriet Tubman had given drugs to babies to keep them quiet. LaTanya, speaking of her third-term exhibition, said she had "wanted to learn something new. . . . Like, . . . nobody knew about the Middle Passage. . . . Nobody knew that women were being used, and, nobody knew that men were jumpin' off ships because they didn't want to be killed by the different colored man. . . . So, I found it kind of interesting."

One of the characteristics of historical topics is that they contain items of information—such as Harriet Tubman's drugging babies or men's jumping off slave ships—that people of all ages find interesting in and of themselves. Simply learning such facts adds to one's knowledge. Interest in such items does not necessarily lead students to do further research and analysis. Students may feel spurred to obtain more such information, or to explore associated issues (such as the ethics of giving drugs to infants or how Africans resisted the slave trade). Or they may not. Whether such further inquiry takes place depends in part on students' habits and skills, as well as on the boundaries of their interests.

Students' interests marked what they would not pursue as well as what they would. Wayne, for instance, when doing his second-term research, acted eager to learn about the Cherokees' forced relocation. Once he found out some details about their actual journey westward, though, he ceased reading. There was much more about the topic that I wanted him to explore—various issues that lay behind or accompanied the relocation. Wayne's comments at the time suggested that, in part, the issue to him was how much work he wanted to do, regardless of the topic. But it also appeared that by the time he stopped reading, he had found out what he most wanted to know: the fact that the Cherokees were forced to move, and a basic description of their trip and its attendant hardships.

In Jorge's third-term project, one of the issues, in terms of whether or not his interest led to extended inquiry, was that his interest was broadly defined and the topic vast and amorphous. He had proposed the topic of Latin American slavery on his own and expressed a general interest in it. During most of the time that he was preparing for the exhibition, though, Jorge seemed uncertain as to exactly what he wanted to know. One day toward the beginning of the project, he shared with me a table listing the numbers of slaves in various countries, and said he had not known there had been so many. When I asked him what else he could address in conjunction with that, he said he thought the class would be most interested in the rebellions that occurred. In a subsequent conference with me, he defined his interest as "the abolition of slavery" in Latin America. Throughout the project, though, the information, from his books, that he shared with me as having caught his eye continued to span a variety of topics, including Spain's and Great Britain's involvement in the slave trade and the racial classifications mestizo and mulatto. During his exhibition, when Gloria asked why he and his partner Danilo had picked the topic, Jorge answered,

> We wanted to know more about it. . . . What did Latin America have to do with slavery. That's what we wanted to know. We only knew about . . . North America . . . , but we wanted to know what

other countries did. How they controlled slavery, for what they used the slaves.

While Jorge (Danilo barely contributed to the preparation of the exhibition) never settled on a more specific area of focus and pursued information within it, his exhibition was nonetheless, in Diane's and my view, one of the strongest in our class. He projected a sense that the topic was worth talking about, he presented a range of information that was new to him and to his classmates, and he also touched on some thematic issues. His interest was a contributing factor to these achievements.

STUDENT CONCERNS AND THE NEGOTIATION OF STANDARDS

To a significant extent, the process whereby standards evolved from students' interests and perceived challenges was one that took place within each student or as a result of the student acting independently. The student, himself or herself, made meaning of exhibitions and his or her experiences with them. Some pursuits, also, were undertaken largely on the student's own initiative—as in the case of Renée's preparing her propaganda presentation or Fred's practicing oral reading.

The development of classroom standards around students' concerns is also a process that involves teachers. Students' interests and perceived challenges can influence a teacher's decisions about the location of *joint* activity. I responded to Anwar's signals, for instance, by using conference time to address his concerns about how to structure his presentation. I guided Bruce to a resource that would help him investigate an issue he was curious about, and I tried to help Jorge map out an approach to a topic that interested him. Diane's and my work with Pierre over the course of the year also illustrates this principle. We concentrated on the mechanics of written language more than we did with other students, both because we recognized this as a learning need of his and because he regularly solicited our help in composing and editing.

Students' input in the negotiation of classroom standards includes both their establishing standards on their own and their influencing teachers. In addition, it includes their influencing one another, as the next chapter shows.

9

Students Creating Standards, Through Peer Interactions

While interactions between students and teachers lie at the heart of the negotiation of classroom standards, interactions among students are also significant. Both the formation of students' thoughts, and many of the classroom activities that students undertake, are social as well as individual processes, involving classmates as well as teachers.

One way in which peer interactions contributed to the formation of standards at Powell was that students' observations of each other's exhibitions helped to shape their ideas about what constituted good work. A second way was that students considered their audience when thinking about how to present exhibitions. A third way was that dialogue with peers during exhibitions gave the contents of those exhibitions added meaning. These are considered, in turn, below.

STUDENTS' OBSERVATIONS OF ONE ANOTHER

Fellow students' work embodies standards in concrete form. As a source of knowledge about possible attributes of a performance, such work is an alternative to one's own efforts and experiences, yet still close to those experiences—closer, perhaps, than what adults might present.

When I interviewed students about exhibitions, their notions of what constituted a quality performance sometimes emerged, or became more focused, through their comments about classmates' work. At times, too, they described how observations of peers had given them ideas about how to do exhibitions. Those ideas sometimes translated into new standards-in-practice for the observer, although they did not necessarily do so.

When students spoke favorably of classmates' exhibitions, the attributes they cited were likely to be among those discussed in the previous two chapters: in particular, how a student had obtained information about his or her topic, given his or her own explanations, and/or had an effective manner of presenting. In terms of the quality of work in these areas, students' impressions of classmates' performances often appeared to reinforce, or help establish, the conceptions of competence that they were forming through their own experiences as well.

LaTanya, for instance, described Paul's exhibition on Jefferson Davis—which consisted primarily of a biographical summary, presented comprehensibly with some embellishments—as a successful example of both finding information and explaining it: "That was interesting 'cause I never knew who Jefferson Davis was. . . . I think Paul did a real good job on his exhibition. 'Cause when it comes down to Paul, he tries to explain, in depth. . . . He makes sure he gets his point across." Deniece, similarly, said of Brett's exhibition on the Battle of Gettysburg (described in Chapters 7 and 8), "It was good. He had a lot of information and stuff. . . . Brett's a very smart boy, . . . he's very knowledgeable." Luis, in praising a classmate's propaganda presentation on Dr. Jack Kevorkian, noted the quality of her delivery as well as her explanations:

> I think it was a good exhibition. 'Cause she didn't say, "Ah, he was born this and that, and died—." . . . She just came out and said, "This is Dr.,"—said his name and said this is what he does, this is how he does it, and this is how he helps people be doin' it and stuff. Y'know she just got out there and did it.

Several of the students with whom I spoke cited Eva's exhibition on Harriet Tubman (described in Chapter 7) as one that had been done well. Some mentioned that Eva appeared to be well informed. Others mentioned the drawings of Harriet Tubman she had made. Of the drawings, Carlita said, "I never seen anything like that before. Out of all the exhibitions I've seen so far." This attribute of Eva's exhibition fit within the general principle of having visual aids—a principle that many students had recognized, and applied, on other occasions. In this case, Eva had also come up with a specific innovation, which impressed Carlita.

Students noticed other ways, as well, that classmates integrated visuals into their third-term presentations. Brett said of Luis's exhibition on the Gettysburg Address, "He did a good job on it. He handed out, like handouts, which is also a good thing to have." Carlita said that Brett's exhibition was "really good," and when I asked if she remembered what was good about it, she replied, "When he showed the video, because a lot of people don't show videos when they do exhibitions. Just like, one in every ten shows videos."

These latter remarks illustrate how in some instances students noted qualities of classmates' performances that distinguished them from their own. The practical impact of those observations depended on whether students derived lessons that they could apply to their own work, and whether they in turn attempted to apply these lessons.

The specific nature of some observations made them potentially useful in this regard. Harlan, for instance, when experiencing exhibitions for the first time (during the third term, as a new Powell student), noticed that other students had prepared visuals. "And I just had the little paper in front of me [when presenting], so I said next time, if it includes that, I'll do it." He also thought about how he might have used a visual in the context of his exhibition topic: "I could've, like, drew, or had a board of, showin' how Harriet Tubman—y'know, which routes they took. . . . I thought that would have helped a lot. People to see which way." Harlan did not have an opportunity to act on this insight during the remainder of the year, though, because there was not another exhibition scheduled in which students were expected to use visuals.

Brett also drew a fairly concrete lesson when he compared his propaganda exhibition to Luis' and Eva's. All three students had chosen the same topic: legalization of marijuana. Brett noted how the others had done more research than he had, and also the particular kinds of information they had obtained. He was somewhat dismayed at the comparison:

> I didn't really do a good job on that one. I just threw mine together at the end 'cause I had to get it done. Like, 'cause I really hadn't researched a lot. So like—well, Luis had all the facts about George Washington and stuff sayin' it was good, so they should legalize it if the father of our country y'know did it. Eva did all the medical uses, sayin' it should be legalized and—I really didn't do that good on that. I did horrible on that compared to the others.

In his subsequent exhibition on the Battle of Gettysburg, Brett was sufficiently informed so that he did not do "horrible compared to the others."

A series of observations that Eva made contributed to her evolving standards-in-action. She contrasted some classmates' third-term exhibitions with Beth's:

I noticed other people sittin' up there reading the whole report—
and I'm sittin' there, I'm like, "I'm not gonna be writing everything
down. He's not really giving clear facts, he's just mixing it up in
one big report, that he's just reading off right now." . . . And it did
not attract my attention so I figure it didn't attract anyone else's attention either, 'cause I saw people fiddling around not paying attention. [But when] I saw somebody like Beth get up and she drew
this chart on the board, with all the information right there, and
she's like, "This is what happened, boom boom boom," I saw a lot
of people taking notes, and I saw a lot of people copying whatever
she was writing on the board.

Eva brought up this observation when describing how she had learned
to leave out what she called "in-between stuff" when presenting an exhibition:

It's like, when you write a paper. . . . When you read it, there's intro-
duction, there's all those little unnecessary paragraphs that truly
are, they're not—they're significant for the paper itself, but they're
not gonna serve any purpose in exhibition.

In this vein, Eva explained, "I found in exhibitions that the less you
talk, the better it is. But when you talk less you have to get your facts
straight." Indeed, the difference between her second-term research-in-
progress presentation, during which she read all her notes on Joseph Sta-
lin, and her third-term exhibition, which took place after Beth's, indicated
that she had applied this principle in evolving her approach to her own
exhibitions. Her thinking about presenting differently may not have occurred only as a result of observing Beth, and the other classmates whose
work contrasted with Beth's, but those observations contributed to that
thinking. Her actions aligned with her thoughts, also, furthering the development of standards.

Eva's remarks also show how negative images provided by peers'
work helped to define what students wished, and attempted, to avoid in
their own performances. LaTanya made a statement that combined some
of the most common such images: students appearing unprepared, nervous, and unable to "explain," and students reading from a book or piece
of paper:

Sometimes I wonder if people actually, when they come to do their
exhibition, do they actually know what they're doin'. 'Cause you
got the people that get up there, twiddle their thumbs and stuff,

and, "Da da da da da." And then you got the people that get up there, and do what you have to do. But people that get up there and go, "Da da da da da," I find it a little hard to see—I feel that they're not prepared. But, maybe it's either they're nervous, or they're not prepared, or they just don't know how to put what they wrote down in words short enough that they're not up there for 3 hours. Then you got the people who read straight from the paper. Which I can't stand those type.

LaTanya indicated that she had worked to meet the standards that these remarks suggest: "I used to read straight from the paper. But then, like, after that I started developin' skills." However, speaking of her third-term exhibition, she noted that she "really wasn't prepared" and "was partly readin' from the book, and I wasn't payin' attention to what I was actually sayin'." In this instance, she had not put in the effort needed to reach the standard she had thought about.

There were some observations that, in contrast with those discussed above, were so general as to be of little direct utility. What one emulates need not be fully understood. But it matters whether one has some clear sense of what it is one is trying to replicate—and of how to replicate it.

Gail, for instance, appeared to find it difficult to pinpoint what Beth had done to make her third-term exhibition seem especially good:

I don't know, Beth's just—I liked the way she talked and how she presented herself and, like, how she talks, like the words she used and stuff. I don't know, it was just interesting, and it made me want to listen to it, and she sounded like she knew exactly what she was doin', and what she was talkin' about, and she was ready—and it was just interesting so I listened.

Sean, to give another example, remarked that Eva "knew everything about" Harriet Tubman. His observation was in a sense more specific than Gail's, since he identified the attribute of being well informed. Behind Eva's accomplishment, though, lay skills that Sean had yet to acquire. His broad impression of her knowledge did not offer guidance as to how to develop those skills.

ACCOUNTABILITY TO THE AUDIENCE

Linda Darling-Hammond and associates (1995) refer to an oral presentation as "an act of public accountability" (p. 95). Julia also invoked this concept when comparing Powell exhibitions to the research papers she had written at her previous school: "So that's the difference here, you gotta explain it to somebody and be ready for the questions. When you have to say it to somebody, you have to know what you are talking about."

It was not uncommon for a Powell student, while presenting an exhibition in class, to have his or her eyes aimed directly at the teacher. On the other hand, many student comments about their exhibitions placed the peer audience in the foreground. By participating in an act of communication with the peer audience, students in a sense entered into an agreement to try to say something that was intelligible and informative—and perhaps impressive—to that audience. Being accountable in this way, students considered their audience when thinking about what was good to include in a presentation.

Deniece, for instance, portrayed her decisions about what information to present as based on what she thought her classmates would want to know and what she thought would be sufficient explanations to them:

> You have to explain things to the fullest, to the point where you would answer all their questions before the end of the exhibition where everyone's raising their hands and asking questions. You have to try to sit down and ask yourself, "Well, what type of question would I ask about this?" Because other people will ask these questions too, so if I answer them for me, then [I can] answer them for other people, 'cause I know they'll ask the same thing. So you try to just explain it to the fullest so that you wouldn't have, you know, people raisin' their hands sayin', "I'm confused about this."

Students' estimations of how the audience would receive particular pieces of information helped them assign value to items that they might present. LaTanya, for instance, recounted her rationale for including certain material in her exhibition on the Middle Passage: "At first I thought I really didn't need to say, or show, what kind of chains they used to lock the people up—all they need to know is they were locked up. But then, I realized it was necessary to show it. Let them see how they were locked up." Likewise, Harlan's belief, after his exhibition, that his classmates would remember what he had told them about Harriet Tubman's giving drugs to babies reflected an assessment of what kinds of information they would be likely to find meaningful. Harlan saw a distinction between this item and some other types of information: "I think that, like, some of the other exhibitions, like I said, [the presenters] read the material—the kids don't remember the dates. They don't remember those exact details."

Eva had thought about what kind of broader presentational strategy might best engage her audience; this was evident when she spoke about leaving out "unnecessary paragraphs" in her presentations:

> Unnecessary paragraphs . . . are not gonna serve any purpose in the exhibition because nobody really wants to hear it. They want to hear just the facts. . . . Just about her life story as quickly as possible. . . . What happened to Harriet Tubman, like when she was born, when she got remarried, when she ran away—what happened, how many slaves she led to freedom.

Marcus's description of Eva's exhibition suggests that Eva was on target with her judgment of her audience. To him, Eva's presentation was clear and focused on significant information:

> She explained what she was gonna do and she described it, and it's like she just went down the line, and explained everything. . . . Like from top to bottom, from beginning to end, like what [Harriet Tubman] did. Like she started off—like she would . . . tell Harriet Tubman's, when she was born, like what her life was about, how was her childhood. Then what she accomplished, and then she had little pictures showin' her. . . . So I think hers was probably one of the best ones done.

Marcus's remarks also outline a biography script—a format for telling about a person's life with which students may have been familiar from previous school experiences. His comments suggest that Eva's use of this script, and the skill with which she used it, helped to make her talk accessible and comprehensible to him. The format Eva used also restricts what is shared in an exhibition. In an exhibition on Harriet Tubman, there are kinds of knowledge and analysis a presenter could offer that extend beyond what fits neatly into such a script. One could give a much more comprehensive description of the Underground Railroad and its history, for instance. One could make connections to other topics or historical eras, explore issues about how people organize and resist oppressive systems, or highlight questions that arose during one's study. Eva's central perception of her audience's needs did not press her to develop her presentation in these ways.

To some extent, accountability to the peer audience meant a desire to distinguish oneself, through demonstrations of skill. Paul, as noted in the previous chapter, referred to an exhibition as "a showcase of your talent," while Julia talked about how if one effectively made a point and illustrated it with an example, "They'll just look at you and be like, 'She know what she's talkin' about.'" Deniece described her propaganda poster as a way of making an impression on her classmates. The poster, as she explained it, was deceptive in a clever way: It featured a large picture of a marijuana leaf and had "Marijuana" written across the top, but "then when I flipped the thing down . . . it said, 'Abuse,' [and] then they was like, 'Oh, and she against it.'" She pointed out that all the other marijuana-related exhibitions in her class favored legalization, and said, "So I said, 'Well let me be different and do—go against.' . . . That sort of made me stand out."

In some cases, accountability to the peer audience brought forth not so much a motivation to excel as a motivation not to "look stupid," as Anwar worried he would do in his exhibition on David Walker. This concern could be quite intense and was a major part of some students' fear of presenting. When Sean felt unable to understand the book he had obtained for his third-term exhibition, he proceeded with the exhibition because he did not want to fail for the term, but he was distressed by how he might appear to his classmates: "I didn't want to do it. . . . I was too nervous. I didn't want to make a fool out of myself, 'cause I didn't know what I was doin'. 'Cause the book wasn't any good." In the first term, by contrast, he was less worried about feeling embarrassed because he believed he would show a basic degree of competence: "I knew what I was doing. Just basically doing what everybody else did. I didn't care if they laughed or not that time."

Accountability to the peer audience also helped to establish standards through limits to the kinds of achievements that students thought would be well received. Eva's judgment about what presentational strategy to use offers one illustration. Some students, also, expressed concern about the prospect of making an unfavorable impression by demonstrating too much ability or engagement. LaTanya said, "Oh it's hard to get up there in front of your friends, and talk about something, and it'll be like, 'Oh. She's smart.' Y'know. And then they call you 'teacher's pet.'" Beth, whose academic knowledge and experience, on the whole, exceeded that of any classmate, said, "I don't like to come off as, 'I think I'm all that.' So that would be the only thing that I have to be mindful of." Perhaps this consideration was one reason she viewed leading a class activity during her third-term exhibition as "putting herself out there"; by leading such an activity, she would have risked distancing herself, in a way, from her peers.

Concerns of this nature entered into Anwar's feelings toward presenting. Indeed, "looking stupid" could mean appearing overly engaged as well as appearing incompetent. Anwar's efforts to avoid being in each of these situations were evident on a day when Diane and I spent a lunch period with him, watching the video of his exhibition on David Walker. He had willingly forgone a trip off campus with two friends in order to see this video. During the viewing, when Diane and I offered suggestions as to how he could present more effectively, he appeared to be absorbing them earnestly. At one point, however, he showed to Ronald, who was also in the room, a much different affect toward what we were doing: he abruptly turned toward Ronald and said, "Yo R., this is mad corn." At another point in this conference, Diane said to Anwar, "You have a lot of latent knowledge, but you're not letting it all out." Anwar responded, "I don't want to let it out."

In their relationships with peers, adolescents harbor desires to stand out as well as desires not to stand out. Peer cultures in different schools vary in the extent to which certain kinds of standing out are rewarded and in the extent to which certain kinds of behaviors constitute fitting in. The peer culture at Powell did not encourage a drive for academic excellence as much as it might have. However, accountability to peers did contribute to the building of certain standards of achievement.

AUDIENCE INPUT

Audience participation was a means through which students validated each other's work. By asking questions of a presenter, audience members indicated that the presenter had attracted their interest and brought them into a communication event; by not participating, the audience sent an opposite signal. Exchanges with the peer audience, furthermore, could be occasions through which significance was attached to particular aspects of students' work.

Limits in Audience Input

On the whole, there were notable limitations to the audience participation that occurred during Powell exhibitions. Often there was minimal audience response during an exhibition or response from only a small portion of the audience. There were a number of reasons for this. Carlita spoke for others as well as herself when she said she did not ask questions because she was quiet and shy. The phenomenon she felt she observed during her propaganda presentation—students not asking questions because they were more concerned with their own upcoming exhibitions—was acknowledged by some students when they described their experiences as audience members. Gloria gave another reason for nonparticipation: "I know sometimes I be dozing off during the exhibition; . . . it's like, sometimes I kind of lose focus." She suggested that this response could be caused by a lack of interest in the presenter's topic: She told Diane and me that she "would've paid more attention" to classmates' third-term exhibitions if, at the time when those exhibitions took place, she had "understood the importance" of the Civil War–era history. Renée described a more general disinterest that she felt periodically and that led to her disengaging during classmates' presentations: "Y'know, even though somebody's gettin' up talkin' to you, sometimes you're not into it, y'know. And especially in the morning and stuff, you're just like, 'I don't want to hear this person.'"

Sometimes the presenter's ineffective presentation methods or apparent lack of preparation was partly responsible for the lack of audience input. I sat next to Warren, the student who had led the challenge to Gail's statement that John Brown was "boring," during an exhibition about the New England Antislavery Society in which a classmate simply read from a book. When he was uncharacteristically quiet during the time for questions, I turned to him and said, "You don't have any questions?" He answered, "If she were tighter I would. This way I'd probably ask her about something she didn't know." Eva's remarks cited earlier in this chapter describe how those who presented in this manner were often unable to hold the audience's attention.

Discussions were most likely to emerge around topics—such as legalization of marijuana or Bibles in schools—that had some current, personal meaning to the students. On the other hand, when students in the audience had little or no prior knowledge of the presenter's topic, an attentive response could very well be as Renée described: "If you know nothing about it, you're like, 'Okay, well that's good to know,' and take a few notes and learn something new and that's it."

When audience members did ask questions, furthermore, the questions were sometimes of dubious significance to both questioner and presenter. Had I kept a tally, "When was (s)he born?" probably would have proven to be the most frequent student-asked question. Marcus's and Eva's comments, cited earlier in this chapter, suggest that information about a person's birthdate was part of a biography script that served an orienting function, at the least, for some students. Luis's observations provide additional perspective on students' use of this question:

> That's just a thing— . . . it's not, y'know, they're not askin' that because they want to know, y'know. . . . It's just something they do for, like, probably to confuse the other person and make theirself look good or whatever. But it's not like they're gonna leave out there sayin', "Oh y'know they were born, nine–." . . . It's just like some-

thing to ask whenever you don't have anything else to ask, y'know. It's like, the last thing to do or whatever.

He laughed and added, "I ask that a lot too."

Because of these tendencies on the part of the audience, interaction with the audience did not contribute to the growth of student achievements to the extent that it might have. Indeed, at times the audience appeared to have a depressing effect on students' efforts. Jorge, a few days before his third-term presentation, told me that he did not want to get especially concerned about the exhibition because the class was "so ignorant." He explained that he meant how classmates did not act interested when someone was presenting, adding that he had heard others in the class say the same thing. When students perceived the audience in this manner, audience input was affecting standards by helping to establish boundaries on what would be considered worth doing.

Engagement Between Presenter and Audience

Despite these limitations, there was audience–presenter interaction that lent positive meaning to Powell exhibitions. Several of the students I interviewed made remarks suggesting that they had anticipated some audience input as they prepared for their presentations. And in describing exhibitions they had done, several students indicated that exchanges with audience members stood out as significant events.

Of the questions that students in the audience asked, a fair percentage asked the presenter to repeat or clarify points already made or to provide additional facts. Some of the students I interviewed reported having received such questions and described the questions as indicating that the audience had been interested and paying attention. Furthermore, they described having successfully answered these questions as instances of competence they had experienced. Recollections by Brett and Nadine, cited in Chapter 7, illustrate. The questions Brett and Nadine mentioned called for further details: generals in the Battle of Gettysburg, and slave codes in different states. These questions affirmed a purpose that these students had in their work, by directing some serious attention to their attempts to be knowledgeable about a particular subject. By supplying the requested information, Brett and Nadine used their knowledge in a way that met peers' expectations.

There were some instances of more passionate or probing questioning. There was, in fact, a strain of outspokenness among some Powell students, which could emerge during exhibitions. Renée observed that Powell students will "criticize you in your exhibitions." Julia concurred:

"People at this school, yes. They give you their idea." Presenters were likely to be apprehensive about receiving such input. All the same, it functioned as a kind of positive feedback. As Gail said about her third-term exhibition, in which audience challenges had indeed made her uncomfortable, "Like when you argue, it's usually people are interested."

On some occasions, the more passionate questions went beyond what the presenter knew or had thought about—just as some of the more modest factual requests did. When Warren and Beth challenged Gail about John Brown's "boringness," for instance, Gail defended her position, but her statements ("He could have done more") did not address issues of abolitionist tactics as specifically as Warren's and Beth's did. Another example occurred during Harlan's exhibition on Harriet Tubman. One classmate persisted in inquiring whether slave owners noticed that their escaping slaves were missing—implying that she thought they would have and that this would have complicated Tubman's efforts. Harlan did not have information with which to answer her directly. He groped for a response at first, and finally replied that Tubman did not take all the escapees at once. The positive meaning that Gail and Harlan took from these exchanges centered around how, as each told me, the audience "got into it," rather than around what they themselves had said.

There were other instances, though, when the ideas expressed in exchanges with peers remained memorable to students I interviewed. LaTanya described how classmates had challenged her during her propaganda campaign for literacy, and also recounted the reasoning she had offered in response:

> One other girl at the same time did one about—not being literate, just getting pregnant and earning money for every baby you have. So, and mine was in opposite of hers. Don't get pregnant—go to school, learn. . . . We had like a minidebate. . . . Someone was sayin', "Why should I go with your campaign instead of hers—I'm getting money. I'm getting money right away just to have a baby." But then, my theory was, who's gonna take care of the baby, when you want to go out and party? Who's gonna finance your money, if you don't have a high school diploma? So in a way, my thing contrasted hers.

Marcus recalled an exhibition from the previous year, when classmates had responded to his raising of an issue. Like LaTanya, he placed certain ideas in the context of a conversation that peers took seriously, thus giving those ideas added significance and meaning:

I posed a question that asked, like, what do you think they should do with juveniles when they commit homicides, and then the class was having a big discussion about it. It was like, "Well I think they should do this, and do that," and then people—one person said, "I feel that they should be as—locked away like an adult," another person would disagree with 'em like, "Well, they young," and then, other person would be like, "Well if they young, if they know what they doin', then they should be able to be tried as an adult, instead of lettin' them just go to [Department of Youth Services] for like, six months or a year, and then come back out again." . . . I kind of agree with the person who said that if they know, if they at an age where I could say they knew what they did—

Questions carried other messages besides interest in the presenter's topic. As Luis suggested when talking about the question about birth date, a question could reflect a decision to participate—to enter the social event, or perhaps to comply with teachers' directives to the audience—as much as, if not more than, it reflected involvement with the content of the exhibition. Questions that were motivated thusly—and perceived by the presenter as such—could still carry significance to the presenter. Some students, for instance, spoke of questions from the audience as a deliberate testing of the presenter. Carlita said, "When they ask questions, I guess [they're trying to] see if the presenter knows what they're really talkin' about." She added, "Sometimes a [presenter] gets stuck and says, 'Well, I didn't read that far' or 'I don't know that.' 'But I thought you studied it,' something like that. That's why I think people ask questions." Luis took this idea another step, describing exhibitions as a game:

The audience is there to prove that [the presenter] didn't do enough studying or research. Y'know? It's kind of like competition. Like, the audience is trying to bring the presenter down, so they can get a good grade, y'know? And the presenter is tryin' to get the audience calmed down, so he can get a good grade.

Having framed the questioning process in this way, Luis experienced a direct hit of success in his encounter with Warren at the end of his exhibition on the Gettysburg Address. He spoke with pleasure as he described what occurred:

I kind of answered all the questions [with the initial presentation]. I only got a couple questions from Ms. Jennifer. . . . You know Warren, right? How he's always tryin' to be the wise guy and stuff, in the class? He was gonna ask me [a question], and he started, and then he said, "Ah, forget it." He didn't have any questions. He said he couldn't think of one. He said, "Give me a minute, and I'll ask you one."

Here, ultimately, it was the absence of questions that was experienced as an accomplishment. Renée described the effectiveness of her propaganda presentation in similar terms: "I expected everybody to be pro-abortion. . . . And I was gonna be standing there like overwhelmed with these questions, but everybody just took in what I had to say." But as with some of the verbal exchanges described above, there was an interaction with peers taking place, and some pride, on the presenter's part, in what he or she had done in that interaction.

CLOSING REMARKS

There were limitations in the input that Powell students provided to one another—in the kinds of performances that students were able to observe, in the general encouragement to perform well they received, and in the audience responses to their presentations. Still, peer interactions played a role in the assigning of value to certain pursuits and accomplishments.

What students learn through their encounters with one another is especially real to them, as they construct meanings around the work they are doing. The phrase "know what you're talking about," to give one example, appeared repeatedly in students' remarks about what they needed or wanted to do in exhibitions. "Know what you're talking about" is a principle. Its meaning was developed as students attached it to particular examples they observed, and as students felt they knew what they were talking about in the eyes of their peers.

In these in-class exhibitions, dialogue among peers was a more prominent element than it is in many school activities. However, in any classroom, students observe and talk to one another. In their interactions, concepts are defined and actions are given significance. The standards in a classroom will reflect these processes.

10

Teachers' Standards: What Teachers Thought About Exhibition Work

Powell humanities teachers, like their students, formed and harbored standards in their minds. Those standards were significant in their own right, as the thinking of classroom participants. They also were integral in the shaping of the broader classroom standards. Those broader standards bore the imprint of the standards in teachers' minds through a variety of means. To cite one of the most fundamental: Simply by virtue of teachers' designating the assignments, classroom activity reflected teachers' ideas about what was worth working on and what was good work.

Teachers had given questions about the quality of student work more explicit consideration than their students had. They not only had many more years of experience with academic work; it was also their profession to think about it. Still, because of the student role in creating standards, because of processes of negotiation, and because of the imperfect correlation between thought and action (which applies to teachers and students alike), the standards in teachers' minds were not the same as those that prevailed in the interactive classroom environment. Rather, these standards underlay—and/or were outgrowths of—actions that teachers took in that environment.

The standards in teachers' minds included general aspirations for student work, which I discuss in the first part of this chapter. They also included ideas that emerged when teachers viewed work their students had done. Those ideas reflected the influence of the classroom context on teachers' standards. The last part of the chapter explores that process of influence and its significance.

TEACHERS' ASPIRATIONS

Teachers' aspirations were in a sense the starting point from which teachers entered the classroom negotiation process. These were the conceptions of good work and student achievement that teachers would have most liked to see realized in their classrooms.

Teachers expressed their aspirations to each other when talking about curriculum and pedagogy or about their students' instructional needs. Most of the teacher comments cited below were made in interviews with me. Those interviews were part of a larger, ongoing conversation involving all the members of the humanities department. At department meetings and on other occasions, we discussed issues of what we wanted our students to be doing in their exhibitions and other work. The ideas expressed in the interviews are indicative of that larger conversation.

Powell humanities teachers' aspirations reflected our professional concerns as well as our own academic histories. All of us had graduate degrees, and our thinking as well as our dialogue with one another drew on knowledge we had acquired as students. In addition, as part of Powell's long-term project of developing curriculum and pedagogy along the lines promoted by the Coalition of Essential Schools, we were actively engaged in considering what it means for students to have a richer educational experience than has conventionally been the case in high schools.

Teachers' aspirations spanned the areas of student performance that are discussed in Chapter 7: content knowledge, understanding and thinking about a topic, work habits, and manner of presenting. They also pertained to students' reading, writing, and researching skills.

The general goal that students "learn content" was expressed periodically by all of the teachers. This teacher purpose was often in evidence during the humanities department's curriculum-planning sessions. Teachers discussed which components of the broad unit topics—the Jewish Holocaust, Civil War, civil rights movement, and Vietnam War—were most worthy of study and potentially engaging to students. We selected readings and videos partly on the basis of what information we wanted students to learn. Teachers did not designate specific bodies and amounts of information that all students would be expected to know in each unit. The third-term unit guide expressed a more general intent: "We will need to know a certain amount of general information to be able to draw appropriate conclusions about the era." It then added, "For example: What do you know about the following?" and listed items such as the Compromise of 1850, *Uncle Tom's Cabin,* John Brown, Abraham Lincoln, and the Confederacy.

Since exhibitions were individualized projects, the specific content goals that teachers considered were not meant to apply to each student's exhibition. In the kind of exhibitions teachers most hoped to see, though, students would incorporate and make connections to knowledge they were acquiring in class.

Teachers also thought about particular thematic understandings that they hoped students would attain during each unit. For example, Barry Sheehy said:

> Always the interesting thing doing the civil rights movement . . . I think, is the difficulty there is trying to help your students understand—not necessarily agree with but just understand—what nonviolent direct action was. Because they see no model of that.

Likewise, there were conceptual threads running through the whole year's work that teachers wanted students to consider. For instance, the question "What makes people be brutal?" was emphasized in the Facing History curriculum. Diane referred back to it later in the year on a number of occasions, including a student's exhibition on the Middle Passage and a planning meeting on the Vietnam War unit.

Essential questions (see Chapter 2) occupied a significant place in teachers' thoughts about curriculum. A fair amount of time during curriculum-planning meetings was spent deciding on the essential questions for each term. The essential questions we designated represented both issues we wanted students to think about, and a kind of thinking—looking into large questions that do not have simple answers—that we wanted to occur in our classrooms. Barry said, "I think what we've really said is that asking these essential questions is where eventually we want to be." Charles Touchstone, when I interviewed him, pointed to a role essential questions could play in exhibitions: When students have to "do something with that broad question, or answer it in *a* way," he said, they do more than simply present information.

When Barry talked about what he most wanted to see in exhibitions, he emphasized the thinking that students displayed. He said, "I guess the aspect of really thinking about it is, in many ways, to me what the exhibition is all about." He explained:

> We could give multiple-choice tests, and kids could answer them, and they could know the facts without really thinking about it.
> And really thinking means having some content knowledge at your

disposal to really think about, but then asking some questions that are hard, that aren't so clear.

Like "know what you're talking about" and other student descriptors of good performances, "really thinking about it" is a broad principle. It can be defined somewhat more specifically through possible ways that students can demonstrate "really thinking." Charles, for instance, indicated what he thought good questions during exhibitions would do:

> Make [students]—y'know like, "Why do you think they'd do that?" or something like that—make them make a slight leap from where they're at. . . . Or, "Is this related to you in some way, shape, or form?" Y'know, those kinds of questions, that make them draw some conclusions from something.

Barry, too, provided some examples of "really thinking" when discussing the kinds of questions one might ask students. He felt that some of the questions asked during the propaganda campaigns were good because they led students "to kind of take stock, and relate [their exhibitions] to what we were studying in class." In reference to Gail's statement, in her third-term exhibition, that John Brown was "boring," he said that one might ask her,

> "Okay what's the alternative?" . . . What could he do to show his opposition to slavery? What are the alternatives open for him? How would you judge those different alternatives? . . . It does seem to me that perhaps really thinking means, among other things, not accepting that just the way things happened is the way they had to happen, or the decisions someone made were the only decisions one could make.

In presenting another example of what might qualify as "really thinking," Barry evoked Sizer's notion of "using" content knowledge (see Chapter 2) and talked about students exploring connections to their own lives:

> I hope that that's what the purpose of some of these, of all of these exhibitions are—eventually to get kids to have the ability to understand different content, use different content, think about different content, and think about it not just in terms of the content itself, but in, kind of, broader perspective. . . . So if it was about, let's say, the civil rights movement . . . it would really say something about

"What does the fact that four kids sat-in in North Carolina in 1960, what the hell does that have to do with me?" Well, it may have a lot to do with you. And it may be that you have to wind up thinking about whether you think that kind of action, kind of civil disobedience, is proper, whether you think that nonviolence is a worthwhile philosophy of life or strategy, or nonsense—and that it's something that you study in the context of that period but something that you also use to think about how *you* act, and what *you* think about, and what *you* think is important.

Because "really thinking" could take different forms and occur on different levels, teachers' aspirations in this area contained a certain amount of ambiguity. This ambiguity was illustrated in an exchange I had with Diane during our interview.

Diane first made a statement about what she wanted to see in exhibitions:

I think exhibitions have to have an idea. . . . And all of the ones that were propaganda campaigns that were good, they had an idea, they had like a controlling idea. And that's what the kid is working on: "Here's my idea. Now I'm gonna give you evidence for this." Instead of information, where there's no idea.

She elaborated on this concept when talking about a particular student:

Maybe he's not yet able to rise above all that data and to pull out of that some new, interesting insight. Maybe insight's a better word [than idea]—there has to be an insight there, that controls the information the kid's [putting] out, so that it comes out as some kind of whole with meaning. So many exhibitions have no meaning.

A little later in the interview, she gave an example:

I'm talking about a kid getting insight. Insight is when you go, "Whoa. Hmm-m. Harriet Tubman's brother turned her in. Hmm-m." Which isn't true—it was in one source but it isn't true. "Wow, I wonder what it must be like to have your own brother turn you in. Gee, I'd like to find out more about this."

I suggested, "Wayne did that. When he did the thing on the abolitionists. When he said, 'Now here was a guy who ran the gaming house, and he made his money illegally and then he used it to help the cause; what do you think of that?'"

Diane said, "Yeah. That's a good example of it. That's an insight that he made with that information."

I then thought back, though, to Diane's earlier use of the phrases "controlling idea" and "whole with meaning." I offered, "But it wasn't an overall idea that tied the whole thing together." Diane responded,

> But that's not what makes it interesting. What makes it interesting, both for the listener and the person doing the research, is that little thing. So, I guess what that means is you have to do enough background reading [so] that you do find that thing. And then when you do get it . . . you recognize it—you get excited about it.

Although "controlling idea" and "whole with meaning" represented a form of thinking that Diane valued in students' work, she described other possibilities for how students could demonstrate "insight," which she valued as well.

Teachers' aspirations also pertained to how students approached the task of preparing their exhibitions, and how they approached school work in general. A phrase that Barry often used, when talking with colleagues about what he wanted to see in his classroom, was "being a student." "Being a student" involved, first of all, a commitment to the enterprise of school. Barry said that "to have all these other things happen the way we want them to happen," it was necessary

> that by the time they're doing exhibitions, they have in a sense bought into what's a student. Which more and more, as the year went by again, is the question I kept coming to: How do we excite kids about education? Or, . . . how do we somehow work with our kids so that the idea of being a student becomes primary?

"Being a student" also involved habits—from working quietly in the library and doing homework, to habits of inquiry that would lead to thoughtful analysis in an exhibition. Revisiting one's work was one habit that Charles thought was very important. Charles also discussed how successful exhibition-type work, to him, required students to function independently:

> At some point, they have to have time where [the teacher says], "Okay, now, do this." And that "this" is, take a look at what we've done, studied . . . y'know, do some of those habits-of-mind things.

Make some connections, do some what-ifs, y'know, do that stuff which is very internalized, and not very teacher-directed, and not very kind of, "I have to sit on you to make you do your work."

Diane, throughout the year as she and I discussed approaches to our class, often emphasized a more fundamental goal for student-workers: students' completing the products required of them, or "getting work done," as she put it. "Good work is when you do the work," she said, stating the obvious but suggesting that this was not a trivial issue. She observed that when we coached our students, we often emphasized their working in an efficient and timely manner, and she believed this was a worthy focus. She also remarked that one value of the portfolio system was that it gave students the experience of having a list of things to do and doing them, and then being able to mark their accomplishments by saying, "I did that, I did that," and so on.

Judging by what was emphasized in teachers' conversation, the particular presentation skills students might display during exhibitions figured less centrally into teachers' goals than students' knowledge, thinking, or ways of working. Teachers did express aims and desires for students' work as presenters, though. Most fundamentally, we considered it valuable for students to learn to speak before a group of people. Once when I mentioned to Diane how Wayne had seemed to become more comfortable as a presenter during the year, she offered that this was a worthy benefit of requiring students to present before their classmates. Teachers also hoped that presenters would project themselves in a way that demonstrated engagement in their work. Barry spoke of students crossing the "barrier" between "'I'm just sayin' these words'" and "bec[oming] part of their project."

In addition to the aspirations discussed thus far, teachers expressed desires that students learn academic skills that have more traditionally appeared among secondary school English objectives. When talking in general terms about what she wanted her students to become, Diane periodically used the phrase "competent readers and writers." Teachers spoke about the research paper assignment as an opportunity for students to learn reading, writing, and researching skills. When the humanities department, at a March retreat, discussed what students might be required to do in a system of "graduation by exhibition," teachers' nominations included performances that would demonstrate some quite specific skills: writing a compare-and-contrast paper; going to the library, finding four sources, and summarizing them; keeping a notebook; reading and discussing the first two pages of a newspaper; and others. Diane brought up the notion, on this and other occasions, of students' being able to write an "error-free paragraph." She explained that if students were asked, on the spot, to write on an employment application, their writing mechanics would affect how they were judged.

These latter aspirations for the most part did not pertain as directly to exhibition work as those described previously. However, in their projects students practiced reading, writing, and researching in a variety of ways, and these were among the multiple purposes that teachers saw in exhibition work.

RELATION OF TEACHERS' ASPIRATIONS TO STUDENTS' STANDARDS

The concepts of good exhibition work that marked teachers' aspirations differed from those that appeared in students' comments, as reported in Chapter 7. The teachers wanted students to be more broadly knowledgeable about the unit topics than the students were intent on becoming, and they were more concerned that students integrate such knowledge into their exhibitions. They spoke of kinds of thinking—such as exploring large questions, making connections, and having controlling ideas—that tended not to be among students' stated purposes. They wanted students to demonstrate solid commitments to "being students," while many students were more concerned with being "prepared" for an exhibition in a more minimal way.

It is not uncommon, in teacher–student relationships, for teachers' goals for students to extend past the students' goals for themselves. Teaching involves leading students into territory that students had not previously imagined. By virtue of experience, teachers know their field more intimately than do students and have a fuller vision of what their students might learn to do. In public schools, furthermore, where the students are not voluntary participants, the students are likely not to share the same passion for the field of study as the teachers. They are also, of course, younger.

At Powell, in addition, teachers' aspirations involved elements of what would be considered, anywhere in the nation, outstanding academic performance. The students' educational histories, on the other hand, were such that performances of that nature would have to be built toward gradually.

In any event, there was *tension* between what teachers wanted students to pursue and what students hoped to achieve, and between teachers' and students' notions of what good exhibition work comprised. This created a fundamental condition for negotiation.

Because teachers' standards were multifaceted, though, and in some cases based on principles that were by nature ambiguous, it was possible for their standards to overlap with those of the students. When students talked about what went into "explaining" their material, for instance, they were not envisioning all the forms of "really thinking about it" that Barry had in mind. However, they were envisioning more than the kind of "knowing the facts without really thinking about it" that Barry said characterized multiple-choice tests. From such areas of agreement, the process of building standards together might proceed.

TEACHERS' ASSESSMENTS OF STUDENT PERFORMANCES: STANDARDS IN CONTEXT

Teachers' ideas about what characterized good exhibitions emerged from their interaction with students as well as from independently held beliefs. One way that this occurred was through their assessing students' work.

As teachers thought about the quality of their students' work, they drew on their own ideals. But they did not simply regard the work in light of standards they already held. Teachers also observed what students were learning and achieving, within the framework of particular assignments and activities, and derived concepts of good work from these observations. In this way, the classroom context helped to shape teachers' standards.

The assessments discussed below were not formal evaluations of students' work. They were teachers' perceptions and thoughts about that work, shared with me in interviews or conversations. These same assessments may or may not have been communicated to the students whose work was in question.

Both Diane and Barry spoke more enthusiastically about one group of propaganda campaigns in the class they co-taught than about any other exhibitions. Eight months later, Diane recalled the day when Paul and several of his classmates presented:

That day was stunning in the number of kids who were really ready and had some kind of original presentation that was well crafted and well thought out. Every part of them was good. And that was amazing—and then we never had a good set from them again, the whole year.

I asked her to say more about what was good about these exhibitions. She replied:

> The objects in the exhibition were well done. You didn't get any of these dippy little drawings that somebody did 5 minutes before. They were really crafted pieces. They had interesting, original angle[s], each person. Like, Paul had these little tear-offs, if you wanted more information about owning a gun. And Frances had some survey, something about religion—I forget what it was. But there were surprises; that was what was cool. There were surprises. Where you would go, "Oh wow, that is cool. I wouldn't have thought of that."

In describing the same set of exhibitions, Barry emphasized some of the same qualities that Diane did: how they were interesting, original, "thought out," and well prepared. In addition, he spoke of how Frances's exhibition, which advocated teaching about religion in schools, "really did clearly come from the material [about the Jewish Holocaust] we got in class. . . . It was really based on the fact that, as she studied history she learned that religion was very important, but she didn't know very much about religion."

Barry described how Paul's and Wanda's exhibitions were successful, in his view:

> Probably the most outstanding was Paul's. Which was . . . the Protect Yourself Campaign. And it was in favor of everyone carrying a handgun. And his slogan was a very effective "Don't Be a Victim." Which had a pretty damn good ring to it. He had a logo, a very powerful logo, . . . he had a good poster with some, y'know, eye-catching photos of people carrying guns. People you wouldn't expect to be carrying guns, y'know: pretty women, mostly. And, then he had a rap. . . . It was very effective. And it was he who took the most heated questions from . . . guests and classmates and teachers, because I think this really, y'know, hit people where they live. "Are you really saying this?" And he had his answer down pat. I mean he was good. And he had facts. . . .
>
> The other one . . . which really jolted our [adult guests] I'll tell you, was Wanda's, which was . . . "Get paid to have a baby." It was fomenting teenage pregnancy. And she had her poster, and she had her line, she had her 1-800-QUIK-LOOT. Her phone number, 1-800-QUIK-LOOT: very effective, still in my head. Three weeks later. . . . And she handled all those questions—it was really an interesting

presentation. . . . The next day, two of the [guests] called me, expressly to ask whether Wanda was serious. That's how good she was. Because, under relentless questioning . . . she stayed in character. . . . Paul was much more of a performer. . . . But she stayed in there. She didn't giggle, she didn't let anybody sway her.

The two teachers' enthusiasm in part reflected how the exhibitions met criteria they had thought about previously. For instance, Barry had said, in a department meeting before the propaganda exhibitions, that he hoped students would demonstrate the skill of articulating a position. Posters, slogans, and logos were required components of the assignment, and the teachers had wanted these to be imaginative and effective. But Barry's and Diane's enthusiasm was also a direct response to the performances themselves, on the performances' own terms. As they made their assessments, Barry and Diane were discovering what students could do with an assignment.

One way that these students fulfilled teachers' concepts of good work was by demonstrating engagement and independent thinking. As Barry said, "[These students' exhibitions] really had a life of their own, in that it was . . . more than our assignment. It became something that they got into." When students meet this teacher standard, they are liable to create their own images of excellence at the same time. The particular forms of presentational skill and flair that distinguished Paul's and Wanda's exhibitions, for instance, had not been included in any preliminary profile of outstanding work.

Barry's comments about these propaganda campaigns show, also, that he recognized different attributes in different individuals' work. Paul's and Wanda's presentation techniques stood out in a way that Frances's didn't, and while Barry noticed this difference, he also saw a strength that distinguished Frances's work.

The third-term exhibition assignment provided an occasion for students to realize some teacher aspirations to a greater extent than they had in their propaganda campaigns. However, it also posed greater difficulties to the students—and challenges to the teachers—in terms of the academic skills and the amount of preparation involved. The result, in Barry's view, was that "it was probably the term we had the worst exhibitions." When I interviewed them, the teachers did not identify any third-term performances that had been especially good. Their responses to this set of exhibitions demonstrate that they did not simply direct their enthusiasm for student work toward the leading candidates. Rather, a recognizable element of creativity, care, or competence, as well as some convergence with teachers' own standards, was required.

One other performance of which Barry spoke very positively was a fourth-term exhibition for which a student had interviewed her grandmother. In the exhibition, the young African American woman, after recounting what her grandmother had talked about, said the interview had made her more aware of her own attitudes toward White people. She observed that if a Black person bumped into her on the bus she would probably be accepting and exchange "Excuse me's," whereas if a White person bumped into her she would be ready to fight. Barry noted how engaged her classmates, including White students, became in discussing this with her. "What made that powerful," he said, "was that she was able to take real content and think about it."

Barry's assessment of this exhibition involved criteria that he mentioned when discussing his aspirations for exhibitions: In "taking real content and thinking about it," the student "used" her knowledge and thought about "What does that have to do with me?" At the same time, because this student's performance stood out to him as a concrete embodiment of "thinking about" content, it was helping to define that standard. Her performance met the standard in a particular way: There were other forms of thinking about content that Barry mentioned when I interviewed him—exploring essential questions, for instance, or making connections to other subject matter in the course—that this student did not do. These other forms remained in his thoughts, but they were not as crystallized into an image of student work.

Teachers' concepts of good work were multifaceted and multilayered; this meant that it was difficult to consider them in their entirety at any one time. It also meant that when students met teachers' standards, they were likely to do so partially. Teachers were therefore in a position in which they could view a figurative glass as "half full" or "half empty." Diane often said to me that she thought it was important to focus on the "half full" side of students' work.

Some teacher assessments of student exhibitions were clearly unfavorable. Regarding the first term, for instance, Barry said that on one particular day in his class, "many of [the exhibitions] were not of broadcast quality." He mentioned one young woman's: "There was very little, there was no substance there. There was no poster there. There was a poster but there was no poster. I mean, she slopped together [some] stuff." Charles, similarly, said that in his class some students' propaganda projects amounted to "10 minutes of work." Diane described Winston's third-term exhibition on Frederick Douglass in terms of basic elements of understanding and purpose that appeared to be absent: "He had no concept of any kind of significant controlling idea that he could put out to the class. So he very pathetically read this totally incomprehensible poem that nobody understood. . . . He had no idea. He wasn't working on anything." In these cases, teachers did not view the exhibitions on their own terms. Rather, they held up their ideas of good work—or adequate work—and found the exhibitions wanting in comparison.

Even in some of the least accomplished performances, though, teachers saw progress that individual students had made, and viewed the work favorably in that respect. Barry, for instance, cited simply doing an exhibition as a positive step that some of his students had taken during the first term. Similarly, Diane said that while Winston was poorly prepared for his propaganda presentation, he thought well on his feet, "which is progress for him"; in his previous year's exhibitions he had made little attempt to respond to the questions asked of him.

The assessments teachers expressed varied when they were made from different vantage points. A distant and panoramic perspective could result in the teacher's comparing the work to what he or she had hoped for—and therefore emphasizing the work's shortcomings. Thus in June, Diane shared a reaction to a group of third-term exhibitions: "We saw, time and again, kids get up and explain the slave trade, and you could tell they didn't have any idea how the statistics they were giving, or the knowledge they were putting forward, was in any way connected to any principle about slavery." She also said, during this interview, that she had to "think for a while" to remember any individual third-term exhibitions—an indication, she said, of how "soft" they were compared to the propaganda campaigns, many of which remained fresh in her mind. When she spoke about third-term exhibitions close to the time when they had been presented, on the other hand, and when she considered individual performances, she was likely to mention qualities that made them "half-full."

Juan, for instance, was apparently one of the students to whose work she was referring in the above assessment of exhibitions on the slave trade. While Harlan (see Chapter 7) admired the clarity of Juan's speaking and was impressed by some of the information Juan provided, Juan appeared to teachers as having an uncertain command of his material. For instance, he distributed a chart entitled "The Magnitude of the Slave Trade," with figures for different countries and regions but no dates; in response to a question, he said that the "124,000" figure next to "United States" was for the entire period of slavery. When Barry told him that number "seems low," Juan consulted his source and seemed to become further confused. On the day of his presentation, Diane remarked to me afterward that Juan wasn't able to do more than "skim the surface." Yet she also, in the same conversation, observed that Juan had put more work into his exhibition than Mario, another student who had presented that day. She added that it was interesting how Juan had selected certain information from his book to present, even though he relayed some of it erroneously.

As for Mario, his preparation was "really thin," Diane said. He had had no materials with him when he presented his exhibition on Reconstruction, and no plan for his presentation. His research had consisted of a few pages of reading. Yet he was a student with a fair amount of historical knowledge, and skill at discussing historical topics. Aided by Warren's input, he had touched on a number of issues during the session. Diane spoke of how he was able to "make good experience out of something really thin" and "run with" what he had. She referred to Mario's as a "good exhibition" at one point.

The student strengths that such assessments identify are relative in nature: relative to individuals' abilities and histories, and/or relative to other students. They may take into account challenges that students appear to be addressing. Positive assessments such as these did not reflect "teachers' standards" in the sense of what the teachers, independently, thought of as good exhibitions. However, they did reflect "teachers' standards" in another important sense: They reflected standards that were being constructed, in practice, in the classrooms of which teachers were a part. These assessments recognized positive attributes of students' performances, in aspects of the work that teachers considered important.

Teachers' favorable assessments sometimes centered on what made an exhibition unique in a classroom. Diane, for instance, thought it was good that Frances had worked to draw answers from the class as she presented her third-term exhibition. Involving the class in one's exhibition was a standard to which several of the students I interviewed alluded but which most Powell students did not try to meet to the extent that Frances did. Frances's performance, to Diane, was not so much an accomplished one as a reasonable first effort. It opened a new area of endeavor, for herself and perhaps for her classmates, and was a potential step toward the further development of standards in that area.

Diane's response to Beth's third-term exhibition illustrates how teachers' views of student work varied according to what they saw as the learning needs of individual students. Prominent in this exhibition was Beth's assertion that ancient Egyptians provided knowledge to their Greek neighbors but are not properly acknowledged for this today. Diane commented later that Beth did indeed have "an idea," and said, "That's what made it interesting." Had Beth been a student with a history, in Diane's eyes, of presenting "information with no idea," the presence of such an idea might have been viewed as a notable achievement. Beth, however, was the most accomplished student in her class, and Diane apparently expected this much from her.

During the exhibition, Diane, in her role as questioner, scrutinized Beth's idea and the evidence behind it. In response to particular comments Beth had made, Diane pressed her with questions about whether she faulted Plato for studying in Egypt, whether Plato himself never acknowledged his Egyptian teachers, and how much of his knowledge and ideas he actually got from Egyptians. Afterward, Diane noted that Beth had little evidence with which to address these issues. She also spoke about what lay behind her pushing Beth as she had:

> I saw that—this term that the British use . . . the idea of the re-
> ceived knowledge? . . . Received knowledge is what the culture pas-
> ses on to the next group. And it's unquestioned, and you're not sup-
> posed to think critically about it. . . . And I see . . . that there's some
> received knowledge that's passed down through, like, [Beth's] par-
> ents and her upbringing, where it's completely uncritical.

This statement indicated a kind of examining of assumptions that Diane wanted all of her students to practice. However, this issue did not come to the forefront with regard to all of her students' work in the way that it did with Beth's, because others did not present bodies of "received knowledge"—or present historical material with a point of view—as Beth did.

A conversation Diane and I had during the fourth term illustrates how thinking about standards for one's students differed from thinking about good work in the abstract. On this day, Diane remarked that when she thinks of how she learns, she notices that her ideas about a subject don't come immediately, but rather take years and years, and "layers and layers." She wondered if, in asking for "understanding" (which she referred to as the Coalition of Essential Schools' emphasis), we were asking for something beyond the students' range. It might be enough, she said, for high school students to absorb the *Eyes on the Prize* (Hampton, 1986) videos we were watching in class during our study of the civil rights movement; adolescents don't have to "come to conclusions" in the way that adults do. I brought up an exhibition Claudia had recently given about the Middle Passage, and Diane's periodic comments that Claudia needed to have more "critical thinking" in her work. "Are you changing?" I asked. She said no—but then added that maybe she was, and that Claudia's problem was more that she "didn't know enough" about her topic.

As the year continued, Diane on many occasions indicated that she

thought it was important for students to do more than absorb information. Where the line was, though, marking what students should show in
their current work, was not a question with a precise answer for her. As
this conversation suggested, addressing that question involved considering her students and how they learn, as well as adults' desires for what
students will produce.

Teachers' and students' direct exchanges with one another are discussed in the following chapter. However, one such event is included here
because it sheds some additional light on how the standards in teachers'
minds were related to the context of their classrooms.

After Juan's exhibition on the slave trade, Barry sat alone with him
at a table. As he talked to Juan about the exhibition, Barry used the word
"good" several times. Of Juan's speaking performance, Barry said, "There
was nothing you said that people didn't understand." He told Juan he
had shown how Africans "weren't stupid" and didn't simply go along
with the slave trade. He also pointed to the table Juan had handed out,
with the misinterpreted numbers, and said Juan could have done better with that.

Later that day, in the teachers' room, I told Barry I wished I had
captured Juan's exhibition on videotape. I was thinking about how the
class had seemed to engage with what Juan was saying. Barry indicated
agreement that a videotape would have been worth having. As he did so,
he rolled his eyes at me and remarked that this exhibition was "exactly
what the reality is"—implying that a videotape would have documented
how poor the third-term performances had been. While Barry had mentioned a weakness of the exhibition when talking to Juan, his overall affect when talking to me was much different than it had been with Juan.

There are reasons why teachers do not express the same evaluations
and feelings to students as they do to other adults. Teachers consider the
meaning students are likely to make of what they say, the relationships
they are trying to build with their students, and the motivational impact
of encouragement as well as criticism. These are educationally relevant
concerns.

At first glance, it would seem that what Barry expressed to a fellow
teacher, who was likely to share many of his perspectives and understandings, would be closer to his "true" opinions than what he expressed
to a teenager. The notion of a "true" opinion, however, implies that Barry's
opinions are uniform, fixed, and developed entirely within him.

Opinions and interpretations of events are the product of social interactions as well as individual thought. What teachers express when they
are among adolescents is therefore "true" in its own way—especially if

teachers are spending their working lives in an environment populated mostly by adolescents. Talking to Juan may very well have made Barry think about how "there was nothing you said that people didn't understand," and the significance of that, more than if he had only talked to other adults. Such a thought can appear valid to a teacher, and enter into the teacher's standards.

At first glance, also, it would seem that the adjusting of a teacher's standards in response to his or her students would mean a weakening of classroom standards. However, it can also mean strengthening them. If a teacher observes, for instance, how "explaining" during exhibitions represents growth on some students' part, then by helping students prepare for exhibitions with this goal in mind, he or she can support student learning and achievement. This does not preclude efforts to meet other standards as well.

11

Teachers' Expectations and Classroom Standards

Teachers' expectations, as the term is used here, are standards in action. Whereas the aspirations and ideas about student work discussed in the previous chapter are standards in teachers' minds, expectations are what teachers somehow project to students. Expectations *reflect* teachers' aspirations and ideas about student work, as those are expressed through what teachers do in classroom interactions.

A teacher's expectations might be formal requirements of students. Or they might be other messages a teacher conveys about what he or she believes it is important that students do. Expectations can be communicated with different degrees of explicitness, can contain different levels of specificity, and can have different amounts of force and consequence behind them.

In Powell humanities classrooms, the process of establishing standards in response to teacher expectations involved explicit, formalized expectations. However, Powell teachers did not convey detailed expectations for the quality of student performances in the manner that some teachers do. Elaborated systems for scoring student work, for instance, featuring rubrics that list criteria and define levels of performance within each criterion, are currently popular among some educators and are one means of making expectations for quality known. These were not used at Powell in 1993–1994.

At some level, though, the process of communicating notions of what good work is must extend beyond such formal means. Previous chapters have shown that when standards pertain to certain matters—thinking deeply or working hard, for instance—they are especially difficult to define precisely and universally. Concepts of valued performances in such areas are conveyed both by direct verbal communication, informal as well as formal, and by a larger context of activity.

With their expectations, Powell humanities teachers attempted to lead students toward habits and achievements that they wanted the students to pursue and attain. To an extent, students took teachers' expectations seriously and attempted to meet them. Students' thoughts about what was important to do could be traced, in part, to teachers' expectations. When responding to teachers' expectations, though, students did not simply adopt the standards presented to them. They made their own meanings of the expectations as they communicated with teachers and as they experienced doing the work in question.

Quite often in contemporary discourse, the expectations projected by those in nominal authority are referred to as the "standards" of a given institution or community. That view, however, ignores the process by which the expectations become translated into community members' purposes and actions. Teachers' expectations, in themselves, are one form of standards that exist in a classroom community. However, classroom standards also include outcomes of students' interactions with teachers' expectations. This chapter highlights those interactions.

WHAT STUDENTS "HAD TO" DO

Several of the students I interviewed talked about exhibitions, at one point or another, in terms of what they "have to" do. "Have to" carried a variety of meanings. At times, it referred to students' own judgments about what doing a competent exhibition entailed. At other times, it referred to students' ideas about what kind of work would please teachers. And at others, it referred to what students were instructed to do in order to complete an assignment. In the latter two instances, students' remarks about what they "have to" do indicated a concern with teachers' expectations.

Such concern developed unevenly. Teachers' expectations differed, and the ways in which they were processed varied from expectation to expectation and student to student.

A fundamental requirement that went with exhibitions—and one that was broadly respected—was that students present before the whole class. Some students enjoyed facing the peer audience. Others were much less enthused by the prospect but agreed to meet this requirement all the same. Brett said, "I'm not comfortable in front of people. But, like, when it's for a grade I'll do it, but like just volunteer I won't do it." Sean felt similarly. He also allowed, "It's all right. Gettin' up, teachin' us how to present things and everything"—indicating some acceptance of the values behind the expectation.

That students present before the class was an absolute requirement: If students did not meet it, they would fail for a marking term. Most directives did not have that large a consequence attached to them. Students were told that their exhibitions were to include certain elements, for instance; the absence of one of these would affect teachers' evaluation of the work, but not in an all-or-nothing manner. There were, in other words, different degrees of required-ness.

With respect to standing before the class, also, it was quite obvious to students what they were being asked to do, and whether or not they had done it could be answered in a "yes or no" fashion. When the distinction between performances that satisfied and failed to satisfy an expectation was less than self-evident—and/or when an expectation was less than absolute—the processes by which students made meaning of the expectation gained importance.

There were more particular tasks specified by exhibition instructions that students spoke of "having to" do. When they looked back on their work, different students singled out different ones of these; the variation in what they identified as significant suggested variation in how they had processed the multifaceted assignments. Regarding the third-term assignment, for instance, students mentioned choosing a topic, gathering information, using visuals, or having an activity for the class at the end of the exhibition.

Renée indicated that she had gained a significant insight into what teachers expected by studying the instructions for the propaganda assignment. She also indicated that her reading of the instructions was not shared by all of her classmates:

> I think a lot of the students didn't do too well 'cause they didn't really understand . . . that you're not supposed to be gettin' up just giving information; you're supposed to be capturing the audience and changing their minds . . . . I don't know, I think the students, sometimes they get lackadaisical. . . . I think they saw that it was just an assignment, so, "We gotta do this assignment." . . . For a moment I thought it was just like writin' a report. . . . But then I read over the paper again . . . and I was like, "Oh, I have to make a campaign." So when I heard that word I was like, "Oh okay, 'campaign,'" so that's what I did.

Renée's remarks suggest that some classmates were not sufficiently concerned to consider the meaning of the instructions as closely as she did.

Nadine also showed a regard for the instructions for the propaganda exhibition, by struggling to understand what they meant. Students were instructed to take a position on an issue, and Diane stressed this expectation in her interactions with Nadine prior to the presentation. Nadine recalled:

> I knew it was about something like a argument, but I didn't really know, so it didn't turn out so good, is what I thought. You know, a lot of kids had the ideas, and I had my first idea, but Ms. Jennifer said it wasn't really a propaganda. So. You know—and I was really confused. I thought I really knew what to do but I really didn't. [I ended up doing] segregated schools, you know: Should schools go back to all Black and all White?

The concern of which Nadine spoke had less to do with what might distinguish a good performance than with knowing "what to do," in the sense of how to be in essential compliance with the assignment. Expectations stated as instructions directly signaled "what to do." Expectations that simply reflected how teachers might judge the quality of a performance had a less immediate significance. The latter were often given less attention by students.

Taking a position on an issue, for instance, was a core part of the propaganda assignment. For their third-term exhibitions, by contrast, students were not instructed to take a position. Whether students had, as Diane put it, "an idea" was an important indicator of the quality of their third-term work, in teachers' eyes, and this expectation was communicated in various interactions with students. It was conveyed less formally and prominently, though, than the expectation that students take a position in their propaganda campaigns. It also concerned a more subtle performance: a layer added to a research-centered task. Brett's remarks about what he "had to" do in the different exhibitions emphasize taking a position during the first term and omit having his own ideas during the third term:

> I think [the propaganda exhibition] was harder to do. 'Cause it was like, you had to prove your point, y'know get your point across. Whereas with the Civil War one, you just researched something and you had your facts there from the books, and you could tell exactly what happened. But with the propaganda campaign you had to sit there and you had to think which side you wanted to go for. And then you had to try and prove it to the class.

His comment about the third-term exhibition resembles Deniece's remarks about the absence of "theories" in her exhibition about the Middle Passage (see Chapter 7).

An interaction with Claudia at the beginning of the third term provides another example of an expectation pertaining to the quality of student work not having made a strong impression on a student. In addition, it shows student understanding and acceptance of such expectations to be significant issues.

Diane and I had an individual conference with Claudia to present and discuss our assessment of her second-term portfolio. At the beginning of the conversation, Diane told Claudia her grade was a "C-plus." Claudia exclaimed, "A 'C-plus'! But I did all my work." Claudia wanted a higher grade; therefore there was an adversarial context to the ensuing conversation that encouraged her to take stances that differed from ours. Nonetheless, as the conversation unfolded, the assessment criteria invoked by teachers and student suggested different underlying ways of thinking about student work.

Claudia looked at her research paper, which was in front of her, and began responding to individual comments Diane had made in the margins. She tried to refute as many of these comments as she could, and then tallied them. She was framing the assessment process as a matter of counting errors, as well as one of acknowledging completion of tasks ("I did all my work"). These were not the central issues in Diane's and my minds, in regard to whether Claudia should receive a higher grade. We felt that Claudia should have put greater effort into her project and that her paper conveyed minimal understanding of her topic. Diane tried to emphasize to Claudia that we did not think she had done enough "critical thinking." This seemed to be an abstract point when we tried to talk to Claudia about it. When we became more concrete by discussing individual passages in the paper that we had found confusing—with Claudia responding by explaining why she had written them as she did—the larger issues on which we had based our assessment seemed to get lost.

While Diane and I had given our students messages that we valued what could be termed "critical thinking," more formal means of telling Claudia of our evaluation criteria, prior to the grading of the papers, might have increased her regard for them. However, more was at issue than our making expectations evident. There were gaps between Claudia's and our understandings of the concept of "critical thinking," the narrowing of which would entail an extended process. Furthermore, her using criteria such as this to assess her work would mean her ascribing to a view of what is important in schoolwork—a view that emphasizes certain dimensions of quality—that is quite different from one that emphasizes submitting assignments and having few mistakes. Apparently Claudia, like many students, had during her history of schooling developed a tendency to see her written products in the latter light. A student might shift between these views as she gains experience and understanding of the work's complexity. The shift also involves, for many high school students, an increased degree of investment in the work.

When students did appear to understand an expectation, factors such as how urgent the expectation appeared, and how much effort and difficulty would be involved, could affect whether they attempted to meet it. Teachers evidently made it clear to some students, for instance, that we expected follow-up research based on questions received during their second-term research-in-progress exhibitions. Nadine, when I interviewed her, recalled my having visited her class during her presentation on W. E. B. Du Bois, and she described my input as an instruction: "You had told me to find out what the debates between him and Booker T. Washington was about." Pursuant to this presentation, though, she did not expand her research in an attempt to find this information: "The encyclopedia I looked at, it didn't tell too much," she said. " 'Cause I didn't read on Booker T. Washington, so. I just read on W. E. B. Du Bois." Julia, likewise, described the research-in-progress exhibitions as if their purpose made sense to her: "They were tryin' to help us. . . . So they wrote like, what we should do to improve. Like, get more information or, y'know, certain questions they wanted to know about that person, they just write it down and give it to you." She recalled one question she was asked, and added that after the exhibition, "I really didn't find out, but I was curious though." To some extent, Nadine and Julia had accepted the principle of further research that teachers wanted them to carry out. It appeared, though, that when they saw that answering the questions they received would mean added research efforts, they decided that pursuing those answers was not a top priority and finished their papers with the information they already had.

One aspect of what they "had to" do that loomed large in many students' minds was answering questions during exhibitions. On the most basic level, this was a requirement that was quite clear to students: They needed to speak in response to what was asked. The more specific dimensions of this expectation, though, were harder to define. What constituted a knowledgeable or thoughtful answer was not a self-evident matter. Also, students were asked to answer a great range of questions and to perform in a range of ways. Students' comments about the questioning process showed that they were constructing their own meaning of the expectation, at the same time that they were respecting the expectation in general.

Some of the students I interviewed shared their perceptions of teacher-questioners' intentions. The fact that teachers had multiple purposes in asking questions was reflected by the variety of student perceptions.

Marcus, for instance, noted that sometimes teachers asked questions "that they probably know you know, just to make you, like, look better— like to pick your mind." Part I shows Diane and me asking such questions of Wayne, Pierre, and Anwar. With this kind of question, teachers were projecting, in a supportive way, an expectation that students fully articulate what they know. We were not necessarily conveying an expectation that students know more than they knew.

Luis, by contrast, described teacher questions as less benign:

> I think the teachers know when you don't know something. So they ask you questions like . . .—they don't hold back. . . . 'Cause they have a feeling of when you didn't study. So I think they, like, ask you a question to make sure that you didn't study. . . . They jump on that real quick.

Whether or not teachers deliberately aimed questions toward suspected areas of ignorance, we did ask questions that explored what and how much students knew. Such questions, and the expectations for knowledge and preparation that they suggested, made an impression on Luis.

Some students described teachers' questions as probing for reflection and understanding as well as information. Gail, when I asked her what kinds of questions she received from teachers, said, "I don't know, like, challenge ones or whatever. They try to make us think." LaTanya said of the questions Barry asked her:

> He asks you to go deep down, and really tell what you know. He will—I think what Barry does, he makes you, after you've done your exhibition, he'll make you redo your exhibition in a shorter way . . . with just a few questions. To actually see if you know what you're talking about.

Gail and LaTanya perceived, in a general sense, that they were being asked to show thinking that went beyond what they had initially presented. Students' perceptions of more specific expectations that lay underneath this sort of teacher question are discussed in the next part of this chapter.

The performance of answering questions was itself a multifaceted one. In the public forum of exhibitions, it included not only the content of one's answer but also one's self-projection while delivering the answer. In Julia's view, both of these elements affected how teachers would regard one's performance. She explained, "You can't give like false information or something. And all you gotta do is look confident and tell them—you know, feeling secure? . . . And I think you'll get a good grade."

Julia said that one did not necessarily have to answer all the questions one received. She indicated one indirect way in which teachers had conveyed this message to her:

> If you can't answer people's questions, all you have to say is, you know, "I'll get back to you, I'll find out a little bit more." . . . That's okay; that's what teachers do. Teachers, you ask them a question and they get stuck, they'll be like, "Oh, can we talk after class?" Y'know. Or, "I'll get back to you with the answer," or something, so if it's good for them, then it's good for us too.

Julia also said the "I'll get back to you" option needed to be used with discretion:

> You can't answer all your questions that way. Just stand there and be like, "Well, can I get back to you on that, can I get back to you on that," because it's a way of saying you don't know your information. . . . You have to be able to know, y'know, off the top of your head, simple things.

"Simple things" was a criterion that could distinguish questions it was imperative to answer from those on which one could pass. This criterion provides but an approximate boundary line, though, and one subject to interpretation. Also, Julia's mention of this criterion did not mean that she would disregard any question that was not "simple."

As students interpreted the expectations that went with the questioning process, they were concerned with more than what the required pieces of the assignment were. "Having to" answer questions led students to think further about what would be a successful performance. They did so in part by considering what teachers would be hoping to see. Teachers' expectations occupied an important position in this process of constructing standards. Students' own role in sorting through a complex set of teacher aims, and perceiving the expectations in a way that made sense to them, was evident as well.

INTERACTIONS DURING QUESTION–ANSWER EXCHANGES

The process of developing standards for answering questions during exhibitions occurred, in part, during the question–answer exchanges themselves. During these exchanges, teachers projected expectations. They did not state what a good answer to each question would be; rather, more subtle processes of communicating intention came into play. Students' responses during the exchanges indicated the meaning they were making of the expectations, as did their subsequent remarks.

A dialogue during LaTanya's exhibition on the Middle Passage, and her later discussion of this exchange, put in context her comment about Barry expecting her to go "deep down." During the exhibition, Barry asked LaTanya why, if packing slaves so tightly on ships created conditions that led to deaths, slave traders packed them that way. "They want 'em to work, so why kill 'em en route?" he questioned. LaTanya answered, "Profit," and explained, "If they can pack in more, they can make more money; if some die they make money on the ones that are there." Barry pressed her: "If people are dying, they're not making money on them." LaTanya reasserted, "They made money on those who lived," and proceeded to another part of her presentation. Barry had wanted LaTanya to consider other possible reasons for tight packing: in particular, methods of social control. Before she got too far away from this issue, he reentered with a statement that terrorizing people was a way to break their spirits. To this a student in the audience responded, "That's like today; they put us in ghettos to break our spirits." Barry and this student exchanged a few remarks, and then LaTanya said, "Can I finish now?"

In response to Barry's question, LaTanya gave an answer that had a plausible logic. She also stood behind her answer, without looking scared or looking in her book, as Julia said it was important to do. Four weeks later, when I asked for LaTanya's recollection of this episode, she confidently repeated the answer she had given. If she was aware of Barry's desire that she consider other issues, she did not indicate so, during either the exhibition or our interview.

LaTanya's remark that Barry's questions asked her to go "deep down" suggested that she felt a general expectation for additional thinking and heightened understanding from questions such as these. The full meaning of that expectation, as she perceived it, also involved the kinds of thinking and explaining that she felt addressed his questions. An experience such as the one described above played an important role in defining that expectation for her, by providing a real example of a way in which she might meet it.

An exchange during Valentina's third-term exhibition illustrates some of the issues discussed in the previous part of this chapter, concerning multiple layers of expectations that teachers' questions carried and selective student responses to expectations. For her exhibition, Valentina (a student in Diane's and my class) had read an article about Black women who moved west after the Civil War. In her talk, she focused mostly on two particular women. She said she had picked those two, out of the several who were featured in the article, because she "found them more interesting, because it talked about their husbands . . . what happened to their husbands." She mentioned that the husband of one of the women, a White man, was executed on a seemingly trumped-up murder charge. Later in the exhibition, I asked her a series of questions about these women's relationships to men:

> JOHN: Did both of the people that you talked about have White husbands?
> VALENTINA: I don't know about the last one but, I know about the first woman I talked about, her husband was White.
> JOHN: Was there something about the second woman's husband too?
> VALENTINA: No. She just talked about that she made an ice cream parlor. She organized her own ice cream social.
> JOHN: Do you think she went out there all by herself, or do you think she went with a husband? Did it say?
> VALENTINA: Maybe with some people, I don't know. . . .
> JOHN: That's interesting, if you think about at the time, women were not as independent usually.
> GLORIA: Probably be dependent on a man.
> DIANE: And, you have to have some cash to start a business. . . .
> JOHN: Yeah. So if a woman went out there on her own and did all that, that's pretty good.

After the exhibition, Diane and I asked Valentina to write what she thought she had done well and what she thought she could have done better. When we asked her to share her assessment orally, Valentina said, "I would've done better if I knew the [second] woman I talked about, if her husband was White, if she went alone and did the ice cream thing. And talked a little bit more about the first person."

The experience of being asked questions about the second woman's husband and answering "I don't know" had given Valentina a clear message that she had not met an expectation. Given that there were other questions that she had answered in this way, Valentina was also exercising her judgment by referring to these particular ones in her self-assessment. Perhaps they stood out to her because they were closely related to what

interested her about her topic. Also, they called for biographical information—what Julia might have termed "simple things" that "you have to be
able to know." Some of the other questions, by contrast, had asked about
historical circumstances surrounding the women's moves west.

My remarks toward the end of the above exchange, about the theme
of nineteenth-century women operating independently, implicitly signaled another expectation: that students discuss broad themes that relate
to their information. By participating in this part of the conversation, a
student—whether consciously or not—would be joining in this approach
to a topic. Valentina did not speak during this part of the dialogue. (It
was Gloria who added a comment about women's independence.) In her
self-assessment, Valentina's mention of not knowing "if she went alone"
perhaps reflected how the issue of independence had seemed significant
to her. On the other hand, she spoke in terms of not having answered a
factual question, rather than not having addressed a thematic point in her
presentation. This was not surprising; in addition to being communicated
quite indirectly, the expectation that she discuss themes was further from
what Valentina had tried to do than the expectation that she have more
information about the two women. It was, similarly, further from what
Diane and I had worked on with Valentina. Valentina had done no preparation for her exhibition until the night before she presented; our comments to her up to that point had centered on encouraging her to do
some reading.

In the above examples, students' after-the-fact remarks indicate how
they processed question-and-answer exchanges. The negotiation of standards can also be observed in the meeting of teacher and student purposes during the exchanges themselves. Particular questions carried expectations for particular kinds of answers. In some cases, students'
responses indicated agreement with those expectations. In others, such
an agreement did not exist, or teachers and students tried to develop one
during the course of the conversation.

In an exchange during his exhibition on slave music, Diane asked
Fred to articulate a point so that she could be sure she understood what
he was saying. This was a purpose that Fred embraced. Learning to express ideas in a manner that would be understood well by teachers was
one challenge that Fred was earnestly trying to meet at that point in the
year. During this interaction, student and teacher were working to bring
a standard to life.

Diane had asked Fred about parallels between slave spirituals and
rap music. In response, Fred focused initially on the group Public Enemy,
noting that their lyrics talk about "breaking out," as slaves' lyrics did.
Then Bruce brought up the name of the group Arrested Development,

and Fred offered commentary that, as he continued, grew less clear to Diane:

> FRED: They have spirituals in their music as well, but more or less of a folk-type, a down-South-type flavor. That's why a lot of Whites like them. Y'know, that's why they won so many Grammies, so many awards, because they're basing their music on facts, and the country, and how Blacks originally—where we originally came from, Black Americans, y'know. And that's down South.
>
> DIANE: So why would that make Whites like the music, I didn't catch that.
>
> FRED: Because I mean, in a lot of ways, they see where we—how could I say. They—in those particular songs, they see more than the majority of Black people because, they see where, they're expressing where we come from as well—sort of like, "Hey." Y'know. Y'know, the rhythm's cool, y'know, it's more of a down-South flavor, and they're talking about like, just like basically I mean—y'know—

At this point Fred, who had turned to face Diane directly during this explanation, laughed and added, "I mean, how—well, you—I mean." He clapped his hands, and spread his arms with hands facing upward. Diane then tried another way of asking the question, and Fred worked further to explain:

> DIANE: So as opposed to somebody that, I don't know, . . . somebody that White people wouldn't like, why would they like that?
>
> FRED: See they . . . have more like an African dance within their stage act, they have a African groove, y'know what I'm saying? Like with Bob Marley, how Bob Marley attracted a lot of White America. Y'know what I'm sayin'. Same as with him, same as with Arrested Development, same as with, um, Ziggy, y'know Bob Marley's son, y'know.
>
> DIANE: So it's . . . just like entertainment, general entertainment, more than a hard message.
>
> FRED: Right.

These exchanges show willing communication across generational and racial differences. Diane encouraged Fred to bring his knowledge of rap music into the curriculum. She also asked him to incorporate it into an analytic framework that she presented to him. Her last statement did not capture all the nuances of what Fred thought and perceived, regarding a subject he surely conversed about in nonschool settings. It did, however, summarize the connection between Arrested Development's style and Whites' acceptance of the group, in a way that Fred's descriptions had not. As Fred agreed with Diane, his manner indicated a receptivity to her way of putting it.

During Gloria's propaganda campaign for "equality in televised sex," Diane posed a question that resulted in more of a standoff. Gloria had made comments during the exhibition that sounded divergent, regarding whether she wanted sexual exposure equalized through a decrease in women's exposure or an increase in men's. Diane asked Gloria to resolve the contradiction: to clarify whether she wanted "less sex in general" or "men to show their stuff more." In the ensuing dialogue, shown in Chapter 4, Gloria did not approach the contradiction as a problem that needed solving. As she respectfully answered Diane's queries, she maintained the duality of her thoughts.

When teacher questions, and the purposes behind them, clashed with a student's intentions, the teacher sometimes made adjustments. Claudia's propaganda presentation provides one illustration.

Claudia's campaign promoted condom usage. In it, she sang her own lyrics to the tune of a popular song—and drew spirited laughter from the peer audience, especially with the line "So pinch the tip and roll it on down." Diane posed a question that was tied to the expectations for this particular assignment. Diane had said to me that one of her goals for the first-term exhibitions was that students show an "understanding of propaganda." In addition, the instructions in the unit guide had asked students to "persuasively promote a controversial political position." Diane's question reflected both of these concerns:

> DIANE: Now Claudia. . . . If you were trying to convince the general public, say, to allow condom distribution in schools, would you use that same rap?
> CLAUDIA: General public? Probably. But then—yeah, I guess so.
> DIANE: You're trying to persuade people like me, to allow condoms and stuff in schools.
> CLAUDIA: Yeah. It has an up beat but it's—y'know, it's giving instructions at the same time.

Claudia challenged Diane's suggestion that the song would not work so well with a different audience. Then, with the point "It's giving instructions," she evaluated the song in terms of the purpose she had defined for her campaign, which was focused on the use of condoms rather than on distribution programs.

Diane's next remarks acknowledged how Claudia had conceived of her campaign:

DIANE: So you're saying you're appealing to women, to always have condoms with them, right?
CLAUDIA: Yeah, just in case.
DIANE: Okay. So you're promoting condom use.
CLAUDIA: Yeah.

Diane did not further pursue the point she had originally raised.

Many teacher questions, like those asked of Valentina and LaTanya, brought up issues and themes that related to a presenter's topic. These questions projected the general expectation that students consider and explore issues and themes, an expectation that students attempted to meet to various degrees. They also projected standards in terms of what particular issues and themes were worth talking about. This too was a matter to be negotiated during the dialogue.

In many instances, the questions introduced themes that teachers thought of, based on their own experiences, conceptual frameworks, and subject-matter knowledge. Gloria was the student in our class who joined most readily and fully into this type of teacher-led discourse. In the following exchange during her third-term exhibition, for example, she shared thoughts that converged with the meaning Diane had made of her material:

DIANE: Did you read this passage on the . . . opinion of the family about [Harriet Jacobs's] having the children with that White guy?
GLORIA: Oh. Well, she was . . . saying that her grandmother said, "Oh this is what it has come to," whatever. Y'know, kind of put her down? And I guess she didn't care, y'know.
DIANE: It sounds kind of familiar though, y'know.
GLORIA: I mean even today they still do that.
DIANE: Today, same kind of thing. And I thought her reasoning was kind of interesting: She'd rather choose a White lover than be forced to have a White lover. I thought that was kind of— y'know it was a dilemma that slave women faced. And she solved it by taking a lover herself, willfully herself.
GLORIA: It's better than to be raped, I guess.
DIANE: Right, that's kind of what she was saying.

Because teachers' experiences, frameworks, and knowledge were quite different from students', it was not uncommon for exchanges to proceed quite differently from the one above. Students, to begin with, often lacked the information they needed to discuss the issues teachers raised. (One reason Gloria was able to converse with Diane as she did was that she had indeed read the passage in question.) In addition, the meaning of teachers' questions was often not perceived as intended. The exchanges, as a result, became a search for a common focus of conversation.

An example occurred during Wayne's fourth-term exhibition. I had asked Wayne to elaborate about his interviewee's civil rights activities in Nashville, which his opening summary had briefly described. In response, Wayne stated that his interviewee, when he started participating in sit-ins, had quit his job working for a White person. I then made a comment intended to call attention to the man's being without the job and to initiate a discussion about how being without it might have affected him—what sacrifices he made, perhaps, in order to pursue his commitment. "So he lost his job," I said.

Wayne responded, however, to the literal meaning of my comment: "No, he quit."

We danced back and forth briefly:

JOHN: He quit it—yeah.
WAYNE: Yeah, he quit.
JOHN: He gave up his job.
WAYNE: And then he started—these sit-ins, and something, but he said, he described most of 'em as being, they wasn't always violent.

I then attempted to state the issue more directly. The conversation still did not go in the direction I had intended, though:

JOHN: Was he a student then or was he, did—
WAYNE: I don't know; he didn't mention that.
JOHN: I mean in other words, did he—was it a real sacrifice that he made, giving up his job? Or did he get another job, or was he trying to support a family, or—
WAYNE: Well I'm not sure, but I would think so. Because there wasn't so many Black businesses as White businesses down there. And he want—and he didn't want to work for the White man, so it would be harder to work for himself. Or, since he was so young. Or,—or a Black business.

Wayne responded to my last set of questions by finding information he had that related to what I was asking, and making a plausible speculation. However, the issue on which he focused—likely employment prospects—was not quite the one I was trying to get to. Perhaps had I more carefully explained what I was asking—or had I not followed my question about "a real sacrifice" with additional questions—Wayne would have addressed the issue I had in mind. On the other hand, had that issue been more prominent in Wayne's own thoughts, he might have more readily detected the inferential meanings of my language. Furthermore, Wayne lacked information to discuss in more detail the consequences of his interviewee's action, not having probed that issue during the interview.

Conversations with teachers, regardless of the context, tended to differ from other conversations in which students were likely to participate, including those that students held among themselves. The formality of the question–answer exchanges during exhibitions accentuated this difference. As Beth remarked when she compared fielding teachers' questions to interacting with the peer audience, "It's on a different level, when you're talking to a teacher, who you have to even just talk to differently."

Powell students accepted teachers' authority to lead these exchanges. They wanted to perform successfully, for the most part, and they tried to meet many teacher expectations: expectations that they supply factual information, for instance, or that they make various sorts of analytic points. Still, students did not always fully understand teachers' expectations, nor did they always value what was being asked for in the same way that teachers did. In some instances, teachers made adjustments as a result. At any rate, the standards that emerged from the interactions were negotiated.

LONG-TERM INTERACTION

The process of constructing classroom standards around teachers' expectations is ultimately a long-term one. It involves teachers and students coming to focus their joint efforts on particular aspects of student performance. It involves the evolution of students' understandings, habits, and achievements. It also, in many cases, involves tension between teachers' expectations and students' intentions.

In many instances, Powell humanities teachers' expectations gave direction to the creation of standards, while the specific contours of the standards were negotiated. This could be observed in individual events such as some of those shown above. It could also be observed in ongoing activity. Negotiations around standards in two areas of performance—getting work done, and reflecting and analyzing—are described below.

Getting Work Done

Much attention in our classrooms was directed toward the issue of students' getting work done. In one respect, the prominence of this issue reflected students' influence on standards: Had students been more committed and efficient in doing their assignments, teachers would have focused more on other aspects of performance. However, it was teachers who assigned the work and who pushed the students to do it. Teachers, in addition, introduced to these classrooms the practice of portfolios, which placed heightened responsibility on students to plan and manage their workloads.

There was, at root, an either–or question of whether assignments were completed. Standards in this area, however, were not one-dimensional. There were questions of how thoroughly the work was done and how students went about getting it done. Standards in these regards formed through the interaction of teachers' and students' efforts. This is shown by the cases of some individual students in Diane's and my class.

During the second half of the year, Fred seemed to make a significant change as a student: He began trying to do successfully the work assigned him, whereas earlier in the year he had mostly tried to avoid it—largely, it seemed, out of fear of failure. Fred also built new standards in terms of how to go about doing the work. Fred needed coaching in order to get the work done—in order to interpret directions, structure the pieces of writing he was assigned, and manage the mechanics of written language, among other things. In his first few months in our class, he avoided not only doing the work but also talking to teachers about his work. As Diane and I got to know him better, we continued to make efforts to work with him individually. Fred gradually reconsidered his stance. One day he asked me, "What do you think of a student who asks you for help all the time?" I told him I thought that was an intelligent student, one who made it possible for me to teach him. By late in the third term, Fred was regularly using available coaching.

Building standards involved experiences of accomplishment. A week after turning in his third-term portfolio—the first one he completed that year—Fred approached me at the end of class. Somewhat obliquely, he said that some classmates complained about my getting on them, but he saw how Diane and I kept telling him to do things and he got them done. I felt that there was something more that he was trying to express, and I asked if he was saying that it felt good to have completed the portfolio. He brightened and said, "Yeah." Then we pumped hands, with large grins on both of our faces. It was a very rare affect for one of our students to display toward schoolwork. It reflected Fred's spirited personality; it also showed how the experience had left him with a pleasing feeling of "I did it"—or, perhaps more accurately, "we did it." He valued what he had accomplished. This and subsequent experiences also helped him gain confidence in his ability to complete portfolio assignments, which affected what he would expect of himself.

Anwar's standards with regard to getting work done reflected a different kind of response to our expectations. He did not find most of the assignments as difficult to do as Fred did; getting them done therefore did not present as great a challenge to him. He had, in fact, gained a sense of competence that was problematic to Diane and me. This was exemplified in a conversation I had with him 2 weeks after he had chosen David Walker as his third-term exhibition topic. He told me he had yet to do any research for the project, and added self-assuredly, "I always do it at the last minute. You know that." He exaggerated somewhat: Anwar had developed a habit of attending to his work far enough ahead of time so that he was not scrambling at the last possible moment. However, he often allocated only enough time to produce something that could be turned in, as opposed to devoting the amount of effort that Diane and I hoped for.

During the last 2 weeks of each term, Estella, Gloria, and Danilo would remain in the computer lab until 5:30 on successive evenings, and would be starting from scratch on assignments that Anwar had already done or begun. With the energy they exuded during these late afternoons, these students demonstrated that they had embraced Diane's and my goal of completing the assignments—just as Anwar did by starting earlier. However, their efforts, like his, defined the meaning of getting work done in a way that did not please us. We wanted them to work on individual assignments over longer periods of time and to put more thought into each assignment. We wanted them to bring drafts and other intermediate pieces to class more regularly and promptly, so that their ongoing efforts could serve as a foundation for daily discussion and instruction. We cajoled them to work in these ways, usually to no avail.

The negotiation of standards is a continuing process, and results such as those that occurred with Anwar, Estella, Gloria, and Danilo need not be permanent. Diane's and my response was to think about how we might make some of our expectations more consequential to the students. During the fifth term, we attached deadlines to some individual written assignments, and in these instances there was more prompt work from some of our students. However, these were relatively small changes in terms of those students' overall approach. And while the negotiation process need not reach a fixed conclusion, the time in a given school year does expire.

Reflecting and Analyzing

Another set of expectations teachers attempted to project concerned the development of habits of reflection and analysis. These expectations were often conveyed in coaching interactions with individual students. Our attempts to convey them revolved significantly around questions: our asking certain kinds of questions of students, and encouraging students to raise questions and explore issues that stemmed from them. Questions occupied a significant place in certain assignments as well as in informal interactions. Students were directed, for instance, to address an "essential question" in their research papers and to think of questions to ask as audience members during exhibitions. In addition, some in-class exercises were designed in which students posed questions for themselves and to one another.

As Brett's remark about the third-term exhibitions, cited earlier in this chapter, illustrates, meeting expectations for reflection and analysis often was not a primary student concern. Nonetheless, there was activity through which standards developed around such expectations. Wayne's experience provides one of the strongest examples. It also shows a student determining the particular ways in which he would approach teachers' standards.

Wayne's propaganda campaign, promoting hypothetical 80-ounce bottles of beer, did not demonstrate distinctive reasoning or analysis in the way that some students' did. During the second term, some of the questions he listed before writing his research paper—"Why did some Cherokee agree to leave?" for instance—suggested explorations that he did not pursue. In the third and fourth terms, though, his own questions, and the thoughts that underlay them, assumed a more prominent place in his work.

In my individual conferences with Wayne prior to his exhibition about the local abolitionists, I tried to coach him to raise and consider broad questions, or questions generative of inquiry and discussion. When he showed me what he had first written after his interview, for instance, I told him that he needed to do more than list names. I suggested to him some overarching questions, with which Wayne seemed unimpressed. I also told him he needed to go beyond having information to having ideas. The latter point was the essence of what I wanted him to do. In this case as in others, finding meaningful terms in which to communicate it to a student seemed challenging to me.

By the time he presented, Wayne had thought of some questions of his own. He asked how the audience viewed John Coburn's supporting abolitionists with illegally earned money, how Frederick Douglass should have reacted when a crowd of anti-abolitionists shoved him from his speaker's podium, and whether it is helpful to have powerful people such as Charles Sumner involved in a movement. These were questions he considered engaging. His questions about John Coburn and Frederick Douglass also drew interested responses from several audience members. These questions connected to issues Wayne knew his peers thought about: the moral status of drug dealers and whether to fight back when confronted with violence. These questions engaged the class more than the questions I suggested to Wayne—about the methods of and relationships within a liberation movement—probably would have. They also engaged the class more than the question about power, a variation of which ("Is power always good?") had been selected by teachers as an essential question for an earlier term.

Wayne's formulating his own questions, rather than using those I suggested, was quite consistent with my expectations. In other respects, though, tension between Wayne's standards and mine remained. I would have liked to see a question lead to a much deeper investigation prior to the exhibition, for instance, than what occurred in Wayne's case. This was a matter to be addressed as the negotiation process continued.

During the fourth term, Wayne thought of a question to ask a civil rights panel—"Would you choose nonviolent, or violent, when it came down to defending yourself when crowds would be around you?"—that functioned as an essential question, in terms of the discussion and reflection it provoked. Wayne raised this question without coaching. He told me later that this was a question he had wanted to address in his own exhibition the previous day. By this point in the year, he seemed to have internalized the notion that discussions around generative questions were good to have during exhibitions. This was a standard that Diane and I had hoped our conduct of exhibitions would convey.

My interactions with Jorge prior to his exhibition on Latin American slavery were similar to those with Wayne, in that I tried to steer Jorge toward raising and addressing broad questions. Eventually I suggested these: Why did it take a civil war to end slavery in the United States and not in Latin America? How was slavery different in Latin America than in the United States? In a couple of our later conferences, I talked about some of the issues behind these questions. Jorge offered some input to these conversations, demonstrating interest and finding applications for some of his knowledge. He then used these questions directly in his exhibition.

My concerns encompassed not only whether students addressed such questions but also the analysis they offered when doing so. In the latter regard, Jorge's performance had what Diane and I noted as limitations. Regarding the comparison of Latin American and U.S. slavery, for instance, Jorge made a basic distinction among different ways of regarding slaves, but did not explore more complex evidence and issues. He contrasted Spanish and Portuguese slaveholders with those in the United States by saying that the former "thought of [slaves] just as regular human beings who just lost their freedom." He also said, "[The] Spanish and Portuguese didn't have any racial prejudice against their African slaves. They had slaves because it was economically rewarding to them. That's the only reason they had slaves."

The kind of analysis Diane and I wanted Jorge ultimately to do would entail learning new skills, a process that could not occur all at once. On this occasion, Jorge added a conceptual layer to his exhibition by raising a question and speaking to it. He began to adopt the habit of including these sorts of contents in an exhibition, and to develop a sense of what it meant to use such questions. These were steps in the building of standards.

In Estella's case, Diane's and my promotion of standards for reflection and analysis was less successful. Among our students, Estella was a relatively skilled reader and writer. However, she showed less engagement in her projects than Jorge or Wayne did.

Questions and ideas are generated more readily when one is interested in a subject or undertaking. In our interactions with Estella, Diane and I often found ourselves searching for a spark. For instance, after Estella chose her topic (Sojourner Truth) for her second-term research paper, she asked me, "What do you want to know about it?" I replied, "What do *you* want to know about it?" She thought for a few seconds, and then answered, "I don't know, like when she was born." In this exchange, as was not uncommon, my search for a spark led no further.

On some occasions, Estella did become more involved in thinking about a subject. For instance, one week before the second-term research-in-progress exhibitions took place, we divided the class into small groups so that students could share what they had found out about their topics and ask questions of one another. I formed a group with Estella and one other student. This classmate spoke about the 1976 student uprising in Soweto, South Africa. After I asked some questions, around the theme of children's role in a social movement, I asked Estella to offer a question. She said she couldn't think of one because she didn't know anything about this topic. I continued conversing with the classmate for a couple of minutes more, as Estella listened. Then Estella entered, and asked about the relative numbers of Blacks and Whites in South Africa. Informed that Blacks were the majority, she then asked how the Whites could control them. By attending to a discussion on a topic from which she initially felt disconnected, she found something that made her curious. She acted in a way that fit the standards embedded in the activity.

There were other moments such as this one, when Estella's spirit of inquiry emerged in our class. On the whole, though, the extent to which Estella posed questions and explored issues reflected her lukewarm participation in schoolwork. She did the work for her exhibitions in short periods of time very close to her presentations, restricting both the amount of material she had to think about and the amount of time she had to think about it.

Pierre, at times, did not perform as Diane and I hoped he would, despite his best intentions. Various tasks' requirements of English language and other academic skills posed problems for him that they did not pose for Wayne, Jorge, or Estella. Yet while some of our attempts to lead him to include more reflection and analysis in his work seemed not to connect very well with him, over the course of the year he gradually came to meet this expectation to a greater degree.

The week after our students presented their propaganda exhibitions, I distributed a set of "Exhibition Reflections" questions for students to answer in writing. These asked students about their hypothetical campaigns: the purpose, the audience, the techniques used, and the prospects of success. I thought these questions might elicit one layer of analysis that the students had not thus far displayed—or been asked to display—in their projects. I spent some time with Pierre working on this assignment, and afterward I felt that the activity had not been very productive. I noted that he had answered some of the questions in a literal sense without addressing the issues they were intended to raise. One question asked who would favor his position (that there be an organized effort to kill Hitler), and why. Pierre wrote that "Jews who want freedom" would be likely to favor it, and then said he could not say why. When I asked him to consider why some Jews, or some Jews who want freedom, might favor his proposal and some might not, he offered no reasons. Later, he wrote, "Their reasons would be because I drew a Jewish man who's trying to kill Hitler."

A conversation Pierre and I had one day during the fifth term contrasted with the interaction after the propaganda campaign. During this term, the students wrote "position papers" on whether the United States should get involved in foreign wars. Pierre chose to focus on Haiti: That spring, the U.S. government was considering military intervention to help restore the elected Aristide regime. He said he favored U.S. involvement. As I conferred with him about his paper-in-progress, I asked him what an argument against his position might be. He mentioned his cousin who was in the military, and said he might be in danger. Then he paused, looked at me, and said, "This is hard." Subsequent to this discussion, he did not do all I suggested in terms of reconciling the two perspectives in his paper. But he had thought about an issue from different angles and recognized its complexity—as he had not when asked why "Jews who want freedom" might support or oppose his campaign. We had learned to communicate with each other in such a way that our joint activity began to encompass new kinds of thinking.

TEACHERS' EXPECTATIONS AND THE NEGOTIATION OF STANDARDS

Expectations in some instances concern the quality of student output: levels of achievement teachers want students to attain in their products and performances. However, it is possible for students not to reach those levels and still to meet teacher expectations. This is because expectations also concern aspects of performance teachers would like to see students *address*. Furthermore, teachers' expectations for quality are likely to be multifaceted and multilayered. Thus, if students are *working on* something, they are likely to be in concordance with some teacher expectation.

Examples in the preceding pages show teachers' expectations initiating joint endeavors and, in so doing, giving direction to the process of building standards. We gave Fred assignments to do and approached him with the idea of using coaching as he did them. We gave a certain emphasis to questions in our conduct of exhibitions and specifically encouraged Wayne and Jorge to incorporate questions into their presentations.

At the same time as teachers are leading in this manner, though, students—and the sort of student concerns discussed in Chapter 8—can be giving direction to the collaborative building of standards. Completing his assignments posed many challenges for Fred, and Diane's and my work with him involved seeing what those challenges were and helping him address them. In a sense, what he was doing was signaling *which* teacher expectations we should focus on: the expectation that a student be able to construct a paragraph that responds to a written prompt, for instance, as opposed to other ones. With Wayne and Jorge, by contrast, we focused more on certain issues concerning the analytic content of an exhibition. At the same time, we acknowledged their expressions of interest as we searched for areas of pursuit, and we took the development of their skills into consideration as we assessed their work.

In classrooms, teachers can assert their purposes to varying extents and with varying degrees of skill. Students can show different amounts of compliance with teachers' wishes, different abilities to do as teachers wish, and different degrees of independent initiative. There is, nonetheless, a certain inevitability to the overall pattern of negotiation—with its two-way lines of influence—in a situation in which people are seeking a basis on which to work together and in which those people's experiences diverge.

12

Teachers' Role: Five Theories Revisited

The five theories of standard setting presented in Chapter 1—demanding, informing, teaching, negotiating, and arising—represent both frameworks for understanding how classroom standards are determined and strategies for teachers to pursue when attempting to establish new or higher standards. This book has explored negotiating as a framework.

Using the framework of negotiation, I have examined what the standards in Powell humanities classrooms were and analyzed how they were formed. In addition, I have looked at standards in a more dynamic sense. Terms such as *building* and *developing*, which appear in earlier chapters, suggest ongoing motion of standards. They also suggest motion in a direction that is connected to the growth of student learning. Teachers' concern is with the creation of standards in this sense.

This book has highlighted students' role in the creation of standards, but it has also shown teachers in a vital role. As teachers consider how they might have an effective impact, the demanding, informing, teaching, and arising theories—as well as the negotiating theory—suggest strategies they might employ. The experience in Powell humanities classrooms sheds some light on issues that accompany each approach and on what each has to offer.

DEMANDING

Powell humanities teachers insisted, unequivocally, that students do their exhibition and portfolio assignments if they were to pass. These demands had an impact. Brett expressed it simply: When it was not required of him, he would not speak in front of the class. Deniece spoke about how the demand that students do exhibitions played out in her mind:

> [Exhibitions are] very important, because it's a big part of our grade. . . . And, sometime I just don't, I really don't like it, but I know I have to do it. So there's no sense in really arguing about it. So, you know, I get to like it. I have to like it because I have to do it because I really want to get a good grade.

The effects of teachers' demands could also be seen when students stayed after school in the computer lab, toward the end of a term, urgently working on their portfolio assignments.

Powell humanities teachers may have been able to use demands to greater effect than we did. Teachers face constraints, though, regarding the use of this strategy. For one, some things are inherently easier to demand than others. That students present an exhibition or submit a portfolio is relatively easy to demand because it is unambiguous. The meaning of what is being demanded does not need to be negotiated as students attempt to meet the demand. When demands pertain to the quality of the work done, this is often not the case. For instance, if teachers were to demand that students not only include essential questions in their presentations but also explore them thoughtfully, it would not be self-evident when this demand has been met and when it has not. The process of establishing what is a "thoughtful answer" would have to play out through the work students do.

It also does not follow, from the fact that most of our students tried to meet the aforementioned demands, that students would respond in the same fashion to all others. If demands too far exceed what students are initially inclined to go along with, students will refuse to satisfy them. Indeed, even our demands that students do their assignments were followed by a great deal of reiterating, cajoling, and encouraging on our parts before students in fact met them. In addition, if students have little experience doing the kind of work being demanded, they may not understand what it is that teachers want them to try. Furthermore, if demands too far exceed what students are presently able to do, students' most earnest efforts to meet them will be unsuccessful. These points apply to demands made by outside authorities as well as to those made by teachers.

The effectiveness of demands depends in part on the effectiveness of the consequences attached to them—which were students' grades in our case, as they are in many schools. It often appeared to Powell teachers that grades were not a very powerful negotiating tool. Barry remarked that the "traditional motivation"—meaning grades and college admission—seemed to have little influence on our students. Charles observed that many of his students seemed to care about their grade if they thought it was too low after they received their report card, but that they did not appear very concerned, day to day, with how their efforts would affect their grade. Diane felt that more students were "comfortable failing" than in previous years.

Certainly most of the students wanted to pass and expended effort at certain times in order to do so. Their concern for grades was not necessarily a concern for doing work that teachers would consider excellent. Julia told me that she had received a "good grade" for her third-term exhibition: a "B." When I asked her if she knew why it was not an "A," she said, "I never asked myself that question before. I was happy with my 'B,' but I don't know."

Diane and I often found ourselves in the position of being displeased with the standards that students worked toward yet at the same time affirming those standards with passing report card grades. The students in question had, however, done some work that we recognized as legitimate. In the third term, for instance, they had obtained information about their topics, prepared visuals and class activities, explained some of their material in ways that conveyed understanding, and fielded questions.

In these cases, much of our concern pertained to whether the work surpassed minimum thresholds of acceptability, as opposed to whether it met such thresholds. Perhaps raising the formal thresholds could have induced some changes in student performance. On the other hand, if our students were to do what we most wanted them to do in their exhibitions—that is, take initiative in developing their projects, raise and explore questions, become broadly knowledgeable about their topics, analyze as well as record information, and engage their audiences, and do such in continually expanding ways—it would reflect a concern on their part, as well as ours, for more than whether the work was passable.

INFORMING

The informing theory of standard setting contains an important principle: that if students are to know what kind of work teachers want them to do, and focus their efforts toward producing it, teachers must communicate their expectations to students.

Informing strategies in which teachers articulate detailed performance expectations and make them consistently visible to students, in printed and other forms, were not followed in Powell humanities classes;

this study therefore cannot comment on such strategies' effectiveness in establishing classroom standards. Earlier chapters do, however, show how communicating expectations is not always a simple and straightforward process. They also show that communicating expectations does not necessarily result in student performances that meet them.

Diane made some remarks during our interview that emphasized these points:

> When you say communicating, what people interpret when they don't know about kids is they say, "Well you just tell 'em. You just tell 'em what the standard is, and then they know." Like, [last year] there was a woman who was—I don't know if you remember her, she drove me so crazy. She was only there for 2 weeks, I was so glad she left. A woman who was shadowing [the assistant director]. . . . Aw, golly. She was like, "Well, you just tell them what they do wrong, and then, the next week they do it right." You're like, "Shut up! [laugh] Go away, go away, I can't deal with you. If that's the level of analysis that you're doing around kids."

When Diane made this remark, I offered in response, "But I think you still have to tell them."

Diane replied, "You still have to tell them. But the question is, does that work? Does it change the behavior?"

I concurred, "Not by itself."

"Yeah," she said. Then she added, "So some other things have to be going on. Lots and lots and lots of other things have to be going on."

The "other things that have to be going on" include students' assent to engage in a particular pursuit and students' learning how to do the work involved. They also include the development of students' understandings of what teachers mean by a given expectation. Good work, as teachers conceive of it, is often most easily described in terms of principles that teachers and students understand differently.

Presenting an expectation in the form of a specific subtask or set of tasks, as part of an assignment's instructions, can be a way to heighten that expectation's significance in students' eyes—to establish its priority standing among what they "have to" do. Gloria's paragraph about the essential question in her research paper—a response to a concretized expectation for reflection and analysis—demonstrates, though, how addressing the expectation can entail more than simply carrying out the subtask (see Chapter 4).

Some of our expectations for "critical thinking" were communicated in indirect ways that seemed to make little impression on students. It is indeed conceivable that had we taken more care to explain what we wanted in this area, and found accessible language with which to do so, students would have been more mindful of these expectations. On the other hand, effective communication of expectations is not always a matter of explicating them. Important messages are also built into the nature of ongoing activities and the ways in which teachers conduct themselves. Wayne had been encouraged to pose questions during exhibitions by such implicit messages, as well as by what Diane and I told him.

Informing is itself an interactive process. In that process, teachers' communication is influenced by our perceptions of students' needs and by students' responses. A sample exhibition that I presented to our class a month and a half before the students began their third-term presentations illustrates these points. I thought that this exhibition might function as a model, and convey Diane's and my standards in that manner.

My exhibition was about slavery in the Caribbean. Before presenting, I wrote statistics on the chalkboard showing the number of slaves in Cuba, Puerto Rico, Haiti, and the United States in different years. I then began by asking the students to study these tables and ask me questions based on what they noticed. When one student asked about the sudden appearance of "0" in the column for slaves in Haiti, I explained about the Haitian Revolution. I solicited questions and comments about the other statistics as well, and talked about why and how slavery increased in Cuba and Puerto Rico.

Toward the end of the lesson, I made the point that slaves had a greater mix of roles in these Caribbean countries than in the United States and that systemic racism was less absolute there. This was a large idea that related to but transcended the facts. I did not, however, state to the students that such an idea was an important—or necessary—component of the exhibition. Nor did I call attention to this idea in other ways: by establishing it at the beginning of the exhibition, for instance, or by centering questions to the class around it. Reflecting on the lesson later, I thought about how I had not emphasized, through word or deed, that addressing a broad theme or question was a characteristic of a good performance. I had missed an opportunity to project what I considered to be an important expectation, in terms of building the standards in our classroom.

One reason my lesson did not better highlight a large theme was that I did not plan it as carefully as I might have. It was not only a matter of my forethought, though. The lesson also took part of its shape through my verbal and nonverbal exchanges with the students. I responded to students' questions and to their selective displays of attentiveness. Thus, when some students said, "There were slaves in Puerto Rico?" I reiterated the fact that there were. I then gave some further pieces of information—what these slaves did, what parts of the island they lived on—that developed this notion of Puerto Rican slavery. When I asked the students, at the end of the lesson, to state what they had learned, most indicated that fundamental facts were what had struck them most. A couple of students, for instance, mentioned that there were large numbers of free Black people in these countries—as opposed to some of the implications of that fact, about which I had also spoken.

Another reason I did not stress my large theme more was that I was focusing on presentation issues as well as the exhibition's content. There were many expectations associated with the third-term assignment, and I could not attend to all simultaneously. The presentation issues were of immediate significance to the students, who had been given the assignment to "teach a lesson to the class," as well as to Diane and myself, who were especially concerned about how these exhibitions would function for those in the audience. I viewed much of what I did in this lesson—using a chart, inviting questions from the class, and asking students to write and share orally something they had learned—as an attempt to model teaching techniques and to lead students to consider how they might do more than simply talk to the class.

After the lesson was over, I led a discussion that focused on presentation methods. Some students' responses indicated that issues my lesson had raised seemed significant to them. Wayne said it did not seem like an exhibition, because I did not just get up and talk. Jorge asked if presenters had to have a chart—to which I replied that they needed some form of visual and that a chart was one way to meet this requirement. When I emphasized that we did not want students simply to read from a sheet of paper, Fred said, "You mean you want us to talk off the tops of our heads?" Yes, I answered, adding that they would need to be prepared in order to do this.

The impact of informing, in terms of the building of standards, is not simply a matter of whether teachers convey the full range of their expectations. I might have expanded some students' aims by creating, and artfully delivering, a stronger exemplar. However, the students also had a say as to what kinds of information would be meaningful. Using nonlecture teaching methods was largely a new undertaking for most of our students, and some, in their own exhibitions, took specific cues from my demonstration. Jorge wrote a chart on the chalkboard, for instance, while Bruce began as I had done, giving information in response to questions. Also, facts such as those which I gave about Caribbean slavery, controlled well by a presenter, could make for an enlightening exhibition from the students' perspective—and in this sense represent standards they might aspire to attain in their presentations. When I interviewed Luis a month and a half afterward (I presented this lesson in his class as well as ours), he brought up my sample exhibition, unsolicited:

> Remember that? When you teach the class? . . . I like the way you did that. . . . You had a lot of good statistics and stuff. About Haiti and stuff? And how it just went down—I didn't know Black people took over Haiti. That was a lot of good stuff there. I didn't even know there were any slaves in Cuba and Puerto Rico and stuff.

His remark suggested a negotiated way in which the informing function of this lesson had contributed toward the development of classroom standards.

TEACHING

My sample exhibition shows the communication of expectations not as an isolated activity but as part of a larger process of teaching. We had already provided the students, verbally and through printed handouts, with information about what we wanted them to do for their exhibitions. My modeling was an added step in this informing process: an effort to reiterate and further specify this information. However, it was also an attempt to help students understand how to go about meeting the expectations.

Through teaching, teachers attempt to address the issues of student assent, meaning making, and skill that intervene between the communication of teachers' standards and students' pursuit and attainment of them. This is a complex project. Powell humanities teachers' experience highlights certain elements of that project and certain issues that accompany it.

The instructional activities in a classroom, in themselves, are one tool in the teaching of standards. Through those activities, students gain experience doing particular kinds of work, and classroom standards develop through that experience. Exhibitions were, to some extent, effective as this sort of tool. Talking publicly about one's work, for instance, entailed presenting one's own thoughts and understandings as opposed to more disembodied information. Becoming prepared to present involved research. Presenting meant attempting to communicate to an audience in a variety of ways. Both before and during exhibitions, students asked questions—of themselves and each other. Powell students learned, albeit not to the extent that teachers had hoped, in all of these areas. One can easily imagine other school activities that would not elicit these kinds of performances and efforts.

The specific design of an activity affects the extent to which it channels students' and teachers' energies toward certain standards. As the year progressed, the humanities teachers thought about a number of issues regarding how they might design exhibitions, and the work leading up to them, more effectively. Charles, for instance, wanted larger-scale projects that were assigned less frequently and that asked students to synthesize what they had previously learned in class. He thought less frequent exhibitions would seem more like "big deals" to students, and he thought students might show deeper thinking in exhibitions if they were adding layers to work they had already done. Barry was interested in how Central Park East Secondary School had identified five "habits of mind"—examining viewpoints, using evidence, making connections, exploring suppositions, and judging relevance—and made these a focus of its entire academic program. He thought that explicitly teaching students to practice these habits might lead to improved exhibitions.

Powell teachers also encountered the issue of how much structure to provide as students prepared their exhibitions. Our assignments asked students to exercise initiative in choosing and formulating their projects and in planning their preparation activities. In theory, this approach could foster students' growth as independent workers and thinkers. However, it often left our students showing little impetus to work on their projects. Most of our students did not appear to view their projects as work to be done in stages to nearly the extent that we did, although some did take steps toward working in such a manner. Many floundered, also, because of uncertainty as to what to do next.

Too much regulation of students' efforts can stifle students' decision making and their involvement with the ideas in their work. Too little direction from teachers can also undermine the development of standards. Teachers' initiatives often provide a focus for student effort—or a reason for students to work—that students do not supply on their own. Also, activities that teachers structure and lead can be invaluable to students' successful completion of a task and to students' learning how to do a particular kind of work.

In Powell humanities classrooms, there were periodic activities in which students wrote or shared what they had learned from their exhibition research, or asked questions of one another. These served at least to call students' attention to their assignments, and in some instances to help students clarify aspects of their work. There might have been more sessions in which students were guided through the production of intermediate products on the way to their exhibitions. Alongside exhibition preparation, there might have been more lessons aimed at the development of particular competencies—from interviewing and public speaking to the use of "habits of mind"—and more repeated occasions for students to practice those skills. One of the challenges that Powell teachers faced was how to balance the many competing pressures for class time in establishing such priorities.

While the activities teachers design clearly affect what standards develop in a classroom, those standards ultimately depend on what teachers and students do within and around the activities. With exhibitions, coaching individual students was a crucial part of teachers' role. Through coaching, teachers guided students toward performances in which they could begin to put new standards into practice.

Sometimes coaching involved leading students through the steps of doing a task. "How'm I gonna do it?"—the question Anwar asked me, with considerable urgency, as we met before his exhibition on David Walker—was the operative question in many coaching sessions. On other occasions, teachers introduced new considerations to student projects that were under way. The outcomes of coaching interactions were usually negotiated ones, as students determined the particular ways in which they would act upon our advice.

Coaching sometimes meant thinking of suggestions regarding how to shape a project. This entailed judging what activities would best facilitate an individual student's pursuit of standards. My advising Pierre to focus on the story of Nat Turner's actual uprising appeared to accomplish its purpose, which was to give him a manageable set of information over which he could demonstrate some control in an exhibition. By contrast, after Anwar's exhibition on David Walker—during which he had solicited classmates' responses to excerpts from *Walker's Appeal,* as I had suggested—I wished I had thought of a lesson plan that would have given him a better chance of engaging his audience.

When I interviewed Diane in June, she emphasized another aspect of working with individual students. "It's all about finding the thing that makes the kid want to do it," she said. She had found fostering assent, engagement, and work to be especially challenging—and especially crucial—with a number of her students. She believed that understandings of her students as individual learners were central to that effort:

> So that's always for me the key . . . is how do you get them to do it? How do you get Winston to go to the library? And I've seen him do it. I saw him do it once, in the [city's main] Public Library with me. And that's the location of success for him. . . . For him, now, my obligation, if I'm really doing the right thing by him, is finding a way

for him to do that a lot, or more—because I saw that worked for him. So that's what it involves, it involves that level of insight about the kid, if you really take the obligation seriously that everybody has to do [the work]. That level of insight about that really hard-to-motivate kid. And the ability to act on that.

Even with a total of 60 students in her classes—considerably fewer than the number assigned to most public school teachers—Diane found it difficult, in terms of the time and attention required, to, as she put it, "get the nuances around [each] kid" as continuously and thoroughly as she would like.

One more aspect of teaching that deserves mention in a discussion of classroom standards is the teacher's ability to inspire students in a personal way. This relates to the issues of motivation Diane raised, as well as to all the other functions of teaching—and demanding and informing—discussed in this chapter. Popular movies portraying heroic teachers—from *Stand and Deliver* in an urban public school to *Dead Poets Society* in an elite boarding school—tend to overemphasize this component of teacher skill, at the expense of a fuller view of teachers' craft and its relation to student learning. However, it is true that students will, to a significant extent, work for *you*—in relationships that range from the familiar to the authoritarian. It is difficult for me to assess my own and my close colleagues' performances in eliciting such student responses. There were occasions—for instance, the exchange with Fred on completion of his third-term portfolio, reported in Chapter 11—that suggested Diane and I had in fact contributed in this manner to the building of standards, just as there were times when I felt we were not doing a very good job of inspiring the students. At any rate, this factor can be extremely important. Students' respect and regard for individual teachers are a means through which students can find new standards compelling and feel inclined to pursue them.

ARISING

Various experiences in Powell humanities classrooms affirmed the value of the arising process. Renée's propaganda campaign, for one, illustrated that standards connected to strong interests can be among the most powerful to an individual student and can lead him or her to pursue groundbreaking activity largely on his or her own accord. As a teacher, too, Barry showed his regard for such standards. He remarked that the best exhibitions in his class were ones that had "a life of their own, in that it was . . . more than our assignment. It became something that [the students] got into."

Students also acted on more moderate interests, and on challenges they identified as significant, in ways that were less striking but that still contributed to the construction of standards. In such instances, students' thoughts and efforts became more focused on particular goals as a result of their concerns.

Nonetheless, the arising process was not, on the whole, especially effective at generating high standards in Powell humanities classrooms. Generally, the crucial factors of interest and engagement—both individual and collective—were not strong enough to lead students into territories where they expanded the existing standards to a significant degree. Teachers, also, had not found ways to elicit such interest and engagement.

One way in which teachers might have attempted to facilitate the arising process would have been by giving the students freer reign to determine their curriculum. Indeed, some of what we asked students to do—research on Civil War topics, for instance—was not especially inspiring to most of our students' creative imaginations. Luis offered a suggestion as to how exhibitions could be structured differently, which reflected these considerations:

> I think that, if you just do, for humanities . . . like everybody has
> to pick a subject, that is like, that they know about. . . . It's just, it
> could be totally different from anything else we've studied,
> y'know? . . . Anything at all. . . . Then you could show that you do
> know, you do know a lot about one specific thing.

Luis said that he thought such projects, while enabling students to use their prior knowledge, would also "motivate [students] more, on studying. . . . 'Cause there's a lot of things that you would like to learn about, that you just don't have the time to do."

For Luis's strategy to lead to performances markedly different from those that occurred in these classrooms, students' interest in topics would have to translate into a desire or willingness to work concertedly at school projects. This does not necessarily happen, because desire or willingness to work in such a manner is more than a simple function of interest in a topic.

In addition, even in projects that stem from students' passions, the making of classroom products often entails skills that students need to learn. A student may have strong interest in a topic, but limited knowledge of how to write a paper or lead a class session. A student may be attracted to the medium of video, but have no experience working with editing technology and find organizing one's material to be a similar problem as it is in written work. A student might learn such skills on his or her own. He or she is often well served, however, by another's teaching. That teaching may very well involve presenting some standards—notions, for instance, of what makes a good paper or editing job—in addition to guiding the student in pursuit of his or her own goals.

This study cautions against overreliance on the arising process as a route to higher standards. At the same time, though, it suggests that students' interests and self-generated pursuits can play a vital role in the building of standards. It is worth a teacher's vigilance to make maximum room for those interests and pursuits, in the context of whatever demanding, informing, and teaching strategies he or she may also be using.

One reason that teachers often reject Luis's strategy—in those instances in which their own decision-making about subject matter is not precluded by state or district requirements—is that they usually have curricular goals that they consider important. We wanted our students, for instance, to learn about the Jewish Holocaust, slavery and the Civil War, and the civil rights movement. When it appears that a subject might not be especially appealing to students, teachers must weigh whether it is worth proceeding with it just the same. And when teachers do commit to a curricular goal, they can attempt to approach it in ways that are most conducive to students' extending their efforts on their own. Students can be granted discretion regarding the content and nature of their projects. Care can be taken, given a subject such as the Civil War, to determine what topics and questions will connect most strongly to the students' interests and curiosity, and to determine what kinds of activities will provide the most engaging approaches to the content for the students. Goals of teaching humanities skills can be pursued in the context of topics that have contemporary standing with the students. Finally, in day-to-day interactions, teachers can be flexible enough to recognize purposes that students engender and support efforts that stem from such purposes.

One way in which we attempted to align our curriculum with our students' concerns was by devoting much of our attention, during the third term, to how slaves coped with and resisted slavery. For a student body largely of African descent, predominantly non-White, and predominantly low-income, this framed the study of a historical era from a perspective more strongly related to their own, than if we had focused mainly on the actions and decisions of dominant groups. To some extent, this strategy worked as we intended. Anwar and Fred, for instance, connected what they learned about David Walker and slave music to issues that concerned them as African Americans in contemporary society. While this did not lead them to do the amounts of work we had hoped they would do, it contributed to their engagement in their projects and helped them place value on the ideas in their exhibitions. Such efforts at culturally responsive teaching (see Chapter 1) enhance the prospect that standards will arise, and that they will be built through other means as well.

NEGOTIATING

This account of negotiation in classrooms, unlike those of Ira Shor (1996) or Garth Boomer and colleagues (1992), does not describe deliberate power-sharing strategies. Nonetheless, Powell humanities teachers, and the pedagogical approach we followed, were more open to negotiation than some teachers and instructional methods are. We conversed with students individually, and in those conversations we tried to elicit and understand students' thoughts and thought processes. The projects we asked students to do could to some extent be shaped by what students found interesting and challenging. We invited students to take initiative and make decisions in their work. We recognized a variety of student accomplishments.

To say that we *were open to* negotiation in these ways, though, is not to say that we *allowed* negotiation to happen. That is because negotiation, as it is presented in this book, was not ours to allow or disallow. In any learning situation, students determine what standards best connect to the endeavors in which they are prepared to engage. Students exercise this power whether or not teachers acknowledge that they do.

Negotiation, as it is presented in this book, also is not an unfortunate set of compromises that teachers are forced to make. Rather, it is a vital part of the process of building classroom standards. Classroom standards, ultimately, are what students and teachers pursue and attain together. It follows that the standards that represent the greatest commitment and achievement may differ from teachers' predetermined goals.

An understanding of the process of negotiation suggests two broad ways in which teachers can further the development of standards in their classrooms. These are divergent approaches, but they can be mixed judiciously.

One way is for teachers to be strong and effective negotiators on behalf of their own standards. This can mean a simple "no"—when, for instance, students attempt to bargain for more time or less work. It can also entail the more complex aspects of teaching and informing. As teachers proceed in this manner, there is an element of tension in their interactions with students, because students and teachers enter the negotiating process from different starting points.

The second way stems from acknowledgment of the necessary role students play in creating the standards they themselves work toward and the standards that prevail in a classroom as a whole. By paying attention to how students are forming standards in their minds, and how they are bringing standards to life through their actions, teachers can identify avenues that provide strong potential for learning. By appreciating the value of the standards students are creating, teachers can shape their collaborative pursuits with students in productive directions.

Epilogue

In spring of 1999, as I was completing this manuscript, I got back in touch with some of the students whom I had taught, observed, and interviewed at Powell. It was a special pleasure to speak and/or meet with the four students portrayed in Part I, with whom I had worked closely. Each came across to me as a composed young adult.

Wayne Gallaton was in the third year of a 6-year program to acquire a degree in pharmacy. Gloria Ruiz was working as a secretary in an insurance office and beginning to take courses at a community college. Pierre Cyrille was in his second year at the state university, majoring in business. Anwar Martin was in his senior year at a historically Black college in the South, and was preparing to take the Medical College Admission Test.

This book devotes a significant share of its attention to what these students, and their peers, did not do in high school. It is important to recognize that their shortcomings as Powell students—and the shortcomings of their teachers—were not ruinous to their future pursuits. Such recognition does not diminish the importance of trying to create as strong an educational experience as possible with one's students. It does, on the other hand, challenge the apocalyptic visions of contemporary public school graduates' life prospects that one often hears when mass testing and other "standards" initiatives are being promoted.

The four students' abilities to move forward do not suggest to me that they underwent drastic transformations. Rather, it appears to me that Wayne and Pierre continued applying themselves conscientiously, and expanded their knowledge and skills in the process; that Gloria figured out how to function competently in the work world and continued to sort out what is important to her; and that Anwar approached school in a more serious manner as he simply matured. They followed logical processes of growth, in other words, building on the strengths they had displayed in high school.

References

Aptheker, Herbert. (1965). *One continual cry: David Walker's Appeal to the Colored Citizens of the World (1829–1830), its setting and its meaning: Together with the full text of the third and last edition of the Appeal.* New York: Humanities Press.

Berger, Ron. (1991). Building a school culture of high standards: A teacher's perspective. In Vito Perrone (Ed.), *Expanding student assessment* (pp. 32–39). Alexandria, VA: Association for Supervision and Curriculum Development.

Bisson, Terry. (1988). *Nat Turner.* New York: Chelsea House.

Boomer, Garth, Nancy Lester, Cynthia Onore, & Jon Cook. (1992). *Negotiating the curriculum: Educating for the twenty-first century.* London: Falmer.

Boykin, A. Wade. (1994). Afrocultural expression and its implications for schooling. In E. R. Hollins, J. E. King, & W. C. Hayman (Eds.), *Teaching diverse populations: Formulating a knowledge base* (pp. 225–273). Albany: State University of New York Press.

Brown, Dee. (1970). *Bury my heart at Wounded Knee: An Indian history of the American West.* New York: Holt, Rinehart & Winston.

Carini, Patricia F. (1987). *Another way of looking: Views on evaluation and education.* North Bennington, VT: Prospect Archive and Center for Education and Research.

Carini, Patricia F. (1988). *Another way of looking: Views on education and evaluation, talk 2.* Talk presented at North Dakota Study Group on Evaluation meeting, Grand Forks, ND.

Carini, Patricia F. (1994). Dear Sister Bess: An essay on standards, judgement and writing. *Assessing Writing, 1*(1), 29–65.

Clinton, William J. (1997, September 29). The president's radio address, September 20, 1997. *Weekly Compilation of Presidential Documents, 33*(39), 1371–1372.

Coalition of Essential Schools. (1989, June). Asking the essential questions: Curriculum development. *Horace, 5*(5). Providence, RI: Author.

Darling-Hammond, Linda, Jacqueline Ancess, & Beverly Falk. (1995). *Authentic assessment in action: Studies of schools and students at work.* New York: Teachers College Press.

Du Bois, W. E. B. (1989). *The souls of Black folk.* New York: Bantam Books. (Original work published 1903)

Fox-Genovese, Elizabeth. (1988). *Within the plantation household: Black and White women of the Old South.* Chapel Hill: University of North Carolina Press.

Fuller, Mary Lou. (1994). The monocultural graduate in the multicultural environment: A challenge for teacher educators. *Journal of Teacher Education, 45*(4), 269–277.

Greenberg, Kenneth S. (1996). *The confessions of Nat Turner and related documents.* Boston: St. Martin's Press.

Hale-Benson, Janice E. (1982). *Black children: Their roots, culture, and learning styles.* Baltimore: Johns Hopkins University Press.

Hampton, Henry. (Executive Producer) (1986). *Eyes on the prize: America's civil rights years, 1954–1965.* [Videotape series]. Alexandria, VA: PBS Video.

Heath, Shirley Brice. (1983). *Ways with words: Language, life, and work in communities and classrooms.* New York: Cambridge University Press.

Jacobs, Harriet. (1988). *Incidents in the life of a slave girl.* New York: Oxford University Press. (Original work published 1861)

Ladson-Billings, Gloria. (1994). *The dreamkeepers: Successful teachers of African American children.* San Francicso: Jossey-Bass.

Litwack, Leon F. (1961). *North of slavery: The Negro in the free states, 1780–1860.* Chicago: University of Chicago Press.

Lyons, Mary E. (1992). *Letters from a slave girl.* New York: Scribner.

Marshall, Ray, & Marc Tucker. (1992). *Thinking for a living: Education and the wealth of nations.* New York: Basic Books.

McDonald, Joseph P. (1991a). Three pictures of an exhibition: Warm, cool, and hard. *Studies on exhibitions no. 1.* Providence, RI: Coalition of Essential Schools.

McDonald, Joseph P. (1991b). Exhibitions: Facing outward, pointing inward. *Studies on exhibitions no. 4.* Providence, RI: Coalition of Essential Schools.

McQuillan, Patrick J. (1998). *Educational opportunity in an urban American high school: A cultural analysis.* Albany: State University of New York Press.

Moody, Anne. (1968). *Coming of age in Mississippi.* New York: Dell.

Murrell, Peter. (1993). Afrocentric immersion: Academic and personal development of African American males in public schools. In Theresa Perry & James W. Fraser (Eds.), *Freedom's plow: Teaching in the multicultural classroom.* New York: Routledge.

National Council on Education Standards and Testing (NCEST). (1992). *Raising standards for American education.* Washington, DC: U.S. Government Printing Office.

National Council of Teachers of English & International Reading Association (NCTE & IRA). (1996). *Standards for the English language arts.* Newark, DE: International Reading Association.

National Council of Teachers of Mathematics (NCTM). (1989). *Curriculum and evaluation standards for school mathematics.* Reston, VA: Author.

Nieto, Sonia. (1999). *The light in their eyes: Creating multicultural learning communities.* New York: Teachers College Press.

Noddings, Nel. (1984). *Caring: A feminine approach to ethics and moral education.* Berkeley: University of California Press.

Ogbu, John U. (1982). Cultural discontinuities and schooling. *Anthropology and education quarterly, 13*(4), 290–307.

Powell, Arthur G., Eleanor Farrar, & David K. Cohen. (1985). *The shopping mall high school.* Boston: Houghton Mifflin.

Resnick, Lauren B. (1987). *Education and learning to think.* Washington, DC: National Academy Press.

Shor, Ira. (1992). *Empowering education: Critical teaching for social change.* Chicago: University of Chicago Press.

Shor, Ira. (1996). *When students have power: Negotiating authority in a critical pedagogy.* Chicago: University of Chicago Press.

Sizer, Theodore R. (1984). *Horace's compromise: The dilemma of the American high school.* Boston: Houghton Mifflin.

Sizer, Theodore R. (1992). *Horace's school: Redesigning the American high school.* Boston: Houghton Mifflin.

Strom, Margot Stern, & William Parsons. (1982). *Facing history and ourselves: Holocaust and human behavior.* Watertown, MA: International Educators, Inc.

Technical Development Corporation. (1993). *[Earl Powell] High School Program Evaluation: Executive Summary.* Author.

Turner, Nat. (1975). *The confession, trial and execution of Nat Turner, the Negro insurrectionist: Also, a list of persons murdered in the insurrection in Southampton County, Virginia, on the 21st and 22nd of August, 1831, with introductory remarks by T. R. Gray.* New York: AMS Press.

Waite, Robert G. L. (1977). *The psychopathic god: Adolf Hitler.* New York: Basic Books.

Wiggins, Grant. (1989). Teaching to the (Authentic) Test. *Educational Leadership, 46*(7), 41–47.

Wiggins, Grant. (1991). Standards, not standardization: Evoking quality student work. *Educational Leadership, 48*(5), 18–25.

Wiggins, Grant. (1993). *Assessing student performance: Exploring the purpose and limits of testing.* San Francisco: Jossey-Bass.

Wilson, Thomas A. (1996). *Reaching for a better standard: English school inspection and the dilemma of accountability for American public schools.* New York: Teachers College Press.

Index

About the Author

John Kordalewski teaches writing at Bunker Hill Community College in Boston, and also teaches courses for beginning teachers in the Medford, Massachusetts, public school system. He has taught in public secondary schools in Washington, D.C., and Boston. He has a doctorate from the Harvard Graduate School of Education. He is also a professional jazz pianist.